The Scriptural Commentaries
of
Yogiraj Sri Sri Shyama Charan Lahiri Mahasaya

Volume 3

English translation by Yoga Niketan

On the web at www.yoganiketan.net
Email: yoganiketan@yoganiketan.net

YOGA NIKETAN, INC.
Publishers

The Scriptural Commentaries of Yogiraj Sri Sri Shyama Charan Lahiri Mahasaya

Volume 3

ISBN-13: 978-1-943125-03-6 (pbk)

Yoga Niketan is a registered non-profit organization, run by volunteers who receive no compensation of any kind whatsoever. All proceeds from the sale of this book go towards maintaining our work.

CONTENTS

Yogiraj Sri Sri Shyama Charan Lahiri Mahasaya

TRANSLATION NOTE

The translated books maintain that an almost literal translation of the Bengali words of the original author best serves both seekers and Kriyavans. No attempt has been made for the translations to be poetic or interpretive for the above mentioned reason. If the reader notices irregular English grammar (including non-traditional sentence structure, punctuation, etc.), please understand that it is intentional.

The translator has tried as best as he could to keep the work as close to the Bengali phrasing in the original without it being unreadable or incomprehensible.

Unless otherwise noted, all text within parentheses - "( )" - are in the original, including the parentheses themselves, and are ABSOLUTELY NOT explanations of any of the text by the translators or the editor. Any clarifications, of text or otherwise, provided by the translators or the editor are in square brackets - "[ ]".

Pranam, The Translator: Yoga Niketan Team

Important Information about the Commentaries of Yogiraj Shyama Charan Lahiri Mahasaya

Dear Readers,

A word about the commentaries of Yogiraj Shyama Charan Lahiri Mahasaya –

In his monumental autobiography, the great Paramahansa Yogananda Giri ji has written:

"Lahiri Mahasaya himself wrote no books, but his penetrating interpretations were recorded and arranged by various disciples. Some of these voluntary amanuenses were more discerning than others in correctly conveying the profound insight of the guru; yet, on the whole, their efforts were successful. Through their zeal, the world possesses unparalleled commentaries by Lahiri Mahasaya on twenty-six ancient scriptures."

This is indeed the truth. The Yogiraj himself did not write books.

Swami Satyananda Giriji Maharaj, eminent disciple of Sriyukteshvar, in his monumental biography of Lahiri Mahasaya has recorded the following in regards to these books and their language and manner:

"About the books that had Lahiri Mahasaya as the author, Swamiji Maharaj [Swami Sriyukteshvar] used to say,

xi

'That Gurudev Himself wrote any books - this is not correct, and to say so is to actually demean Him. He Himself did not author any book. What was written down of His words by His devotees while they listened to His spoken commentaries is what has been published in book form. Gurudev's language and manner from time to time were incomprehensible to many; it's not at all impossible that trying to convey that language and manner in written form could produce some errors here and there.'

The Lord [Lahiri Mahasaya] wrote to a certain disciple,

'...the lord work Kriya good language grammatical correction up to you all - wish is print - my name should not be there - good if in secret.'

We have seen manuscripts, in the possession of a significant devotee, of the early versions of the Gita with the Lord's spoken commentaries that were taken to Him that had extra 'notes'*** written on them. Whatever the case may be, the erudition in these books of the experience of the fantastic kingdom beyond the senses will lead the Kriyavan on the path to Supreme Knowledge with the Divine Touch of the Yogavatar in this scriptural material."

**[Translator's note: the quoted text of the letter by Yogiraj is almost verbatim, without any attempt at interpretation.]

***[Translator's note: the word "notes" is stated in English, (although transliterated in the Bengali alphabet) in the original text.]

Satyanandaji also says-

"He [Yogiraj Lahiri Mahasaya] would be absorbed in yoga and give spiritual commentaries on the Gita and other *books of philosophy. Bhattacharya Mahasaya, Mahendranath Sanyal Mahasaya and other disciples would write them down. Some devotees in some cases would receive His concise and abbreviated commentaries on the scriptures via letter. These were writings that began to be produced as the aforementioned books. The explanations of the deep scriptural mysteries which were handed down by the oral tradition of guru-disciple succession were first brought out in book form to the ordinary people because of the power of the Lord's compassion. Half a century ago [from the writing of this biography], this Gita with spiritual explanation circulated mostly among the community of sadhakas. This beautiful body of literature became manifest during this transition of ages in the land of Arya – India – for the spiritual revelation of sadhakas, the progenitors of beneficence for all human beings. With Sriguru's support, His Holiness Swami Sriyukteswar Maharaj ji also began to publish an exquisite Gita, approved by the Lord, chapter by chapter, with his own commentaries based on his own realization."*

- from "Yogiraj Shyama Charan Lahiri Mahasay A Biography" by Swami Satyananda Giri. English Translation by Yoga Niketan Team for Yoga Niketan copyright Yoga Niketan

They are in fact "recorded talks" put down on paper by various disciples from intimate scriptural talks given by the Yogiraj. Some of these were recorded more accurately than others. Some were recorded close to exact as the Yogiraj spoke them from His Samadhi state hence the sometimes broken and irregular grammar and incomplete sentences. In lofty spiritual Samadhi one often speaks like a drunk man (which the English translators have gone to great pains to intentionally maintain in this exacting English edition). Others (such as Yoga Sutra commentary) are more "liberal" and "polished" and only based on Yogiraj's general teaching on the matter while the disciple who recorded them admittedly expanded and elaborated and polished the commentary. For example, in Introduction of Yoga Sutras we find the following:

*"To be able to completely take in the essence of Patanjal is extremely difficult for anyone other than Guru-initiated persons. Although it is possible that an intelligent reader can come to some understanding of the gross matters upon reading [the work] two or three times with a concentrated mind, but the techniques of sadhana, and certain terms that seem to be easy to understand but whose meanings are deep and hidden - comprehending the meanings of those [techniques and] terms are, in a way, impossible. The commentaries on all of the sutras that are presented here - all of those were received from, and by the Grace of, a Certain Great Saint, **and because the language of [those commentaries] was very complex, [those commentaries] are presented here in as simple a language as was possible, and is extended in some places where it was necessary. Thus, it can be hoped that these simplified commentaries can be of use to both initiated and uninitiated people. But if any part of the fundamental essence is destroyed, that is no doubt my fault, done by me. To the best of my abilities, I have taken care to make it understandable for ordinary people."***

So please bear this in mind as you approach these commentaries.

The true teaching as taught by Yogiraj is that by arduous performance of Kriya the truth of these scriptures is known. Hence he never placed undue importance on books. In the Garland of letter we find his cautionary words:

"Practicing Kriya IS the reciting of the Vedas. When, through practicing Kriya over and over, one perceives the state beyond Kriya, THAT is the revelation of Vedanta. That should be perceived by doing Kriya. What can happen by looking at books?"

The REAL "Kriya Books" made by Yogiraj were of course his authorized channels which he established for the continued transmission of Kriya Yoga. It is true that over the course of time some of these channels have died away but yet some still remain continuing the quiet tradition. Although as Sri Gurudev Sailendra Bejoy Dasgupta Mahasaya had written:

"Shyama Charan had completely surrendered himself to the Guru [the Mahamuni Babaji Maharaj] and the ecstasies of Kriya Yoga. He made up his mind that he would never go back leaving the divine company of his worshipful Guru. But when he opened his heart to the Guru on the subject he was instructed otherwise. The Guru ordained that Shyama Charan must return and resume his erstwhile life of the householder; he was told that many important tasks were in store for him while in that life. At the beginning Shyama Charan protested and prayed to be allowed to pass the rest of life in company of the Guru. Ultimately, however, he was persuaded to agree. In the process he successfully bargained for two concessions from the affectionate Guru. One was permission to initiate fellow householders also into Kriya Yoga to help them to achieve spiritual solace. The Babaji apparently agreed with reluctance but after imposing certain strict conditions. Thus when Shyama Charan returned to his old surroundings it was a different Shyama Charan; he was an accomplished Yogi and a profound Yoga Guru of the novel system of Kriya Yoga. Enlightened and accomplished disciples and grand disciples who had been duly authorized for the purpose spread the message and teachings of Kriya Yoga all over the country and abroad in later years. It may, however, be mentioned that minor differences are noticed in the system now being taught by different groups although the basic features still remain intact."

−from "Kriya Yoga" by Sri Sailendra Bejoy Dasgupta, Yoga Niketan

The correct way to practice is always the way that was shown by one's authorized Guru. One must have complete faith in (authorized) Guru.

It is also noticed these days the curious phenomena of the emergence of a whole stream of "Gurus" claiming to be disciples of the Holy of Holies, the lofty Guru of Lahiri Mahasaya, the Mahamuni Babaji Maharaj. To this we can only comment, as Dasgupta Mahasaya used to remark - "Human gullibility knows no limits!" He remarked on the matter saying "Great enlightened beings such as my Swamiji (Sriyukteshvar Giriji Maharaj), Swami Pranabananda Paramhansa, Sri Panchanon Bhattacharya, Keshavananda Paramhansa and others claimed to have had the good fortune to meet the Babaji a few times in secret. To the Yogiraj and his advanced disciples the Babaji was much more than the God. It pains a worshipful heart when it is perceived in the present days that even much humbler individuals are making a bee line at Ranikhet and some even claim to have received benedictions from this superman. Gullibility of men knows no limit."

So saying that let us leave the matter.

These English editions are presented as an offering to the holy Kriya performers of all lines and traditions descending from the Divine Yogavatar Shyama Charan Lahiri Mahasaya, to all His spiritual children worldwide.

Bala
Yoga Niketan
April 2005

KABIR

Spiritual Commentary

Sri Sri Shyama Charan Lahiri Mahasaya

English translation by Yoga Niketan

KABIR

Contents

KABIR

With the original Hindi [transliterated], Bengali [translation – further translated to English here]

and

Spiritual Commentary

(Volume One)

By the Grace of the Supreme, Highest of the High, His Holiness Sri Sri Gurudeva

[Yogiraj Sri Sri Shyamacharan Lahiri Mahasaya] offered at His Holy Feet

**Published by His disciple
Sri Panchanon Bhattacharya**

**Calcutta
No. 11 Baburam Ghosh Lane
Year 1297 [Bengali calendar]**

FOREWORD

Mahatma Kabir Saheb [great soul Master Kabir] was/is a being who was liberated while still in the body. It seems that many have heard of this Mahatma, yet his exact birthplace remains more or less unknown. There is even a legend that says that he did not take birth in any womb. He was raised from infancy by a Muslim fisherman in Varanasi. If one examines the supernatural work of Kabir Saheb during his actual life, the [aforementioned] legend is not impossible to believe. It has been said that upon the passing of Kabir Saheb's mortal life, his Hindu and Muslim disciples began quarreling over his body. Amongst the disciples, the Hindus wanted to cremate the body of their guru and the Muslims wished to bury him. This conflict led to physical fighting, at which time Kabir Saheb bodily got up [from the bier] and stood in the midst of the disciples and, pacifying them, said, "Why are you quarreling over this body of skin and bones? What will you gain by this? All good that is to happen from this [the passing] has already happened. Do not fight anymore. I will lie down with this sheet and cover myself. Whatever you find under here afterwards – distribute that amongst yourselves." Later, the disciples lifted the cover and saw that there were only some jasmine flowers on the cloth, and there was no body.

His heart was ever full, in every way. In every situation and event, only words of Love emitted from him. His compositions of "dohas" [couplets] of teachings that manifested in these ways are uncountable in number. Whether one is a sadhu [sage], householder or sadhak [practitioner], his dohas are nectarous for all. He explained and expressed in innumerable ways how the jiva [individual soul] could attain Peace in this maya-filled samsara [delusionfilled life in the world]. And particularly, all matters that are necessary for the

7

sadhak to know – all of that is in the dohas composed by Kabir. Thus, there is absolutely no doubt [or – no wonder] that these [the dohas] are considered dear treasures and priceless gems [of wisdom] by sadhaks. At this time, by Guru's Grace, we have obtained 2700 slokas [verses – or the aforementioned dohas], and have proceeded to publish them, accompanied by simple Bengali translations [the dohas are originally in Hindi] and the spiritual explanations we received from Satguru [Yogiraj Sri Sri Shyamacharan Lahiri Mahasaya]. These will be published in several separate volumes. Now, I humbly pray that if there are any errors in this [work], please know that it is my fault and I ask for forgiveness, and may you find it otherwise satisfactory.

Publisher
Sri Panchanon Bhattacharya
31ˢᵗ Jaistha, 1297 [Bengali calendar]

8

WITNESS
[OR: DIRECT EXPERIENCE]

jagat janayo sohi sakal, so guru pragate aye jinh
ankhiyanh guru dekhiyon, so guru dehin lakhaye -1
kabir bhali bhenyi jo guru mile, nehito hoti hani
deepak jyoti patang jenyo, barta pura jani -2

[Bengali translation from the Hindi above – re-translated:]

(Witness [or: Direct Experience]) Perceiving

(The world) The One Who makes [the sadhak] aware of all moving objects – it is He Who reveals Himself as Guru. Guru showed the Eye with which we can see Guru. -1

Kabir – it is so wonderful that Guru has been found. If this did not happen, then there would be death, because one would lose all sense of everything and would end up like a flying insect deluded by the flame of a lamp and dying in it. -2

[Commentary:]

The One by Whom the world – meaning all objects in motion – is seen – that Guru Himself is Now revealed – meaning: Stillness has happened. Guru has shown the Eye via which Guru – meaning Brahman – is seen. Guru is Atman [Self] – proof: Veda - "atma vai gururekah" - meaning: Atman is the One and Only Guru. -1

Kabir: "k[a]" = head; "b[a]" = throat; "i" = Shakti; "r[a]" = the seed of fire. The State that comes about after abiding for

9

a long time in Kutastha Brahman with Shakti in the head and throat is called "Kabir." This Kabir is saying that it is so wonderful that Guru has been found ("Guru" – One Who takes one from darkness to Light – meaning Atman). Otherwise there would be death – meaning: there would be no escape from birth and death. The purpose of this body is to be free from birth and death. If the Knowledge of Atman does not happen in this body, then there is death, verily. What kind of death is this? Like when flying insects, upon seeing the light of a lamp, fall into it because they think that there is no other light as complete [fulfilling] as this. Thus deluded, they fall into [the flame] and burn and die. In the same way, human beings, unable to see the Self [Atman], are burning and dying in the flash and filigree of this false samsara, because they think that the pleasures and indulgences of the world make up the most complete happiness, and that other than this there is nothing that is good [fulfilling]. But because of finding Guru, one has seen the delusion, and has been saved from such a death. -2

kabir bhali bhneyi jo gur mile, jinhte payo gyan
ghathi maaha chautara, ghathi maaha devan -3

[Bengali:]

Kabir, it is so good that Guru has been found, from whom Divine Knowledge has been received – because He has shown the King and the Royal Throne in this vessel-like body. -3

[Commentary:]

Kabir, it is very good that Guru Atman-Self has been found, because Divine Knowledge dawns upon knowing Atman. In this body, there is a "chautara" (seat). Within [this body] is a Diamond Throne; within is Kutastha = Supreme Person. All around is Light, Fire, Lightning, Sun and Moon.

Facing Him verily, "devan" - meaning Mind - is witnessing all realized beings (known through the teachings of Guru). -3

kabir guruya mila, baliyaya dhelauyna
jati panti kul metigai, nam dharaoe kaun -4

[Bengali:]

Kabir is saying that Satguru has been found. Having Satguru, like when a rock is pulverized by a crushing power, in the same way, race, lineage, class/ caste have all been terminated. So who can attach a name [to anything]? -4

[Commentary:]

Kabir, within this body, Atman has merged with Brahman; the Universe has become known as Brahman-filled, due to which [only the] Great is. All things have been pulverized like a ground-up crushed rock – meaning: all things have become Brahman. It is that which is the par-avastha of Kriya. Then all race, lineage – all are finished. When there is no division/separatedness, who can attach a name to anything separately? -4

kabir gyan prakashi guru mile, so guru bisari na jay
jab govind daya kari, tab guru mili jay -5

[Bengali:]

Kabir says: If a Guru who reveals Divine Knowledge can be found, then that Guru cannot be forgotten. When Govinda [a name of Sri Krishna; meaning here: the Lord] bestows His Mercy, then Satguru will be found automatically. -5

[Commentary:]

Kabir, within this body is Atman – the Knowing of One's Self in the par avastha of Kriya (known through the teachings of Guru). The Guru Who reveals the par avastha of Kriya has been found. I do not forget that Guru. When Govinda bestowed his Mercy – meaning: when I saw the three worlds in the Particle of Brahman, it is then that His Mercy is revealed verily. And it is verily then that Atman has merged with Paramatman and has become That. -5

kabir guru gobind dvou ek hay, duja hay akar
apan mete hari bhajei, tab paoe kartar -6

[Bengali:]

Kabir is saying that Guru and Govinda [Lord] are both One [or – the same]; the difference is only in form. When the "I" is finished, then it is verily the worship of the Lord, and it is then that one attains the Lord. -6

[Commentary:]

The Atman within the body is Guru. In the Kutastha, the same Atman is the Supreme Person. The two are verily One [or – the same], only the forms are different – meaning: in motion and Still – Kriya and the par avastha of Kriya. When, upon having performed Kriya, there is Stillness in the par avastha of Kriya, then verily there is no "I"; all is ended and "All is Brahman" happens. Then one attains the Lord - "Lord": the One Who is Doing all. -6

kabir guru gobind dvou khade, kake lagon paay
balihari guru apne, jinh gobind diya lakhaay -7

[Bengali:]

Kabir is saying that Guru and Govinda are both here; to whom shall one do pranam [prostration] first? Let me hail the One who is my Guru because it is He who has shown me Govinda. -7

[Commentary:]

Atman = Guru, and Kutastha both have become Still. Now to whose Feet shall I prostrate? One's Guru is Atman, the One who has ended all, and is the One who has revealed Kutastha. -7

kabir balihari guru apne, ghadi ghadi shaobar manukhten debta kiyo, karat na lagi bar -8

[Bengali:]

Kabir says: Glory to my Guru! Moment after moment and hundreds of thousands of times does He makes one into a god from a mortal. It does not take long to do this. -8

[Commentary:]

Glory to one's own Atman-Self! "Ghadi ghadi" [see doha – literally: second after second] – meaning: again and again, hundreds and hundreds of times He makes man into a god. It does not take long to do this. -8

kabir sangshay khaya sakal jag, sangshay koi na khaay jo bedha guru acchar, so sangshay chuni khaay -9

[Bengali:]

Kabir is saying that the entire world is being eaten up by doubt and uncertainty – meaning: [everyone] is living in doubt and uncertainty – but no one is eating up doubt and uncertainty. One who has found out the difference [between the world] and Guru with the Imperishable Self ("bedha" = "bheda" [distinction]) is thoroughly chewing up and eating doubt and uncertainty. -9

[Commentary:]

Upon becoming restless, Kabir the Atman-Self's mind is going in two directions, sometimes to God, sometimes to samsara. Sometimes he thinks that samsara is real and sometimes he thinks that God is real. But in both are doubt and uncertainty. Because of mind being in two places, two yonis [wombs] are there. One is the Brahman-Yoni Lord, but there is a complete movement away from that – meaning: one is moving from being United to another [thing]. When mind moves from One Substance to another thing, then that [second] thing takes birth – meaning: a desire forms in that. It is like when a man and woman become attracted to each other and he enters her, and they themselves take birth in her womb, but find doubt in accepting the child as themselves, in the same way, this [great] doubt is eating up the world. What this means is: Brahman is everywhere; Atman [Self] is also everywhere. Wherever there is Atman, there is also jiva [individual soul]. And within all jivas is this doubt and uncertainty. Engrossed in thinking about this – meaning: does Brahman exist or not – they are dying in the constant doubting of this. But no one is eating up this doubt. When the mind becomes restless, doubt comes around. When man, attracted to woman, enters her, at that time he is restless. Thus, not knowing the True Nature, a doubt takes place. In that same way, because of the constant doubting "is there Brahman or not," birth and death are taking place. When this restlessness becomes Still, then doubt itself is eaten up – meaning: if there is Stillness, then who is there to doubt? The person who, via the Self, has seen Kutastha from the Self, and has entered into the Particle of Kutastha and seen the three worlds along with HimSelf within that [the three worlds], and has made everything One – His name is "bedha" = "bheda" [distinct knowing]. He thoroughly chews up and eats doubt. When one sees that the three worlds are within himself, and within the three worlds sees HimSelf, then Oneness is. Doubt is in the dual – meaning: is there a God or not? When Oneness is, then doubt is eaten up. It is like when a bird opens the two lips of his beak to take food, and at the time of swallowing closes the beak – meaning: it makes the two lips one - "is there a God or not" is when the two lips are open, and when doubt goes away, there is One Brahman Stillness – meaning: doubt is swallowed up. Then the two lips of the beak become one and no longer remain two. -9

kabir budethe pheri ubre, guru ki lahri chamki
bera dekha jhanjhera, utarike bhaye farki -10

[Bengali:]

Kabir is saying that he was drowning for certain, but he received a wave from Guru, and seeing flashes over and over, he rose up again. He saw one boat [bera] that was full of holes, like a strainer. He [Kabir] got off of that vessel and stayed away from it. -10

[Commentary:]

Oneself was under water but rose again – meaning: oneself was completely drowned in the ocean of maya, but Guru sent a wave out of His Grace. Catching the wave, one saw flash after flash and rose above. The boat [bera] was like a strainer. (The type of boat that has a bottom that is held by four pots on four corners is called a "bera.") But upon seeing holes in those pots, he got up off of that boat and stayed away from it – meaning: upon seeing Light and such in the Guru-endowed wave, he also saw that this pot-like body is full of holes, like a strainer – meaning: upon seeing every pore in the body, as well as the nine doors, he separated from this body and went to the par avastha of Kriya and remained apart there. -10

kabir ek namke pattare, devekon kuch nahi
kyale guruhi samdhiye, haus rahe man mahi -11

[Bengali:]

Kabir is saying that there is such a Name, that nothing

remains to be given, because there is Oneness. Is there anything to be given then? If something is there then there are two verily. The wish to address Guru remained in the mind. - 11

[Commentary:]

The "One Name" is verily when Atman merges with Paramatman – meaning the par avastha of Kriya. Then the door from this side is closed – meaning: upon Atman merging with Paramatman and becoming One, the false "I" ceases to be. In that State, there is nothing at all to give, as giving could only happen if there was a separate "me." Now how can I address Guru? If there was a self that remained, then only could someone address someone as "guru." This wish of the mind stayed in the mind only. -11

kabir man diya tinhu sab diya, manke sath sharir
aab devekon kya raha, eo kahe das kabir -12

[Bengali:]

Kabir is saying that he has given mind, and the body with the mind. He has given everything, and what remains to be given is also being said by Kabir. -12

[Commentary:]

The person in whom his self has become Still and merged with Brahman, then he has given everything, because if the self is, then everything is, and offering up the self means automatically everything has been given. If the self is given, then the body is also given. In the par avastha of Kriya (known through the teachings of Guru), what remains to be given? If mind and body are offered then wealth is also given, because if this body and mind were not there then who is there to call anything "wealth?" When mind and body are given, then wealth is automatically given, even without giving. This [what remains to be given] is the giving of self. Kabir's Self is saying, "Das" [servant]– the one who always serves the Lord with devotion and for the sake of pleasing Him – the giving of self – meaning: one who remains always in the Self with devotion, and pays obeisance to the Self [Atman] and serves Atman to please Atman. The Self is not pleased until the self remains in the Self – meaning the par avastha of Kriya (known through the teachings of Guru). -12

kabir shikligar kijiye, shabda maskala dei
manka mayil chodayike, chit darpan kari lei -13

[Bengali:]

Kabir is saying: do "shikligar." Cleaning a weapon [in this case, a sword] is called "shikligar." There is a sound that is made when a sword is being cleaned, and when it is clean – meaning when the impurities are gone – there is no more sound. In this same way, clean the impurities of the mind and make the consciousness like a mirror. -13

[Commentary:]

Do "shikligar" (the term for sword cleaning) to your self. To do "shikligar" upon a sword, go from the base of the weapon to the tip [in one stroke] and again come back to the base. Now do the "shikligar" of Kriya via the Self and clean the self. With the "maskala" ([see doha] residual pellets that remain after straining diluted calcium carbonate [chuna]) of shabda [sound] – when one takes those small pellets and scrubs the sword to clear unclean stuff (rust), a sound is made. You are also unclean. When you clean the rust-laden self via the Self, there will be a sound. When this sound is no more, then the rust of the self is gone. Just as when the rust of the sword is gone there is no more sound, rid the mind of its impurities in this way (impurities of the mind – desires). A sword remains a sword only until one makes effort to strike and then it cuts. In the same way, mind is mind only – as it is. To whichever thing mind takes the mind, the impurities of that thing immediately come upon the mind. When that [type of] mind becomes somewhat steady, the Bindu Brahman [is seen]. That Bindu does not stay still; It moves. One cannot see when there is swinging in this way. It is like when one cannot see one's face [steadily] when a mirror is moved about, but once it is stilled, no matter what reflection falls on it, it is seen; in the same way, if one stills the mirror of Consciousness as Bindu and keeps it steady in front of him, he will see the entire world in That. -13

kabir guru dhobi, shikh kapra, savan srijni haar
surti shilapar dhoiye, nikle jyoti apar -14

[Bengali:]

Kabir is saying that Guru is like the washerman and the disciple is like the cloth – meaning: in the way that a washerman cleans clothes, so does Guru clean the cloth-like disciple with soap – meaning: cleaning the self again and again on the stone of meditation, Boundless Light comes forth. -14

[Commentary:]

Kabir, the Atman-Guru in the body is washing [you] like this: once up and once down. Mind becomes impure upon becoming attached to other things/matters. The One Who cleans this dirt is the washerman-like Guru. And that mind itself is the cloth-disciple. Using the soap of Shakti-Lord Brahman on that [cloth], and cleaning it on the stone of meditation again and again, a Boundless Light comes forth. The particular characteristic of Boundless Light is that It has no end – meaning Brahman. -14

kabir ghar baithe guru paya, bade hamare bhag
soi ko tarsat hate, aab amrat anchaon laag -15

[Bengali:]

Kabir is saying that I am so fortunate that I found Guru while sitting at home. There was a time when even with [great] effort I could not get the smallest, slightest thing. But now I am even dealing out Immortality/Nectar Itself, generously. -15

[Commentary:]

Kabir, Guru was found in this very body, in the Self itself. I am so fortunate – meaning: suddenly I received a Great Thing. Before I used to despair over whether I would even find a throwaway thing like "maad" (starch). Even a little starch can help one to sustain life. Now I am verily distributing Nectar everywhere because my stomach is full – meaning: if one drinks Nectar, fear of death ceases to be. Having drunk Nectar myself, I have become Immortal and I am just giving it away – meaning: perceiving no prejudiced differences between receivers, I am giving away Kriya. -15

kabir guruko lal gadavon kare, matina pakdai het
ek khont laga rahe, vao lagi lahe na bhed -16

[Bengali:]

Kabir is saying that if there was no reason for this earth-body, then I would have made "lal" (precious jewel) out of Atma-Rama Guru. As long as there is no piercing, stay with the One. -16

[Commentary:]

Kabir's Self is saying that if there was no reason for the earth-body, then he would have made "lal" out of Guru ("lal" means "precious stone") - meaning: the Self would make this body a precious jewel – meaning: would make it Brahman.

What this means is: oneself has merged in Brahman, but because of this body being made of earth, it has remained as it was. Now – meaning: because becoming Brahman bodily did not happen, do not fret over it, and stay where the five senses become one. Until the piercing happens then just stay with that [one] – meaning: when the self becomes one-pointed and merges in Brahman, then this body will be "lal" even without being "lal," because the body is with mind – meaning: if there is no mind, who is there to call something a body? When the mind has merged, then the body will also merge. -16

kabir guru ko lal shikh ku bhanyi, gadi gadi kade khotantar hate sahar dei, baher baher chot -17

[Bengali:]

Kabir is saying that Guru actually is "lal," and that the disciple is [often] bad, because time and again he [disciple] makes wrongful statements/ arguments – meaning: becomes engaged in wrong matters. Blows (chot) are hitting from outside and a stirring to awaken is happening within. -17

[Commentary:]

Kabir, Atman verily remains "lal," but mind is bad, because just as mind is going into the par avastha of Kriya, it is also similarly going back into the sense [absorptions]. Although the bad mind is coming away [from the par avastha], the hand within is calling – meaning: one is touching Brahman little by little, yet when coming back outside, he is suffering heavy "chot" - meaning blows. When mind leaves Brahman and comes back to matter, then there is much suffering. -17

kabir gyan samagam premsukh, daya bhakti biswas guru sevate paiye, satguru shabda nevas -18

[Bengali:]

Kabir is saying that if one has compassion, devotion and faith, then Knowledge comes together, and when that happens, one has "Joy of Love" (premsukh [see doha]). If one serves Guru, then Satguru shows the chamber of sound. -18

[Commentary:]

Kabir, the Knowledge of the Self is the Equipoise Stillness, which is the Happiness of Love. Becoming happy in this way, when one then fully attends to others attaining happiness – this is called "compassion." Having such compassion, one sees that through Guru's teachings I have become happy and others are becoming happy. By this, devotion continues to increase. As this devotion continues to increase, faith comes about. Faith does not happen without "Dhruva Jnana" [Permanent Knowledge]. Thus, Dhruva Jnana is verily Brahman. It is attained only by following Atman. This type of person has settledness in sound – meaning: if one abides by what these persons say, Divine Knowledge manifests (known via the teachings of Guru). -18

kabir guru manukh kari jante, te nara kahiye andh
ihan duhkhi samsar me, age jamko bandh -19

[Bengali:]

Kabir is saying: the one who thinks that Guru is human is a blind person. He [the person] is miserable in this world and later he falls to the clutches of Death. -19

[Commentary:]

Kabir! The one who thinks of the aforementioned Satguru as human is blind. He [the person] is miserable in this world. He will fall to the clutches of Death in the afterworld. -19

kabir guru manukh kari jante, charnamrit ko paan
te nara narakhi jahenge, janma janma hoye shoyan -20

[Bengali:]

Kabir is saying that the one who thinks guru is human and thereby drinks the nectar of the lotus feet – that person goes to hell, and birth after birth will be born in a dog's womb. -20

[Commentary:]

Kabir! The one who does not know that Atman is Guru and thinks that guru is human and drinks the nectar of the lotus feet goes to hell and ends up screaming unendingly like a dog. Let him not think of Atman-Guru as human and let him drink the Nectar of the Lotus Feet ["charanamrit" – see doha] ("charan" [literally - feet] – meaning: that by which one is able to move; one who moves from this body to another body – if he becomes Still, there is Immortality/Nectar; enjoying this Stillness is called "drinking the Nectar of Immortality"). This person does not go to hell, and he does not scream birth after birth as a dog. -20

kabir te nar adha hay, guru kon kahte aur hari
ruthe guru smaran hay, guru ruthe nahi thaor -21

[Bengali:]

Kabir is saying that the person who does not know Guru as Guru and calls Him something else is a low person. If God Hari becomes angry, then one can take refuge in Guru, but if Guru becomes angry, then there is no place for deliverance. -21

[Commentary:]

Kabir! Those who do not know that Atman is verily Paramatman [– their selves remain in the lower [consciousness]. If Hari [God] becomes angry, then there is refuge in Guru – meaning Stillness happens. ("Hari" - one who does "haran" [terminates] – meaning "viveka" [discrimination]. If there is no viveka, still if one meditates on Atman there is Stillness.) But if there is wrongfulness with Atman (if mind goes in the other directions of maya), then there is no place for Rest. -21

**kabir guru matheten utre, shabd bihuna hoye
tako kal ghaseti hai, rakhi shake nahi koye -22**

[Bengali:]

Kabir is saying that when Guru came down from the head, the Sound stopped. That person is taken away by Time (Death). No one can save him. -22

[Commentary:]

Kabir, Guru is Atman. Guru = heavy [another meaning]. When that [heaviness] falls off of the head, then the Divine Intoxication leaves. Therefore there is no Sound. That person is [now] with Kal [Time] – meaning: Time will grab and take him away, dragging him on the ground. No one will be able to save him. -22

**kabir aham agni hriday dahe, gurute chahe maan
tinh ko jam naota diya, tom hohumere mejmaan -23**

[Bengali:]

Kabir is saying: One's heart is burning with the fire of ego and he is [at the same time] seeking respect from Guru. Death is inviting him, saying, "You are my favorite guest." -23

[Commentary:]

Kabir, that fire that is of ego (from not abiding in Kutastha Brahman) is burning the heart to horrible despair. That [ego] is seeking respect from Guru Atman. Death is inviting him, saying, "You are my welcomed guest" - meaning: one who keeps his ego-ness will have to die. -23

kabir guru parash guru parash hay, guru chandan subas satguru parash jiuke, jinho din ho mukti neoas -24

[Bengali:]

Kabir is saying that Guru is like the Touchstone. Guru is the Touchstone verily and Guru is Himself the Fragrant Sandalwood. Satguru is Himself the jiva's Touchstone because it is He Who bestows the abode of Liberation. -24

[Commentary:]

"Parash" (that which is called "sparshamani" [touchstone]) = the one who transforms bad to good is also called "Parash." One whose mind always desires to stay in the bad – upon receiving "satkarma" [holy act], he became free of that [bad] – meaning: he became the Touchstone. Becoming the Touchstone, he became Brahman – meaning: the Touchstone Brahman remained as it always was. Becoming like this, the Sandalwood-like Fragrance of Atman came about and he became dear to everyone's affection. The Touchstone for this self is Satguru, by whom all are being Liberated – meaning: the One Who bestowed the par avastha of Kriya, the abode of Liberation (known via the teachings of Guru). -24

kabir guru parash me bhed hay, bado antaro jaan johan loha kanchan kare, ye e karilei apu saman -25

[Bengali:]

Kabir is saying that there is a difference between a touchstone and Guru. Know that there is a great difference. A touchstone turns iron into gold only, but the Satguru makes the disciple the same as Him. -25

[Commentary:]

There is a difference between Atman and the touchstone. There is a great difference. The touchstone turns iron into gold. Guru Brahman takes the self and makes it the same as Himself. -25

kabir guruko kijiye dandabat, koti parnam
ja eyse bhringee keet ko, karle apu saman -26

[Bengali:]

Kabir is saying do prostrations to Guru hundreds of thousands of times. The way a worm makes another insect like itself – in the same way, Guru also makes the disciple the same as Him. -26

[Commentary:]

One should do hundreds of thousands of pranams [prostrations] to Atman Guru via Omkar Kriya [known via the teachings of Guru]. "Pranam" ["parnam" in doha] - meaning: natural bowing – will happen simply from the performance of Kriya. The way a "bhringi" - meaning worm – takes another insect [larva] as its own – meaning that the other insect [larva] also becomes a worm – in the same way, the human larva = the self, by abiding in Guru becomes transformed into the Self, and upon being settled in Paramatman, becomes the same [as Paramatman]. -26

kabir guruko tan man dijiye, mukti padarath jani
guru ki seva mukti phal, yah girihee sahi danee -27

[Bengali:]

Kabir is saying: surrender body and mind to Guru. Know that Liberation is in this only. Liberation is verily in service to Guru. Whether one is a householder or generous benefactor, service to Guru is all. -27

[Commentary:]

Kabir, surrender body and mind to Guru. Know that you are free when that is done. It is certainly the truth that Liberation is in doing Kriya. -27

kabir guruson bhed jo lijiye, shish dijiye daan
bahutak abadhu vahi gaye, rakhe jiu abhiman -28

[Bengali:]

Kabir is saying: one who has received "bhed" [incision or insight] – meaning: Secret Substance – from Guru, had first surrendered his head [to Guru]. Many pilgrims and renunciates have been swept away in this ocean of samsara – those who held on to their ego-vanity. -28

[Commentary:]

Kabir, pierce [bhed] into Atma-Rama Guru Brahman and become One ("bhed" = one substance enters into another substance) – meaning: upon attaining the par avastha of Kriya, give up your head = remain always in Brahman. Many pilgrims have been swept away by the ocean of samsara – those who held on to the vanity that the Atman is the individual self. -28

kabir guruko sarvasya dijiye, aur puchiye arthae
kahe kabir pad par soi, so hamsa ghare jaae -29

[Bengali:]

Kabir is saying: give everything to Guru and know the Supreme Substance. Kabir is saying [that such a person,] upon touching the Supreme Substance, goes to the House of Hamsa. -29

[Commentary:]

Kabir, when the self is in Brahman in all circumstances

and places, it is verily then that all is given [to the Lord]. And, if one abides in the Particle of Brahman, one knows all experiential matters. One who has touched Atma-Rama in that Brahman-Substance has gone to the House of Hamsa – meaning: [he has gone to] Brahman. -29

kabir gurugamya bataoe nahi, shikh gahe nahin khut
lok bhed bhakhe nahin, so guru kayer thunt -30

[Bengali:]

Kabir is saying: one who cannot show the Path of Truth to the disciple and cannot reveal the "post" which the disciple needs to hold onto to become steady – this kind of guru is paralyzed and cannot do anything. -30

[Commentary:]

Kabir, when one goes to Atma-Rama Guru, one becomes Still. One who cannot teach this, and one who cannot tell the disciple to which post he must hold on in order to become steady, and one who cannot teach the way of revelation for every person – this type of guru is useless. Nothing can be accomplished with that kind of guru. -30

kabit guru batayen sadhuko, sadhu kahe guru bujh
arash parash ke madhi me, bhai agam ke sujh -31

[Bengali:]

Kabir is saying: Guru is saying to sadhu [sage/practitioner] that Vision and Touch merged and the inaccessible [or future] was known. -31

[Commentary:]

Kabir, Atman Guru is telling sadhu [practitioner], "Today, be attentive just to what comes forth after performing two hundred Kriyas." Sadhu asks Guru to help him understand –

meaning: wanting to know the par avastha of Kriya. Paramatman and Atman became one and the Inaccessible Abode was seen – meaning: one went on seeing the past, present, future – all. -31

kabir guru saman daata nahin, jachak shikh saman
tin lokki samprada, so guru dinho daan -32

[Bengali:]

Kabir is saying that there is no giver like Guru and no beggar like the disciple. Guru verily gives all that is in the three worlds. -32

[Commentary:]

Kabir! There is no giver like Atman Guru, because everyone else wants something [back] verily. But the One Who is Guru gives truly all things – meaning: no thing remained after "all is Brahman" happened. There is no beggar like the restless-minded disciple, because he is never satisfied with anything [of the world]. Guru has bestowed the Kriya that encompasses all that is in the three worlds – meaning: heaven, Earth and the underworld – the Kriya [also: activity] that is happening in these three worlds is also being given by Guru. "Patal" [underworld] – [is] from the navel to the feet. These feet move so fast that it seems that the feet are not touching the ground. From the navel to the throat is the Earth plane. One abides Still in the heart, and sees all indescribable and wondrous happenings in the head. -32

kabir pahile daata shikh bhaye, tan man arpo shish
pache daate Guru bhaye, naam diya bakshish -33

[Bengali:]

Kabir is saying that the disciple is actually the first giver, because he [first] surrendered body, mind and all to Guru, and afterwards, Guru became the Giver as He bestowed the [Divine] Name to the disciple. -33

[Commentary:]

Kabir, the mind-disciple gave to Atma-Rama Guru – meaning: putting mind in Mind, he went on performing Kriya. The giving of mind means the body was given also. The first is of course giving mind and performing Kriya. Because of surrendering body and mind, the head has also been surrendered to Brahman. Then, abiding in Brahman in the head, Guru – Who is Atma-Rama – became the Giver – meaning: it is Atman who verily revealed Parmatman Himself. "Name" - meaning: that by which "upadhaukan" is known – He bestowed that. "Upa" = "other" – meaning supernatural – heaviness in the head, and the knowing of covering that heaviness is spoken of here as "upadhaukan." -33

LIKHTE GURU PARAKH KO ANG

On the Matter of Testing the Guru

**kabir guru lobhee shikh lalchee, dono khele daon
dono bude bapure, chadi pakhal ki naon -1**

[Bengali:]

Kabir is saying that both the greedy guru and the lust/hankering-filled disciple are trying to strike a profitable bargain with each other. This type of guru and disciple both are on a boat made of stone and will drown in it. -1

[Commentary:]

Kabir, [certain persons'] inner guru is only oriented towards the fantastic visions and sounds within and stays there to satisfy all kinds of wants – meaning many kinds of desires etc., and the [inner] disciple is lustful-greedy – meaning: mind, which wants whatever it sees. Mind is not satisfied with anything. Both are trying to gain from each other. But both fellows drowned aboard a stone boat – meaning: the stone-filled self and mind with all of their desires together gradually became weighted down and sank from the head to the regions below. Sinking to the underworld, they went on to do all sorts of work belonging to hell. -1

**kabir jaako guru hay aandhra, chela khada nirandh
andhe andhe theliya, duno kua pavant -2**

[Bengali:]

Kabir is saying that [some persons'] guru is blind and the disciple is blind as well, and they are standing there together. Both blind persons shoved each other about and both fell in the well. -2

[Commentary:]

Kabir, one whose inner-self guru is blind, his mind-disciple is also automatically blind. As such, both shove each other about and fall into the underworld = "well" - meaning: the self which abides in the Self finds a desire within to help jivas attain elevation, and upon seeing the suffering of jivas, expresses sorrow and says, "the visible things are all nothing"; for him some Self-Illumination comes about. And the one who abides in the mind – meaning: one who resides always in [non-Atman] matters, and, not being empathetic to the suffering of others, drinks liquor and such, and remains ever immersed in the pleasures of indulgence – he is absolutely blind. The blind self is pushing the blind mind and they are going into, and doing, wrongful acts. Because of having to reap the fruits of these acts, they are falling into the well of the underworld. -2

kabir jana nahi bujha nahi, puchna kiya gaon
andheke andha mila, path bataoe kaun -3

[Bengali:]

Kabir is saying: neither is there knowing, nor is there understanding. No one is even there to ask. A blind guide has found another blind person. So who is going to show the path to whom? -3

[Commentary:]

Kabir, [for certain persons] the inner guru does not know himself as Himself – meaning: he does not understand the par avastha of Kriya, where oneself abides in Oneself. He does not even ask anyone which road one should take. The blind self has found a blind mind. Neither of them can tell the other the way to go. -3

kabir mai mudo, us guru ki jaten bharm na jaay
apne buda dharme, chela diya bahaay -4

[Bengali:]

Kabir is saying: I myself am an ignorant fool, and the guru I have found is also not free of delusion. He drowned in the current himself and made the disciple get swept away too. -4

[Commentary:]

Kabir, Atma-Rama is Guru. One whose mind is not on Atman and is going in other directions, and the one because of whom the delusion of maya is not ending – that being [false self] drowned in the current of the mayaforce, and he also made the disciple – meaning mind – also get swept away. Not only did the self go, but the mind moved from one place to another as well. -4

kabir gurunahu bhed hay, gurunahu me bhao
so guru nishdin badiye, jo shabd bataoe daon -5

[Bengali:]

Kabir is saying: there are differences in Gurus and different feelings in Gurus. Speak always to the type of Guru Who can teach Omkar Sound via pranayam and such. -5

[Commentary:]

Kabir, there are distinctions in the way the Atma-Rama Guru manifests within individuals, and the Guru within each manifests with [different] feelings – meaning: some stay "locked"; some listen to the Omkar Sound; some witness Light and such via the Eye – these can be known via pranayam. Speak to this kind of Guru day and night – meaning: always perform Kriya. [This Guru] speaks the Word. "Daon" [see doha] – like when one throws [dice] in a game – meaning: the way the throw is made – by which method restlessness can be Stilled. -5

**kabir pure guru bina, pura shikh na hoye guru
lobhi, shikh lalchee, tate jhajhni duni shoye -6**

[Bengali:]

Kabir is saying that without the help of Guru the disciple does not attain Complete Knowledge, and if the guru is greedy, and if the disciple is also filled with hankering, then both of them are twice as deep in sleep. -6

[Commentary:]

Kabir, if the self does not go and merge with the Supreme Self, the mind does not become Still, because the self is putting mind in other directions. Mind's own nature is restlessness [movement] and to stay in that state. It is going in other directions. Due to this, the self and the mind are enjoined together in the addiction of worldly things and are asleep – meaning: they are intoxicated with samsara. -6

**kabir pura sahaje gun kare, gune naoyaye cheha
sayer pokhe sarbhare, dan na mage meha -7**

[Bengali:]

Kabir is saying: attending to the guna of "Sahaj Kriya" - one came down via that guna. And that which was being always attended to – he took that thing above via the same guna. [When that happened,] then who can be there to bestow or pray? It is like when all rivers automatically come to the sea, and like the cloud giving rain, yet there is no prayer offered to them. -7

[Commentary:]

Kabir, the Atma-Rama Guru creates good qualities via the "Sahaj Kriya" attends to guna (known via the teachings of Guru) – meaning: the body – which is Omkar Itself – had guna attached to the lower. Upon doing Kriya, [Guru] put that guna above. And there is no place to put a ball on the bowstring – meaning: He began to continuously attend to the very powerful deer-like mind and continued to inject the Shabda – meaning: continued to put [the disciple] in the sushumna via Kriya. The cloud does not ask for any offering; it gives away water on its own. The sun attracts the water and brings it up, and the moon, via its cooling quality, condenses that water and in time cools the Earth via rainfall. In the same way, in the navel is the sun and in the skull [or – palate] is the moon. With the union of the sun and the moon, and thus attaining Settledness in the Rain of the par avastha of Kriya, the mind merges in Brahman and becomes cool (known via the teachings of Guru). -7

kabir pura sat guru na mila, raha adhura shikh
sva gajteeka parheekai, ghar ghar mange bhikh -8

[Bengali:]

Kabir is saying: Satguru was not found. Thus, the restlessness of the disciple also did not end. Mind, swaying side to side like an elephant, has become filled with addictions/attachments and is begging for alms from house to house. -8

[Commentary:]

Kabir, Atma-Rama Guru is the Totality. One was not able to remain in the Atman. One was not also able to remain in the

Parabrahman, which is the par avastha of Kriya – meaning: after not attaining, mind remained anxious – meaning: doubts were not ended. The elephant-like mind was not straight – swaying left and right, abiding in good and bad, went on begging at every house. The mind in the self became desirous of everything - "iccha" [desire] – that to which the addicted mind goes, and bringing it to one's own possession is called "iccha." -8

**kabir pura sat guru na mila, raha adhura shikh
niksatha haribhajan ko, bajhi gyaye maya bik -9**

[Bengali:]

Kabir is saying: Neither was Satguru found, nor did the restlessness of the disciple go. One went outside to worship the Lord but again became bound to maya. -9

[Commentary:]

Kabir, Atma-Rama Guru is Omkar Itself. One did not find Guru. Because of this, mind remained in doubt. One went outside to worship Hari [God] - "Hari" (One Who kills the three intense afflictions ["taap"].) Not finding the "sahaj path" [natural path] within in the form of Kriya – the path that has come along with natural birth [or – natural life] – that is called "sahaj path" - not finding that, one [took] the crooked path. One went on the path of worldly matters and became bound. -9

**kabir guru ki bahar dehaka, satguru chinha nahi
bhau sagar ko jalme, phiri phiri gota khai -10**

[Bengali:]

Kabir is saying: I only know a body as guru, but I do not know Satguru. Because of this one is being hit, bound in the snares of the world-ocean. -10

[Commentary:]

Kabir, the person who does not know Atma-Rama Guru and knows [only] the bodily guru – not knowing the Guru as Atman – is again and again going on being engrossed in the world-ocean. -10

kabir johi gurute bhay na mete, bhranti man ki na jaay guruto eysa chahiye, jo dei brahm darshaay -11

[Bengali:]

Kabir is saying: I do not want a guru that cannot rid me of fear and the confusion and doubt of mind. I want a Guru that can show me Brahman. -11

[Commentary:]

Kabir, if from one's own guru there is no Settledness in Fearlessness, and, not having received the Stillness via the Kriya of Atman, mind remains confused and mind goes in bad paths – this type of guru is not Guru. The type of Guru that I want is One Who can make one see the Kutastha of Brahman in Atman. -11

kabir kan phuka guru haddaka, behaddaka guru aur behaddaka guru jab mile, tab lahe thikana thaor -12

[Bengali:]

Kabir is saying: the guru who blows into the ear has his limits – meaning: those who are finished after revealing a mantra in one's ear. And a Guru that is "behadda" [without limits] is another type – meaning: when "behadda" Guru is found (Guru that has Infinite Power is called "behadda Guru") - when this type of Guru is found, then one will find Brahman's location. -12

[Commentary:]

Kabir is saying: The ear-mantra-giving guru has his limits – meaning: this type of guru tells one the seed [mantra], the [associated] deity and the method of worship. The "behadda" Guru is of another type. When "behadda" Guru is found, then one attains the Stillness in the par avastha of Kriya, and one remains in That. Because of remaining [in That], one becomes That Itself. -12

kabir jane guruko bujhiya, payda diya bataay
chalta chalta tahan giya, jahan niranjan raay -13

[Bengali:]

Kabir is saying, Guru has understood and shown the road. Now, by moving along I ended up where "Niranjan Raay" (God) is. -13

[Commentary:]

Kabir, upon knowing Atma-Rama Guru, I moved along on the road that He showed me and I came upon the place of "Niranjan Raay" - meaning Kutastha. -13

kabir bandhe ko bandha mila, chute koni upaay
karu seoa nirbandha ki, palme lei chodaay -14

[Bengali:]

Kabir is saying: the bound person again became bound. There is no chance of escape. Serve the One who is unbound. If this is done, then He will free one from bondage in the blink of an eye. -14

[Commentary:]

Kabir, Atma-Rama – good and bad are on two sides – when one finds a guru who is fallen, now there is no way of being free from bondage. This means: serve the One Who is unbound – meaning sushumna – the One Who is all-pervading. Upon continuously serving, in the blink of an eye in the par avastha of Kriya – from the bondage of the self – He makes one absolutely free from bondage. The re-birth of the person after one hundred years and absolute bondage – meaning: the bondage which has no end – one is free of that bondage in the par avastha of Kriya. -14

kabir jaka guru hay grihee, chela grihee hoy
kich kich ke dhnoe, daag na chute koy -15

[Bengali:]

Kabir is saying: one whose guru is a "householder" - meaning one who leads a life of attachment in samsara – that is [the meaning of] "householder" [in this case] – his disciple ends up as a "householder" also. Just washing with water alone does not get rid of the stains. -15

[Commentary:]

When one's inner self-guru is "in the house" - meaning he did not stay in Atman – because of the disciple-mind going in other directions, washing the mind did not rid it of even one of the stains. -15

kabir guru naam hay gamyaka, shikh shikhile soy
binu sanghat maryad binu, guru shikh na hoy -16

[Bengali:]

Kabir is saying: one who does not know the place to go, he is guru by name only. Not learning through company, and not staying in a respect, the disciple does not become like Guru. -16

[Commentary:]

Kabir, if the inner self-guru does not settle in any place,

this type of self is not Guru. Learn that through which the restless disciple-mind will become Still. If one does not keep the company of the Self and if one does not perform Kriya with devotion, then the restless disciple-mind does not become like the Still Mind of Guru – meaning abiding in the par avastha of Kriya. -16

kabir ato saste bhaye, koudike, rapachash apne
tanki shudh nahi, shikh karan ki aash -17

[Bengali:]

Kabir is saying that gurus have become so cheap to get that one can find fifty of them for a pittance. [The guru] has not even purified his own being, yet he desires to have disciples. -17

[Commentary:]

Kabir! Those who have mind in other directions, the value of these deluded gurus is such that one can get fifty of them for a pittance. They [themselves] do not even once think about the self abiding in the Self. How strange it is that still they hope to make disciples. -17

kabir jo nihang acchar paaiya, taaka metika doy
so guru pura kahiye, kadihi grihee na hoy -18

[Bengali:]

Kabir is saying: he found such an ego-less Word, that his doubt [or - "two-ness"] ended – meaning: "two" no longer existed. This type of Guru can be called "purna" [complete]. Even if he is a householder, he is actually not a "householder" [see doha 15 of this section]. -18

[Commentary:]

Kabir, when via the Kriya of Atma-Rama Guru one

attained Omnipresence Kutastha Brahman, then all doubt [or - "two-ness"] ended. One became the Complete Brahman Atman Itself – meaning: in all is Brahman and in all is the Self. He became liberated while alive. Even though He resides in a house, He is not a "householder," because all is Brahman. -18

kabir jhunte guru ki pacchuko, tajat na kije baar
doar na paoe shabdaka, bharme bhao jaldhar -19

[Bengali:]

Kabir is saying: do not wait to leave the company of a false guru. If you do not do so [leave], you will not find the door to the Omkar Sound, and you will fall in the net of delusion and remain in the world-ocean. -19

[Commentary:]

Kabir, the Guru is the Self. When mind goes in other directions, that guru is false. Do not tarry leaving his company. Unless you leave that guru, you will not find the door to the Sound, and, deluded by the net of maya, will remain in the world-ocean. -19

LIKHTE SAT GURU KA ANGSHA

On the Description of Satguru

**kabir satguru sam koi sang nahi, sadhu sam nahi jati
hari samane nahi hita koi, hari jan sam nahi panti -1**

[Bengali:]

Kabir is saying: there is no company like the company of Satguru, and there is no class/race equal to that of the sadhu, and there is no savior like Hari [God]. And there is no society like [one comprising of] those who always abide in Hari. -1

[Commentary:]

Kabir, there is no company equal to that of Atma-Rama Guru. There is no class equal to that of one who does the Kriya of that very Atman. That Hari, Who has finished everything in the par avastha of Kriya, because He makes everything One in the par avastha of Kriya, there is absolutely no savior comparable to Him. There is no level comparable to the level of these types of people. -1

**kabir sad guru ki mahima anant hay, anant kiya
upakar lochana ananta, udhariya dekhab nehar -2**

[Bengali:]

Kabir is saying: there is no end to the glory of Satguru; it cannot be described. Jivas receive endless beneficence from

43

Him. The Eye is Infinite, verily, and via that supernatural Eye, He rescues – meaning: He reveals Brahman within a short time. -2

[Commentary:]

Kabir, as Atma-Rama Guru is all-pervading, His glory is endless. Infinite types of beneficence – meaning supernatural work – go on. Infinite kinds of vision – supernatural – which were not there previously – all of those are fully manifesting. One is seeing the Infinite Depth of all things in just one blink of an eye. -2

kabir sab jag bharmat iyon phire, jayon jangal ka rojh sadguru se shodhi bhei, paya hari ka khonj -3

[Bengali:]

Kabir is saying: the whole world is going about like [those] who do not know the jungles' "rojha" - meaning medicinal herbs and such – yet they are roaming the jungles in search of medicine. When one is cured by Satguru – meaning: when one will Know, then one will find Hari. -3

[Commentary:]

Kabir, the inner self guru was deluded and going about in all mobile things. Like one who does not know the medicinal herbs of jungles, and like the way he puts his hand in all plants and trees and tries to prepare some guessed-at medicine from the juices of every plant and tree, verily in that same way, everyone in the world is roaming about filled with delusion. Omkar – which is the body itself – Kutastha Brahman which is within That He is Truth. All else is totally false. It is He Who is the One and Only Guru. Through Him, all things have become resolved – meaning: because of becoming One in the par avastha of Kriya, no separate objects remained. Thus, because of becoming Pure and extremely Immaculate, all things were received [or – attained]. The One by Whom all became One, His location meaning Stillness – was found. -3

kabir aati paai thir bhayo, sadguru dinha dheer manik heera banijiya, maan sarobar teer -4

[Bengali:]

Kabir is saying: I became Still upon finding the place of Stillness, which Satguru showed me. And I became a trader of jewels and diamonds and found the shores of Manas Sarovar. - 4

[Commentary:]

Kabir, the inner self guru attained this par avastha of Kriya and became Still – meaning: upon abiding in Kutastha Brahman, via Kriya one continued to be Still in Para-Buddhi. The Jewel-Light is Kutastha Himself. And Krishnachandra [literally - "dark moon"] is Diamond. Offering Kriya in this way, gradually increase your own Knowing. "Byapar" [trade] – in the Lake of Mind – meaning: if one abides at all times in Brahman, the mind remains ever satisfied. Staying by this Lake and by giving Kriya, one is himself fulfilled and Still. And one is constantly engrossed in this kind of trade. -4

kabir thita paai man thira bhaya, sadguru kari sahaay ananta katha jeeo ucharai, hridaya ramita raay -5

[Bengali:]

Kabir is saying: the restless mind has found Stillness and has become Still, but this happened by Satguru's help only, and this jiva is now going on uttering words of Infinity because he has found the One Who delights the heart. -5

[Commentary:]

Kabir, one found the Stillness of the Self and his mind's restlessness became Still. With the help of Atman Satguru – meaning: upon abiding always with Atman, this jiva became Shiva Himself and is going on speaking words of Infinity. Through the experiential element, [one found] the One Who is presiding in the heart and delighting about in all things as Brahman. -5

kabir chetan chauki baithi koi, satguru dinhu dheer
nirbhay hoye nihshanka bhajo, keval kahe kabir -6

[Bengali:]

Kabir is saying: sit on the cot of Chaitanya [Spirit or Supreme Consciousness] and meditate without fear upon the stable thing that Satguru has given. Kabir is speaking about kevala kumbhak. -6

[Commentary:]

Kabir, abiding in the Atma-Rama Guru Kutastha, sitting settled on the cot that is in the head, being automatically fearless in the place where That which has been received via Kriya is – when there are two, then only there is fear – [as] Oneness has happened, then there is no fear – there is no fear when [all] has become One. In this way, without any feeling of trepidation, constantly meditate. "Kevala" - abiding in Atma-Rama with kumbhak – Kabir is saying this.

kabir bahe bahane jaat the, lok bed ki saath beech
hi satguru mili gaye, deepak dinho haath -7

[Bengali:]

Kabir is saying: with customs and scriptures, one was being ever carried away by the current. Just at this time, one found Satguru, and in the midst of this He bestowed a Lamp to hold in the hand – meaning: one found out all things upon receiving the Light of the Lamp. -7

[Commentary:]

Kabir, Atma-Rama is Guru. Mind, because of being in other directions, was being taken away by the current of maya, and one was being carried away by the waves in the current. While being carried away by the waves of custom and un-scriptural [ways], one found Satguru Himself in the sushumna. That Lamp in my hand which I received – meaning: then, upon having the Lamp, all unseen things went on to be visible and revealed. -7

kabir deepak dinha labhabi, baati dai aghat poora
kiaoe saha na, bahurina cheri ahat -8

[Bengali:]

Kabir is saying: the Lamp was given, but because there was no wick in the container, it was not successful. When the Beloved came and made Full Realization, then one saw a great deal of Light, but after that one could not see [It again]. One tried again and again but nothing happened. -8

[Commentary:]

Kabir, Atma-Rama Guru illuminated with the Revelatory Light. But the wick of that Lamp is not in the container – meaning: when the all-pervading sushumna becomes fully realized, then there is Light and more Light. I could not find that kind of Light at any other time, and I could not even find Its whereabouts. -8

kabir sadguru nidhi milaiya, sadguru sahu sudheer
nip je me sajhi ghane, bantan haar kabir -9

[Bengali:]

Kabir is saying: the One Who is Satguru has revealed the Treasure of Kutastha. It is Satguru Who is verily "mahajan" [great being], and it is He Who is Supremely Intelligent. Kabir is handing out the aforementioned Treasure to all of its shareholders. -9

[Commentary:]

Kabir, Satguru Atman has revealed the Treasure of Paramatman Kutastha. That Atman is Itself the Kutastha "mahajan," and His Beautiful Stillness is wanted by many. The Atma-Rama Guru Kabir is handing out that Treasure (Kutastha). -9

kabir sat ham so rijhikei, ek kaha parsang
badar barisha prem ka, bhiji gaya sab ang -10

[Bengali:]

Kabir is saying: the One Who is Truth made me fulfilled, and spoke about being united as well. From this, such a Love came forth that my whole body became soaked in the Rainwater of that Love. -10

[Commentary:]

Kabir, as much as I became attracted and attached to Atma-Rama Guru, He became attracted and attached to me just as much. Then He also became attracted and attached with me. Then He became One and "Sohang Brahman." With mind in this kind of state of certainty, the Clouds of Love rained intensely, and because of Brahman being in all things, one attained Satisfaction – meaning: everything verily became One Brahman. -10

kabir chaupar mari chauhate, sari kiya sharir
sad guru dnao bataiye, khele das kabir -11

[Bengali:]

Kabir is saying: with power all around the body, one went on to play the dice-board game. Satguru is advising the throws and moves, and Kabir is playing. -11

[Commentary:]

Kabir, Atma-Rama Guru, via Omkar Kriya, is taking vayu from all sides and moving the selves in all bodies, upon which, He is coaching the throws and moves of the dice-board game in the par avastha of Kriya. Atma-Rama Kabir then went on playing. -11

kabir sad guru ke sad ke kiya, dil aapneka saach
kalyug humse ladi pada, mohakm mera baach -12

[Bengali:]

Kabir is saying: the One Who is Satguru can do good if mind and life are spontaneously [automatically] surrendered to Him. But how will this be possible? Kali Yuga is battling with me: "this is mine," "that place is mine," "this is my directive," "this is what I'm saying and you must listen" – because of these things, it does not happen. -12

[Commentary:]

Kabir, Atma-Rama Guru himself sacrificed Himself in Paramatman – meaning: this experience went on happening: that one was truly Still in the heart. But Kali Yuga began to fight with me. "Kali"* - meaning sin, which happens when mind goes in other directions. "Yuga" - (two = rajo and tamo gunas – ida and pingala). Then one went on to say, "The tree that has grown at my border/limit – I am its rightful inheritor, and the fruits of this tree are mine." -12

[*Translator's note: The word "Kali" in "Kali Yuga" does NOT refer in any way whatsoever to the beneficent Goddess Kali. Her name is actually pronounced "Kaali" with a long "a" [like "ah"] sound but spelled with Western alphabets the same as "Kali" in "Kali Yuga" [which is pronounced with a short "a"].]

kabir satguru sacha sudheeya, shabd jo baha ek
laagat hi bhayi meti gayi, para kaleje chek -13

[Bengali:]

Kabir is saying: within the Perfect Melody that is Satguru, there is an Omkar Sound. With this only [verily], all fear ended and prana also became Still. -13

[Commentary:]

Kabir, Atma-Rama Guru has a perceivable Sound (the Unstruck Sound Omkar Resonance). When that Sound became continuous, immediately the fear of death ended, because as long as the Omkar Sound is heard, vayu is Still for that long. This is spontaneously and automatically experienced by oneself. If vayu is Still, then who can die? It is when vayu goes out that there is death. Thus, the "dhak-dhak" [beating sound] of the heart ended, meaning: became Still (known via the teachings of Guru). -13

kabir sadguru shabd kaman leyi, bahan lage teer
ek jo vaha preeti kari, bedha sakal sharir -14

[Bengali:]

Kabir is saying: Satguru took up the bow of Shabda and went on shooting arrows – meaning: one went on doing the Kriya of pranayam and such. As soon as He shot forth an arrow filled with devotion – it is then that the entire body was pierced. -14

[Commentary:]

Kabir, Atma-Rama Guru took up the bow of Shabda and went on shooting arrows – meaning: one went on doing Kriya. As soon as the arrow was shot with Love, then it entered the whole body – meaning: vayu entered the entire body. Then, one can take the Still vayu anywhere in the body. -14

kabir sad guru mara baan bhari, dhari koi sudhee
muthi anga ughare lagiya, gaya dubhasha phuti -15

[Bengali:]

Kabir is saying: Satguru filled the arrow and shot it. With full concentration it took hold in the "muti" [see commentary below] and struck one's bare body and the dual experience disappeared. -15

[Commentary:]

Kabir, Atma-Rama Guru went on doing the Kriya of sushumna. Catching "sudhu muti" - meaning: devoid of ida and pingala, the form/body began to rise. All forms/bodies – down to the door of the anus – began to rise and the dual types of thought were destroyed – meaning: one went beyond "yes" and "no" and became Still in Para Buddhi. -15

kabir haase na bole unmani, chanchal mayla maree
kahe kabir antar bedha, sadguru ka hatiyari -16

[Bengali:]

Kabir is saying: one does not have any desire to talk after having received the gem of Hamsa. Then all mobile things stop, because Satguru's weapon has penetrated all and made One. This is what Kabir is saying. -16

[Commentary:]

Kabir, with Atma-Rama Guru and meditation on the

"gem" – meaning: abiding in Kutastha – one no longer speaks, because, due to abiding in Kutastha, mind does not go elsewhere. When the stains of mind going in other directions stopped automatically, then the Stillness Brahman-Knowledge entered all – all of which became cut up by Atma-Rama Guru's weapon, and cutting oneself also, became One. -16

kabir gunga hua baura, bahira hua kaan
paonthete pangula hua, satguru mara baan -17

[Bengali:]

Kabir is saying: Satguru has shot such an arrow that one has no desire to speak – like a mad person. There is the power to hear, yet I cannot hear anything at all. There are legs, but like a lame person, there is no desire to walk. -17

[Commentary:]

Kabir, OM Tat Sat is Brahman Itself. Satguru has shot such a Kriyaarrow that upon going on doing Kriya, in the par avastha of Kriya one has no desire whatsoever to talk. And that kind of "eyes pulled" [or – squinted] way of looking that mad persons have – like that, there is no desire at all to look at anything either. He has made me like an insane person. One can hear everything, yet like one deaf, is not hearing anything at all. Even though there are legs and feet, one does not have any desire to lift one's legs and feet – like a lame person. -17

kabir guru mera shooruan, bedha sakal sarir baan
dubhasha chuti gaya, keyon jeeye das kabir -18

[Bengali:]

Kabir is saying: the One Who is my Guru is a warrior. He has pierced my whole body with His arrow. It is because of this that the feeling of two-ness has flown away. Now how is servant Kabir supposed to keep living? -18

[Commentary:]

Atma-Rama Guru, like a warrior, has shot an arrow. The entire body has been pierced – meaning: great warriors can kill several hundred with one arrow. It is when one dies that there is Stillness. Via that kind of Kriya, vayu has entered every nerve in my body and everything has become Still. Upon becoming Still, movement on the two sides – meaning sin and virtue, pleasure and pain etc. - have left. Now how can Kabir the self [person] keep living? -18

kabir satguru sancha shoorian, nakh shikh mara
pur bahar dhaoan dishy, bhitar chakna chur -19

[Bengali:]

Kabir is saying: Satguru is verily the Perfect Warrior. He has struck everything from head to toe. Because of this, although it looks like things are going on on the outside, inside everything is pulverized/destroyed – meaning: there is Stillness. -19

[Commentary:]

Kabir, Atma-Rama Guru is truly the Warrior, not "warrior" by name – by acts. He has struck arrow[s] completely from head to toe – meaning: everything has verily become Still (in the sushumna). Movement is seen on the outside – meaning there is motion on the outside, but within is Stillness. Within, one has no power to do anything at all – meaning: one has merged with the Particle of Brahman and been totally crushed/destroyed. -19

kabir satguru mara baan bhari, tuti gayi sab jeb
kahi asha kahi apada, kahi tasbi kahi kiteb -20

[Bengali:]

Kabir is saying: Satguru has struck His arrow. Just with

that everything has been destroyed. But before this, one used to sometimes hope, sometimes do some things and become surrounded by trouble; sometimes one chanted with rosary, or sometimes one would read the shastras [scriptures] and, not understanding their true meanings, doubts and confusion would form. -20

[Commentary:]

Kabir, via Kriya, Atma-Rama Guru has stopped the moving mind from all of the places [it would go]. Before, it used to hope for something from some place, or putting too much mind in something, one would become filled with [or – surrounded by] trouble. Sometimes one chanted with rosary. Sometimes one would become excited by some book and then be filled with doubt. I used to think that I would merge with the Lotus Feet of the Lord by chanting with rosary, and I used to also think that every confusion would be cleared by reading books and such, but neither of the two things were attained by doing those things. Now, upon doing Kriya, I have attained the par avastha of Kriya. -20

kabir satguru mara gyan kari, shabda surange baan
mera maya phiri jiue, to haath na gahi kaman -21

[Bengali:]

Kabir is saying: Ascertaining with surety the place from where Omkar Sound comes, Satguru struck His arrow there. By this, He killed me – meaning: He destroyed the "I am such and such" idea. But if that again lives, then I will not take up the bow again. -21

[Commentary:]

Kabir, knowing the certainty of Atma-Rama Guru, I went on doing Kriya. If that which I strike with my arrow, while making Sound within, continues to live – meaning: if one does not attain Immortality – then I will never take up the bow of the body again. -21

kabir satguru mara baan, nirakhi nirakhi nij thaor
ram akhilme rami raha, chet nahi aowe aur -22

[Bengali:]

Kabir is saying: Satguru is taking aim on the Self and shooting arrows profusely. And when He sees that the Self is delighting about in all, then nothing at all is coming to the chitta. -22

[Commentary:]

Kabir, in the par avastha of Kriya, one is stringing up arrow after arrow in the Still vayu in sushumna, and aiming and shooting at Brahman. Then all became Brahman; nothing else was in the chitta. -22

kabir satguru wahi preeti kari, rahi katari tuti
aysi ani nasali, taysi chali muti -23

[Bengali:]

Kabir is saying: the cutting weapon used to get into that which Satguru has Loved became broken up. As much Stillness there was in the Thing, one's hold on the Post was that much. -23

[Commentary:]

Kabir, Atma-Rama is Guru. When one became merged in that same Brahman, one did not see anything but Brahman. And the cutting weapon to attain Stillness – in-breath and out-breath – broke. In the way that one became Still upon entering the Thing, in that same way was there Stillness-hold on the Post. -23

kabir man barai urume, ei jag ko byabahar das garibi band gi, satguru ko upakar -24

[Bengali:]

Kabir is saying: respect, honor, self-praise, all these are more or less the ways of the world. And gentleness, calmness and things which are for everyone's good – meaning those things by which everyone is able to take up each one's own dharma – the effort for this – this is verily the beneficence of Satguru. -24

[Commentary:]

Kabir, the way of the world is about doing things that bring respect from people, and about talking to people with the feeling, "I am great." But being everyone's servant – meaning: being small to everyone else and treating everyone with honor and living by the ways of Truth – which is Kutastha – one should do all work in this way – meaning: one should always try do that by which everyone receives Kriya. -24

kabir dilhi maho didar hay, bad bake samsar satguru shabda kam sakla, jise woar hi paar -25

[Bengali:]

Kabir is saying: everything is actually inside Mind, but the people of the world are just uselessly wasting themselves by babbling on and on. When one went on to hear Omkar Sound via Satguru, then one went on to see this side, that side – everything. -25

[Commentary:]

Kabir, with Atma-Rama Guru, Kutastha Himself is in the Mind, but people are just going about wasting themselves by arguing. Going on doing the sound of Kriya, upon abiding in Brahman, one went on seeing this side and that side –

meaning: that which was withheld [from knowing] came about. -25

kabir jo dishe soi binushe, nam dhara so jay kahe
kabir soi tattva gaho, jo sadguru dei batay -26

[Bengali:]

Kabir is saying: everything visible that you see – all of that is subject to destruction. Whatever you hold by name, that will go away – meaning: that which can be materialized has its end. Kabir is saying: get hold of that Substance, that which Satguru has let one know. -26

[Commentary:]

Kabir, all visible things that you are seeing are all subject to destruction. What you can name will go away. Atma-Rama Guru is saying: take hold of that Substance – meaning Kutastha Brahman, which Satguru has let one know. -26

kabir kudrat payi khabar so, sadguru dayi batay
bhaur bilamava kaulme, ab kayse udi jaay -27

[Bengali:]

Kabir is saying: one received news of such a Shakti, which Satguru is letting one know, that it is just like when a bee goes to drink the nectar from a lotus, enters the lotus and becomes intoxicated with drinking nectar – here the jewel of the day [sun] has gone down, the mouth of the lotus has closed up. Thus the way for the bee to fly away has been closed off. In that same way, upon receiving news of this Shakti, mind remained stuck in That. How can it fly away after this? -27

[Commentary:]

Kabir, Atma-Rama is Guru. Keeping sight on the experiential Shakti-Substance – that which Satguru is letting one know – by this, the bee-like mind became stuck in Kulakundalini. Now how can it fly away? -27

kabir ram nam charo nahi, sadguru shikh deyi
avinashi so parash kari, atma amar bhayi -28

[Bengali:]

Kabir is saying: do not ever let go of "Ram-nam" [the name of Lord Rama], which Satguru has taught [you]. Immediately upon touching the Indestructible, the self becomes Immortal. -28

[Commentary:]

Kabir, Atma-Rama Guru is He Who is delighting about in all things natural and supernatural. In the natural, "Rama" is a name only. The essence of the supernatural is Rama – the same Rama Who speaks all supernatural things, because of Him – that Ram-nam is the name in this Ram-nam; [this Ram-nam] does not say anything at all. Thus, everything can be known or heard by the supernatural Ram-nam – meaning Kriya. I will never let go of that – meaning: I will always do Kriya, which Satguru has taught me. Upon continuously doing that Kriya and abiding in the par avastha of Kriya, "avinashi" - meaning: the moving mind, upon touching Stillness, is no more. It has become Brahman Itself. That moving self, merging with the Supreme Self, has become Immortal. -28

kabir chaushati diya jo e kari, chaudaha chanda maahi
tehi ghar kaysa chanda, johi ghar sadguru naahi -29

[Bengali:]

Kabir is saying: I gathered up sixty-four lights, and fourteen moons also were there, but regardless of even this much light, how can the house that does not have Satguru be illuminated? -29

[Commentary:]

Kabir, Atma-Rama Guru is saying: the light that is coming forth from sixty-four nadis going in eight directions – that, in the fourteen worlds within this body, is residing as the moon in the skull. That kind of light is such – meaning: although it is there, there is no revelation. The house that is only of the natural – meaning: one has not become Atma-Rama Brahman in the body (all is Brahman). If one does not become so, all things are not known – meaning: regardless of the appropriate light being there, there is darkness. -29

kabir koti ek chanda ugahi, suraj koti hajaar kahe
kabir sadguru bina, dishai ghor andhaar -30

[Bengali:]

Kabir is saying: millions of moons have risen and a thousand-million suns have risen. Kabir is saying: without Satguru, all ten directions are dark, regardless of all this light. - 30

[Commentary:]

Kabir, Atma-Rama is Guru. In Yonimudra in the Kutastha, millions and millions of suns rise and millions and millions of moons rise. One cannot see that at all without the Grace of Satguru; one only sees dense darkness. -30

kabir satguru mohi neoa jeeya, dinhu su amar bol
sheetal chaya saghan phal, hangsa kar hi kalol -31

[Bengali:]

Kabir is saying: Satguru saved me through a beautiful and immortal saying, and by that, the ripe fruit of a cool shade was gained. The One Who is Hangsa went on shouting ecstatically. -31

[Commentary:]

Kabir, Atma-Rama Guru saved me, and bestowed me with a beautiful and immortal Sound, where there is shade like that which is produced by a wonderfully cooling cloud, and all experiential fruits were gained. And "Hangsa" - meaning Atma-Rama – is ecstatically shouting and is in Bliss (known via the teachings of Guru). -31

kabir satguru sat kabir hay, sankat pare huzur
chuka seova bandegi, kiya chaakree dur -32

[Bengali:]

Kabir is saying: Satguru Himself is Kabir, as He has made and kept one inaccessible to all danger. And if one does not do service – meaning: if one does not do sadhana, then He will remove one from the job. -32

[Commentary:]

Kabir, Atma-Rama Guru is truly Kabir, as He has kept one, via Kriya, away from all trouble. As long as one does not do Kriya, then He distances one from the Bliss that comes from doing the job of Kriya. -32

kabir chit chokkhe man ujle, dayavanta gambhir
sei dhoke bichale naahi, jehi satguru mile kabir -33

[Bengali:]

Kabir is saying: when mind becomes pure and illuminated, one becomes compassionate and profoundly calm. Then one is not disturbed by anything at all – one who has found Satguru Kabir. -33

[Commentary:]

Kabir, the Mind of Atma-Rama Guru is incredibly Pure and Illuminated. Merciful, "gambhir" - meaning: the Subtle

Self-Revealed Being, ready to do good for all – meaning: ready to give Kriya. Upon entering Subtle Brahman, one is not disturbed by even a thousand temptations/distractions – he who has attained the Certainty of Brahman-Knowledge and has Satguru Kabir. -33

**kabir gyan samagam prem sukh, daya bhakti biswas
satguru mili ek bhaya, rahi na duji aash -34**

[Bengali:]

Kabir is saying: when Knowledge comes together, there is the Bliss of Love. There is compassion, devotion, faith. Then, upon merging and becoming one with Satguru, absolutely no want of any kind remained. -34

[Commentary:]

Kabir, when there is the attainment of Brahman for Atma-Rama Guru – becoming like That, becoming Bliss Itself – just like that, all becomes Bliss Itself. Effort [is made] for this, and there is absolutely nothing other than Brahman. If I lose everything, may this Brahman never leave, because through the experiential thing one has complete faith, and one has gone into Atma-Rama Guru and become One. This is also being experienced. But when I am not, it is then that all has become Brahman. When everything has become Brahman, then where is want? Of what? And who is even there to want? -34

**kabir satguru parash ko shila, dekha tattva bichari
ahi paroshini le chali, diya diya so bari -35**

[Bengali:]

Kabir is saying: Satguru is verily the Touchstone. You can investigate the truth of this and see. Just like this, He goes about touching [souls], like a lamp lights another lamp. -35

[Commentary:]

Kabir, Atma-Rama is Guru. Brahman as Satguru is the Touchstone, which has no color. But when I touched Brahman, there was gold-like Brilliance − meaning: the light of the five elements became revealed via Brahman. Others nearby who took initiation also became Illuminated, as if a lamp lit another lamp. -35

kabir satguru gami jo kahi diya, bhed diya aur
thaay surati koyalke antarich, niradhar pad paay -36

[Bengali:]

Kabir is saying: That which Satguru has known and spoken, along with [making one know] the meaning, He has made one penetrate It as well. One attains the Support-less Substance in the Whole Lotus − meaning: in Sahasrar. -36

[Commentary:]

Kabir, that Brahman-Substance which is received via Atma-Rama Guru − He has spoken about That, and He has also said how to penetrate the Particle of Brahman. In Yonimudra, within the Vision of Kutastha, I received the Support-less Substance of the Supreme Space. -36

kabir jeeb aksham bahu kuteel hay, koi nahi gati
aiye tako aigun meti kay, satguru hangsa banaye -37

[Bengali:]

Kabir is saying: the jiva is incapable and filled with twisted thinking; nothing actually is understood by him. Satguru resolves the errors of such people and makes them Hangsa. -37

[Commentary:]

Kabir, the jiva within the body of a human being is

incapable and thinks only in wrong directions in twisted ways, and it also does not trust anyone at all. Making satsang, He has taken this type of jiva and made it Hangsa by keeping the self in the Self. -37

kabir satguru bade sarak hay, parakhe kharao
khot bhao sagarte kadike, rakhe aapne ot -38

[Bengali:]

Kabir is saying: Satguru is the Big Examiner. Upon analyzing one's faults and virtues, He snatches one from the world-ocean and keeps one in the ashram of the Self. -38

[Commentary:]

Kabir, Atma-Rama Guru is the Big Examiner. He checks one's good and bad. The person who, with a simple "antahkaran" [mind in all its aspects], meditates and practices – He takes that person from "bhavasagar" [worldocean] ("bhava" = that which is happening), whose happening is endless = desire – He took [the jiva] out of that and put it in the par avastha of Kriya, in the direction of the Self – meaning: put it in the sushumna. -38

kabir satguru shabda jahaj hay, koi koi paoe bhed
samudra bund ekai bhaya, kako karo nikhed -39

[Bengali:]

Kabir is saying: Satguru is the ship of the Omkar Sound; a few come to know this. When the Ocean and the drop ["bindu" - also means "point"] have become One, who then can restrict such a being? -39

[Commentary:]

Kabir, a few come to find out about riding Atma-Rama Guru's ship of the Sound of Kriya – meaning: upon doing

Kriya and abiding in the par avastha of Kriya – that Sound from Silence, riding which, the entire ocean of samsara enters the One Bindu – the Particle of Brahman – and becomes One. If there is Oneness, then who restricts whom? -39

**kabir satguru mahal banaiya, gyan gilaoa dinha
duri dekhan ke kaarane, shabd jharoka kinha -40**

[Bengali:]

Kabir is saying: Satguru has built a chamber and is feeding Knowledge. And, in order to be able to see things afar, He has purchased a window to listen to the Omkar Sound. -40

[Commentary:]

Kabir, Atma-Rama Guru has made a chamber of Knowledge. That chamber is the head. Rising into that, objects far away can be seen. And He has made a window of Shabda, by which unheard sounds can be heard. -40

**kabir satguru bachan maane nahi, apni samjhe nahi
kahe kabir kya kijiye, kiyo bitha jeeo maahi -41**

[Bengali:]

Kabir is saying: the type of people that do not listen to the teachings of Satguru do not know the Self. Kabir is saying: what are these people doing, wasting the human lives that they have taken up? -41

[Commentary:]

Kabir, Atma-Rama Guru is One Who has gone to Brahman. One does not listen to His words, and, not having the intellect in the Self, one does not understand [anything] either. For what reason has God created these types of people to do sadhana? His life is meaningless like other jivas. -41

kabir satguru bapura kya kare, jo shikh hi mohaay
chuk koti yatan pramodhiye, bansh bajaoe phook -42

[Bengali:]

Kabir is saying: what more can poor Satguru do, if there is wrongness in the mind of the disciple? Even after explaining with great care millions of times, there will be no understanding. It will be like blowing into an empty bamboo, [what will sound is only whatever the bamboo can do]. -42

[Commentary:]

Kabir, what can the Brahman-knowing Atma-Rama Guru do if there is the wrongness of incapability in the disciple? [It does not matter if] millions of careful explanations are given, whatever kind of bamboo he is, only that kind of flute will play. No other kind of holy fragrance will come out – meaning: the jiva is putting out inhales and exhales only, but no other holy fragrance is coming out at all. -42

kabir satguru mila to kya bhaya, jo man pariya bhol
paash beena dhanka para, kya kare baapura chol -43

[Bengali:]

Kabir is saying: what good would it do for someone of a dissipated mind to even have found Satguru? The musical instrument veena [Indian lute] is lying besides one, covered up. What fault is of that poor cover? -43

[Commentary:]

Kabir, what good is it even if one receives a Kriyanvita guru if the mind remains in an ignorant state? The musical instrument veena is close by oneself, covered up. If one does not play it, is it the fault of the cover? -43

kabir satguru ko sara nahi, shabda na bedha
ang kora rahi gya sidhra, shada telke sang -44

[Bengali:]

Kabir is saying: what Satguru has said has not been realized, for this reason the Omkar Sound did not enter the body either. One remained as one was. Regardless of being with oil, one did not get stained and remained white. -44

[Commentary:]

Kabir, you did not do what the Kriyavan person said. The type of sound he said to make – that also did not enter into your body. You remained unbleached and straight. Even while staying with oil, the white remained white – meaning: the cooking [or – congealing] did not happen. -44

LIKHTE SUMIRAN KA ANG

On Doing Remembrance

kabir dandabat gobind guru, abajana bando soye
pahile bhaye parnam tehi, mnojo aage hoye -1

[Bengali:]

Kabir is saying: one no longer prostrates on the floor to, nor does one sing the praises of Govinda Guru any more. One used to prostrate to Him before, but now, via a certain act, one has prostrated and has become "mnoja" (a particular state known through the teachings of Guru) and is remaining as such. -1

[Commentary:]

Kabir, Atma-Rama is Guru. One no longer bows to Guru Who is Govinda Himself, because one has automatically done pranam [reverent bow] via Omkar Kriya and is constantly in Bliss. -1

kabir gyan kathe baki baki mare, kaahe kare upadhi
satguru hamse eo kaha, sumiran kar samadhi -2

[Bengali:]

Kabir is saying: people are wasting their lives babbling on about spiritual knowledge for nothing but honor and title. But Satguru has told me this: do samadhi of remembrance ("smaran" [remembrance] – known through the teachings of

Guru). It is not what is ordinarily known as "remembrance." It requires sadhana. -2

[Commentary:]

Kabir, people are babbling and blathering on about spiritual knowledge and wasting their lives. The reason: one takes on a title to add to one's position in society. Satguru has told me such: constantly practice remembrance in/on the Self. Samadhi will come about automatically. -2

kabir nij sukh ram hay, duja dukh apar mansa
bacha karmana, kabir sumiran saar -3

[Bengali:]

Kabir is saying: Rama is one's happiness. And one who thinks of "two" has endless sorrow. Kabir is saying that remembrance is the essence of all that can be done by mind, speech and action. -3

[Commentary:]

Kabir, Atma-Rama Guru is saying: the happiness that one feels is itself Rama, verily – meaning: in the par avastha of Kriya – meaning: in samadhi there is only the happiness of the Self. In any other state there is endless sorrow. Doing Kriya via mind and talking about Kriya and all actions and work are all because of Atma-Rama only. Abiding constantly in the Self is called "smaran" [remembrance]. This remembrance is verily the One Essential Thing in this world. -3

kabir sumiran saar hay, aur sakal janjal adi
ant sabh modhiya, duja dekha kal -4

[Bengali:]

Kabir is saying: remembrance is actually all [or: that which is the Essence; that which is of value]; everything else is garbage. Within all of the beginning and the end one saw second [type of] time. -4

[Commentary:]

Kabir, Atma-Rama is saying that the par avastha of Kriya is the Real Thing; everything else is unreal [or: worthless]. [Via] the remembrance by which all from beginning to end have been purified – one saw even more – the time that is the par avastha of Kriya. -4

kabir sumiran kiya tab jaaniye, tan man raha samaay
adi ant madhya ek ras, bhula kabihi na jaay -5

[Bengali:]

Kabir is saying: if you practice remembrance, then you will know that body and mind were [existent], but upon entering in a certain place, one could no longer determine beginning, end, middle – none of that at all. That one "ras" - meaning: one feeling – that feeling cannot ever be forgotten by one who has attained it once. -5

[Commentary:]

Kabir, Atma-Rama is Guru. When one went on to abide in the Self at all times, then when the par avastha of the par avastha of Kriya happened, then one came to know that I was in great Bliss. And that place where body and mind entered, when I was in the par avastha of Kriya – in that I could not determine at all the time of entering, and middle and end. There was a Bliss from beginning to end. This is being felt – that Bliss which is impossible to ever forget. -5

kabir adi ant madhya bhuliya, pachtaoa man maahi
kahe kabir hari sumiran, ohoto kiya naahi -6

[Bengali:]

Kabir is saying: one is in Mind, unaware of beginning, end and middle. Repentance is being felt. Kabir is saying that one has not remembered the Lord. -6

[Commentary:]

Kabir, in that par avastha of Kriya, I was unaware of beginning, end and middle. I was repenting silently that I was not remembering Atma-Rama Guru. -6

**kabir sumiran ghor hi bhala, jo kari jane koye sut
na lagi banwani, sahaje sabh sukh hoye -7**

[Bengali:]

Kabir is saying: one who has done and known – for him even a lesser amount of remembrance is good. To make thread, the things that are needed and difficult effort that is necessary – but to weave with the thread of "sahaja," no particular thing is necessary and there is no struggle. All becomes happiness and remains so. -7

[Commentary:]

Kabir, even a little remembrance of the Self is good for the one who knows how to practice remembrance and is able to do it. Like the way the thread-like mind is bound to thoughts of other things – in that remembrance, that type of thread is not needed. To make thread, it is necessary to have cotton, a spinning wheel and a person to work with them, but this thread needs none of those things at all. In the case of clothes made from the thread of cotton, one gains pleasure from wearing the clothes only. But this thread was born with you. The thing that you weave with that – when that thing comes about, all will be happiness. -7

kabir jioban to thor hi bhala, hari ka sumiran hoye
lak baris ki jeeuna, lekha dhare na koye -8

[Bengali:]

Kabir is saying: it is still good if one lives only a short time while remembering the Lord. Without doing that, there is no credit in living even a hundred thousand years. -8

[Commentary:]

Kabir, it is still good even if one lives only a short time, if one remembers "Hari" (the One Who ends everything). If one lives a hundred thousand years, nobody cares [or: it is completely unimportant]. -8

kabir dukhme sumiran sab kare, sukh me kare na
koye jo sukhme sumiran kare, to kahko dukh hoye -9

[Bengali:]

Kabir is saying: everyone remembers while in pain/sorrow; no one at all remembers while in pleasure. One who remembers while in pleasure – what pain/sorrow can be there for that person? -9

[Commentary:]

Kabir, Atma-Rama is Guru. [People] remember when they have put mind in other directions and are crying "alas, alas!" from the self not being satisfied and in pain, or when, bound by the desires of past lives, they perform actions which result in illness in this life and [experience] the pain of this body, mind and speech, but they do not remember in times of ease, because of laziness. [If] one abandons laziness and abides in the Beautiful Brahman, and while going on remembering, becomes Brahman – when all has become Brahman, then how can it be possible that one goes far away – meaning: has sorrow? -9

kabir sukhme sumiran na kiya, duhkhme kiya jo
yad kahe kabir ta das ki, keon lage phiriyad -10

[Bengali:]

Kabir is saying: one did not remember during times of pleasure. One who has remembered [only] after falling into pain/sorrow – Kabir calls that person a servant and in what manner will his judgment come? -10

[Commentary:]

Kabir, Atma-Rama is Guru. When one is in the state of Pleasure – meaning: when one is in Brahman – if one does not remember the Self at that time, and if one remembers the pleasant state when mind has gone in other directions and has fallen into a painful state, then Atma-Rama [oneself] has become a servant of pain. And in the way that one is engaging in sorrow-breeding things because of putting mind in other directions, in that same way one will of course have to partake in its fruits. If one cries "alas, alas!" in that state of experiencing those fruits, how can that cry be heard? At the time He was Lord, He heard that, yet it is exactly then that he fell to other directions – meaning pain. Thus, as the action is, so is the result. When one does not partake in the fruits, it is then that judgment is without power [or: consequence]. -10

kabir sumiran ki sudhi eyo karo, jayse kaami kaam
kahe kabir phukari kay, khusi hohi tab raam -11

[Bengali:]

Kabir is saying: practice remembrance like the way a lustful person feels towards the object of his lust. Kabir is saying loudly: if that happens, then Rama will be pleased. -11

[Commentary:]

Kabir, Atma-Rama is Guru. Make your remembrance

right, like the way a lustful person, addicted to sexual desire, has sexual intercourse and comes to peace – meaning Kriya. Kabir is loudly saying: Rama, the One Who does "raman" [delights], will be satisfied after Kriya – meaning: one will get Peace in the par avastha of Kriya. -11

kabir sumiran ki sudhi eyo karo, jeo gaagri panihaari bole dole surtime, kahahi kabir bichari -12

[Bengali:]

Kabir is saying: like the way a woman keeps the water pot on the head and walks swinging side to side and talks at the same time, yet the pot on the head stays as it is and does not fall, and her mind is actually on the pot itself – one must do remembrance in this same way. It is this that Kabir has discerned and said. -12

[Commentary:]

Kabir, remember Atma-Rama Guru correctly in that way, like the way the water-woman keeps the pot on her head and goes on talking all the time, moves swinging side to side, yet her mind is on the pot on the head. Upon discerning such, so has Kabir Saheb said. -12

kabir sumiran ki sudhi eyo karo jeo surabhi sutchahi kahahi kabir charachari, surabhi bacchuke pahi -13

[Bengali:]

Kabir is saying: do remembrance in such a way: like the way the mother cow is always looking after the calf, yet she is eating grass and grazing about as well, but her mind is always with the calf. Kabir says, "Keep the mind in this way." -13

[Commentary:]

Kabir, do remembrance of Atma-Rama Guru in such a

way: like the way the mother cow's mind is on her calf. Kabir Saheb is saying: people are seeing that the cow is only eating grass, but her mind is actually on the calf. In that same way, abide in the Self and do all work. -13

kabir sumiran ki sudhi eyo karo, jayse daan kangal
kahani kabir bisari nahi, pal pal lei sabhal -14

[Bengali:]

Kabir is saying: do remembrance in this way: like the destitute person who has had no alms given to him. Kabir says that the destitute person remembers the need to receive alms moment after moment; he never forgets. One must do remembrance in that same way. -14

[Commentary:]

Kabir, do remembrance of Atma-Rama Guru in that way: like the destitute person who has no alms – meaning: like the destitute person who has no money yet wants to eat good things, and that want is so extreme that although he is doing all kinds of things but that craving to eat those good things is constantly on his mind. -14

kabir sumiran man lagai naahi, jagso samita jaay
kahahi kabir shuna sadhuya, taaka kahan upaay -15

[Bengali:]

Kabir is saying: the mind does not at all latch on to remembrance. The mind remains attached to all the visible things of the world. What chance is there for him? -15

[Commentary:]

Kabir, the mind does not latch on to remembrance, yet the mind latches on to the moving things of the world. The one who is meditating – Kabir Saheb is saying to him, "Listen sadhu! That person has no chance." -15

kabir sumiranse man jab lagai, jagso hoye nirash
kayako sukh choti key, jagso hoye udaas -16

[Bengali:]

Kabir is saying: when the mind grabs on to doing remembrance, then the mind becomes disinterested in the world. One lets go of the happinesses of the body and one becomes aloof about the world. -16

[Commentary:]

Kabir, Atma-Rama Guru does remembrance when He is locked in the par avastha of Kriya, when He remains without any desire for moving things. At that time one lets go of the happinesses of the body. He becomes nondesirous of moving things, climbs to the top of the head and remains seated there – meaning the par avastha of Kriya. -16

kabir sumiran man laage naahi, bikhe halahal khaaye
kabir haat kana rahe, kari kari thake upaay -17

[Bengali:]

Kabir is saying: the mind is not attending to doing remembrance. Thinking that there will be happiness, one drinks the poison of worldly things. Kabir says: upon haplessly convulsing with the burning pain of the aforementioned poison, one thinks that he will do, yes he will do [remembrance]. But one does not do, yet one does not find any [other] way out either. -17

[Commentary:]

Kabir, one is not keeping the self in the Self after all, because the mind has become satisfied in the poison of desire.

Although one is haplessly convulsing with the burning pain of the poison of desire, one is still thinking that that is pleasure. Sometimes, after being distressed enough in mind, one becomes zealous and says that he will do Kriya, but that also does not remain; it slips away. Making strenuous effort like this again and again, [eventually] one does not do Kriya at all. And letting go of Kriya, one cannot find any other way out either. -17

**kabir sumiran so man jab laage, gyan ankush de
shish kahehi kabir dole nahi, nischay biswas -18**

[Bengali:]

Kabir is saying: when the mind latches on to remembrance, then the hook/anchor of Knowledge pierces deeply in the head. It is this that Kabir is saying. -18

[Commentary:]

Kabir, the mind will latch on to the remembrance of Atma-Rama Guru at the time when Knowledge – meaning: the hook/anchor of the par avastha of Kriya will be in the head. Then the mind will not be moving – meaning: it will be Still. When that happens, there will be faith with certainty. -18

**kabir sumiran soti sab bhala, ghar ban sab hi thaon
kahe kabir sumiran bina, neha bhal ban nahi gaon -19**

[Bengali:]

Kabir is saying: with remembrance, all is good; it is the same in the house or in the jungle. Kabir says, "Without remembrance, neither jungle nor village – nothing at all is good." -19

[Commentary:]

Kabir, if one remains in the par avastha of Kriya, all is

good, in the house, jungle – everywhere. Kabir Saheb is saying: without the par avastha of Kriya, it is not good in either of the two, village or jungle. -19

kabir sumiran so siddhi hot hay, sumiran so riddhi hoye sumiran sai mile, kari dekh sab koye -20

[Bengali:]

Kabir is saying: doing remembrance, one gets "siddhis." One attains "riddhis" as well – "riddhi" – the eight siddhis [extra-rational powers]. One who does remembrance gets the Lord as well. Do this everyone, and see. -20

[Commentary:]

Kabir, from continuously abiding in Atman, when Atman merges with Paramatman all things become One, and this is what "siddhi" is. When every single thing becomes One, then all wealth has become yours. When every single thing is yours, you are in everything and everything is in you, then You are Lord – meaning: Brahman Itself is Lord. Whatever you are doing is Brahman. You are not doing anything at all. Do Kriya, and see this clearly with your eyes [or: with the Eye]. -20

kabir sumiran so sukh hot hay, sumiran so dukh jaay kahe kabir sumiran kiye, sai maah samaay -21

[Bengali:]

Kabir is saying: doing remembrance brings happiness and sorrow goes away. Kabir says, "One can even enter into the Lord." -21

[Commentary:]

Kabir, if one does Kriya, the par avastha of Kriya happens. That Bliss is known in the par avastha of the par avastha of Kriya. In the par avastha of Kriya, mind does not go in other directions and pain/sorrow is not there. Kabir Saheb is saying: if one does Kriya all the time, then the self can enter the Particle of Brahman in the par avastha of Kriya. -21

kabir sumiran so sangshay mete, sumiran so mete shog kahe kabir sumiran kiye, rahe na eko rog -22

[Bengali:]

Kabir is saying: doing remembrance casts away doubt/trepidation. Doing remembrance casts away grief. Kabir says, "If one does remembrance, no illness even remains." -22

[Commentary:]

Kabir, upon doing Kriya and abiding in the par avastha of Kriya, a self-confident certainty is known and therefore no doubt/trepidation remains. And no kind of grief remains either, and no kind of illness remains as well. -22

kabir sumiran maahi ram ke, dhil na kijiye man kahe kabir chan ek mo, binashi jaayega tan -23

[Bengali:]

Kabir is saying: do not be lazy in doing remembrance of Rama, because at any moment this body can be destroyed. Kabir is saying this. -23

[Commentary:]

Kabir, do not be lazy in doing Kriya, because within a flash of time this body will be destroyed. -23

kabir sumiran kare so shanta jan, ahirnishi apne jaagi kahe kabir sumiran tyaje,tako bada abhagi -24

[Bengali:]

Kabir is saying: it is the peaceful people who are staying

awake day and night doing remembrance. Kabir says, "The person who abandons remembrance is truly unfortunate." -24

[Commentary:]

Kabir, peaceful people are staying awake day and night and practicing Kriya. One who did not do that is very unfortunate. -24

kabir sumiran sama kuch hay nahi, yog yagya brat daan sumiran sam teerath nahi, sumiran sama nahi gyan -25

[Bengali:]

Kabir is saying: whether yoga, yajna, charity, vows – there is nothing comparable to remembrance. And there is no pilgrimage that is comparable to remembrance either; not even knowledge is comparable to remembrance. -25

[Commentary:]

Kabir, there is no thing on this Earth comparable to Kriya. Yoga, yajna, vows, charity – whatever types of things such as these that exist – Kriya is greater than all. Kriya is greater even than pilgrimages and knowledge as well. -25

kabir jap tap sanjam sadhan, sab sumiran ko maahi kahe kabir bichari kai, sumiran sam kuch naahi -26

[Bengali:]

Kabir is saying: japa, penances, self-control, sadhana – all these are inside remembrance itself. Upon discerning, Kabir is saying: there is absolutely nothing comparable to remembrance. -26

[Commentary:]

Kabir, japa, penances, self-control, sadhana – all are inside Kriya. Upon discerning, Kabir is saying: there is absolutely nothing other than the Self-contemplation. -26

kabir sahakami sumiran ka karei, paoe ucha dhaam
niha kaami sumiran kare, paoe avichal raam -27

[Bengali:]

Kabir is saying: the person who does remembrance with desire attains heaven. If one does remembrance without desire, one attains the Immutable Rama – meaning: the Stillness Substance. -27

[Commentary:]

Kabir, if one does remembrance of Atma-Rama Guru with desire, one attains a high abode, and if one does remembrance in a way without desire, one attains the Stillness Substance Rama. -27

kabir sahakamee sumiran kare, phiri aoe phiri jaay
niha kamee sumiran kare aoa gaman nashaay -28

[Bengali:]

Kabir is saying: the one who does remembrance with desire comes back and goes. If one does remembrance without desire, coming and going end. -28

[Commentary:]

Kabir, if Kriya is practiced with desire, there is rebirth, and if Kriya is practiced without desire, there is liberation. -28

kabir, raja rana na bada, bada je sumire raam
taahi mo so jan bada, jo sumire nihakaam -29

[Bengali:]

Kabir is saying: Neither is the raja [king] great, nor is the rana [another type of king] great. The one who remembers

Rama – that is the person who is great, and the greatest among such persons is the one who does remembrance without desire. -29

[Commentary:]

Kabir, neither raja nor rana are great. Great is the one who meditates on Atma-Rama, and the one who is great even among such persons is one who practices Kriya without desire. -29

kabir saheb ka sumiran karei, tako bando deo pahile aaye digabayi, pache lage seo -30

[Bengali:]

Kabir, the one who does remembrance of Rama – the gods even sing the praises of that person. First they come and try to fool [the sadhak]; afterwards, they serve [the sadhak]. -30

[Commentary:]

Kabir, one who does remembrance of Atma-Rama Guru – the gods sing his praises – meaning: everyone [gods] comes in front [of the sadhak]. At first, they try to fool [the sadhak] – meaning: they present temptation, fear etc., because of which mind becomes distraught. Afterwards, they serve [the sadhak] – meaning: they obey the orders [of the sadhak]. -30

kabir sumiran surti lagaaike, mukh so kachuo na bol baher ke pat dei kei, andar ko pat khol -31

[Bengali:]

Kabir is saying: when remembrance has caught on, then there is no desire to speak anything. Do not say anything with your mouth. Drop the outer curtain and open the curtain within. -31

[Commentary:]

Kabir, while remaining in the par avastha of Kriya, do not speak anything at all. Abiding in the par avastha of Kriya, close the curtain of external sight and open the curtain that is within. -31

kabir jo bole to raam kahi, aorehi raam kahaoe
ja mukh raam na niklei, ta mukh pheri kahae -32

[Bengali:]

Kabir is saying: whatever you are speaking is actually being spoken by Rama himself, and it is actually Rama Who is making one speak, and the one from whose mouth "Rama" does not come forth – that mouth is not a mouth at all. -32

[Commentary:]

Kabir, whatever is being said is being said by Atma-Rama Guru Himself. The One Who is loving – it is He Who is speaking and making one speak. And from the one whose mouth the Name of Rama does not come forth – meaning: one in whom the Supreme Person is not – because it is He Who is making everything happen – how can that mouth be called a mouth – because that mouth is not at all a mouth. -32

kabir mukh to soi bhala, ja mukh niklei raam
ja mukh raam na niklei, so mukh kone kaam -33

[Bengali:]

Kabir is saying: the mouth that is good is the mouth from which the Name of Rama is uttered. And the mouth that does not utter the Name of Rama – what reason is there for that mouth [to be]? -33

[Commentary:]

Kabir, the mouth that is good is the one from which the

Name of Rama comes out – meaning: Atma-Rama. The mouth from which the Name of Rama does not come out – that mouth is not good for anything. It is like a mouth of stone. -33

kabir hari ka naam me, surti rahe ek taar
ta mukhte mati jhare, heera anant apaar -34

[Bengali:]

Kabir is saying: remain as One by practicing the Name of the Lord. Pearls come forth from that mouth, and one gets diamonds and such jewels in infinite amounts. -34

[Commentary:]

Kabir, Atma-Rama Guru does Kriya and extinguishes all. Afterwards, He resides in the par avastha of Kriya and the Self merges with the Supreme Self and becomes One. Then all speech is like pearls – serene and priceless. Then the Infinity of Brahman is known, and one is unable to find Its end. -34

kabir hari ke naam me, baat chalaoe aur
tis aparadhee jeeuko, tini lok nahi thaor -35

[Bengali:]

Kabir is saying: the person who speaks other things regarding the Name of the Lord – meaning: says bad things [about the Name of the Lord] – there is no recourse at all for that type of wrongdoing person in the three worlds. -35

[Commentary:]

Kabir, the person who says, "Of what use is it to practice Kriya?" - meaning: he himself will rot in hell from not doing Kriya, and by deterring others from going on the path of Truth, he becomes even more of a wrongdoer. That wrongdoer jiva has no place [anywhere] in the three worlds – meaning: Heaven, Earth and the Underworld. "Patal" [Underworld] –

meaning: not being able to attain Stillness at the Muladhar, and thus always being distracted in mind and desiring always to conduct illicit behavior, one continuously falls further and further in the vortex of evil ways. "Martalok" [Earth] – meaning: [because of] becoming deluded by saying "I" and "mine" in the heart, and thus doing unruly [or incorrect] acts, one has to experience living and dying, and one's self is [caught] in the vortex of delusion life after life. "Svarga" [Heaven] – meaning head – in that very head, having the whim to perform many kinds of evil acts and thus not knowing the Supreme Feeling, one becomes enslaved to lust, anger and greed, and thus becoming engaged in illicit behavior, one gradually falls into the vortex of evil ways – meaning: [because of such conditions] not in any one of the three abodes in the body does one attain Stillness. -35

kabir ratan sumiranee raam ki, poye man mastul
chabi laagi nirakhat rahe, mit gaya sangshaya shool -36

[Bengali:]

Kabir is saying: mind is threading a garland/rosary made of the Rama Himself as the jewels. In this state, one went on seeing a certain picture. By this very thing the piercing doubt/conflict became resolved. -36

[Commentary:]

Kabir, Atma-Rama Guru is taking the self (mind) and threading it to the "Sumeru" [North Pole or top of the Earth] (Kutastha) in the garland/rosary of contemplation – meaning: He is performing Kriya. That Self, becoming locked in the Supreme Self Kutastha Itself, is seeing That Itself. Then the "shula" [stake or piercing feeling] of "samshaya" [doubt/conflict] became resolved. "Samshaya" - a term which means: the intellect not being able to have certainty of something that is unclear because of the thing being at a distance, or because of darkness [and such]. ("Shula" = the illness called "shula) – which is always churning in the belly. When that pain expands and rises to the heart, there is death. That shula of samshaya is again and again causing the downfall of jivas into hell. When the Self has become locked with the Supreme Self and is seeing That Itself, then the shula of samshaya is resolved/finished. -36

kabir meri sumiranee raamki, rasana upar raam
aadi yugadhi bakthi je, sabko nij bishram -37

[Bengali:]

Kabir is saying: the "Sumeru" [top of the Earth, or North Pole] of my rosary of the Name of Rama is above sensuality. It is He Who is the beginning and the yugas, and it is by residing in Him that devotion blossoms. Everyone's place of rest is also There. -37

[Commentary:]

Kabir, Kutastha is That which is above sensuality, Who is the beginning and the yugas – meaning: before ida and pingala; and devotion – meaning: the place where faith comes forth upon going there, and That which is verily everyone's own place of rest – meaning Kutastha Brahman. -37

kabir raam naam sumiran kare, brahma bishu mahesh
kahehin kabir sumiran kare, narad shukdev shesh -38

[Bengali:]

Kabir is saying: even Brahmaa, Vishnu and Maheshvar are practicing the remembrance of the Name of Rama. Kabir is also doing remembrance, and sages such as Narada are also doing remembrance. -38

[Commentary:]

Kabir, the Self, Who is Lord of creation, sustenance and destruction/ resolution, He has become Kabir and is doing remembrance of Himself by Himself, listening to the Omkar Sound, becoming "all is Brahman." [He is] in every place as the Self Itself. -38

kabir sanakadi sumiran kare, naam dhruva prahlad
jan kabir sumiran kare, chori sakal bakbayat -39

[Bengali:]

Kabir is saying: sages such as Sanaka are also doing remembrance; Dhruva and Prahlad are also doing remembrance. Persons who have been sheltered by God throw aside all incessant talking and practice the Name of God. -39

[Commentary:]

Kabir – the four Vedas – doing remembrance in the four directions. In absolute certainty and contentment, Kabir Saheb is doing remembrance, having thrown away all kinds of other useless talk. -39

kabir ram namke sumirte, jvare patit anek
kahe kabir nahi choriye, ram namke tek -40

[Bengali:]

Kabir is saying: if one practices the remembrance of the Name of Rama, those who have fallen and people of low character burn up with envy and say many things. Do not listen to what they say, and never let go of the Name of Rama. -40

[Commentary:]

Kabir, because of one practicing Kriya, those who are below the "manibandha" [union jewel] die of jealousy. Kabir Saheb is saying, "Do not let go of the refrain of the Name of

Rama." Let the hypocrites say what they want. -40

kabir raam naam ke sumirte, adham tare samsar
ajamil ganika supach, seori sadan chandar -41

[Bengali:]

Kabir is saying: even the despicable and low persons can be carried [safely] across the ocean of samsara if they do remembrance of the Name of Rama. Many people of low character like Ajamila and other such types have been carried across. -41

[Commentary:]

Kabir, [even] the lowest is carried [safely] across samsara via Kriya. Many [low] people – Ajamila, Ganika, Supacha, Seori, Chandar and such types – have been carried across. -41

kabir raam naam man laaile, jayse paani meen
pran tyaje pal bichure, daas kabir kahi deen -42

[Bengali:]

Kabir is saying: keep mind on the Name of Rama in this way: like a fish in water. Just as a fish dies from being without water even for a few moments, keep mind [on God] in that way, Kabir is pleadingly saying. -42

[Commentary:]

Kabir, remain merged in Brahman in that way, like the way a fish is in water. The fish dies from being out of water even for a few moments. This means: upon remaining as merged in Brahman and being Brahman, whatever you are seeing is verily all Brahman. If that person's mind leaves Brahman and even for a few moments goes in other directions, immediately there is death – meaning: when one leaves the intoxication that happens from being locked [in Brahman] that

[Divine] kind of Bliss of Intoxication is no longer there. He does not find that kind of Bliss by ingesting liquor and taking hashish and such which are the opposite [of Divine Bliss]. There is death within just a few days. -42

kabir raam naam man laaile, jayse naad kurang
kahe kabir tare nahi, praan tyaje tehi sang -43

[Bengali:]

Kabir is saying: keep mind in the Name of Rama in this way: like sound and the deer – meaning: when hunters go to hunt deer in the forest, they first go to the forest and play the flute. Deer love to hear the sound of the flute. Hearing the flute, the deer gradually come near the hunter. Then hunters catch them with their nets. Kabir is saying that the deer still do not move [or: fight], and [then] die. They die verily with [or: while listening] to the sound of the flute. -43

[Commentary:]

Kabir, do Kriya in this way: like sound and the deer. Like the way the deer die while listening to the sound, yet do not stop listening to the sound, in that same way, even if prana comes up to the throat [or: if life is at the throat], do not abandon Kriya. -43

kabir raam naam man laile, jayse keet bhring
kabir visraoe aab ko, koye jaay tehi rang -44

[Bengali:]

Kabir is saying: keep mind in the Name of Rama in this way: like the bug and the worm. Kabir is saying that the worm forgets itself and takes on the color of the bug – meaning: the worm becomes enchanted upon seeing the bug's color and forgets itself. When, like the worm, one puts his mind upon the Name of Rama, the jiva itself attains Shiva-ness. -44

[Commentary:]

Kabir, remain in the par avastha of Kriya in this way: the way the worm and bug are. [The worm] forgets itself and becomes the bug – meaning: always in the par avastha of Kriya – meaning: always abide as bodiless in Brahman. -44

kabir raam naam man laile, jayse deep patang
pranatyaje chan ek mo, jvarata na mode ang -45

[Bengali:]

Kabir is saying: keep mind in the Name of Rama in this way: like the moth and the flame. It falls in the burning flame and dies within an instant yet it does not struggle and fight even once. -45

[Commentary:]

Kabir, in the par avastha of Kriya – upon doing Kriya – one becomes merged in Brahman in an instant – like that – like the way the flying insect enters the flame of the lamp and in an instant sacrifices even it's very self yet it does not cower even once at the time the body is burning – meaning: it does not struggle and fight. -45

kabir raam kahe sabh rahit hay, tan man dhan samsar
raam kahe bin yat hay, laak chaurashee dhaar -46

[Bengali:]

Kabir is saying: if one speaks the Name of Rama, body, mind, wealth, life in the world [samsara] – all of these stop. If one does not speak the Name of Rama, one has to travel through eight million four hundred thousand wombs. -46

[Commentary:]

Kabir, everything stops in the par avastha of Kriya, because when there is One, nothing separate remains.

Automatically everything has stopped. The body goes: thus the mind goes; mind goes; thus wealth goes, because if there is no mind, who is there to say "wealth"? When the body becomes still, the mind becomes Still. If the mind becomes Still, who [is there to] crave wealth? When all that is moving becomes Still, then samsara becomes Still. (The name of moving things is "samsara.") This means: one gets the Stillness – That Brahman – in the par avastha of Kriya. The one who did not get the Stillness went on traveling eight million four hundred thousand wombs. -46

kabir raam naam ruchi upje, jiu ki jvalani bujhaye
kahe kabir ek raam naam binu, jiuke daha na jaye -47

[Bengali:]

Kabir is saying: when one acquires "ruchi" [deep interest, like a gourmet for food] for the Name of Rama, all of the "jvaala" [afflictions, agitationburnings] of the jiva are cooled off and settled. Kabir is saying, "Without the singular Name of Rama the jvaala of the jiva does not go away" – meaning: all jvaalas continue to remain. -47

[Commentary:]

Kabir, if one does not do Kriya, the ruchi [see above paragraph] to do Kriya does not develop. Upon continuously doing Kriya and going to the par avastha of Kriya, the jvaalas [see above paragraph] of samsara are ended. Kabir Saheb is saying that without Kriya there is no way for the burning of the jiva to end. Being burned up by the fire of desire in samsara, the jiva becomes cindered [like charcoal]. Although the flames are no longer there in the cindered state, the "daaha" - meaning the searing heat - does not go away. The more that water is applied, the more that heat increases. It is like that type of person, upon whose son's death, grief burns up the body and makes it cindered for sure, but when thoughts about that son come to mind, immediately at that time feelings [for the son] keep on coming up – meaning: the body gets heated up. It is like in a fever-oriented illness, the body is inflamed and burned up, and though the fever left for certain, the searing heat of the illness did not go. The only way of ending the searing heat of worldly joys is the par avastha of Kriya. -47

kabir raam rijhnaile, jihbaso karu mat hari
saagar nahi visarei, nar dekhi anant -48

[Bengali:]

Kabir is saying: do not just try to appease Rama via the tongue – meaning: do not do it with empty words [or: only words]. Keep the Ocean of God always in mind. Do not ever forget. When it will be like this, then the human will see Infinity. -48

[Commentary:]

Kabir, take Atma-Rama with "rijha" in Brahman. Do "rijha" - meaning: like a man expressing physical affection with a woman again and again and making the woman as full of desire as himself, and upon both becoming filled with the same feeling and becoming full of lustful desire, they lose sight and awareness of anything else. Doing Kriya in that way, the Self goes to Brahman again and again, becomes filled with Brahman-Feeling, and losing sight and awareness of anything else, becomes Brahman. Doing this way, make "rijha" with the Self. Do not talk with your tongue. If one does rijha with the Self in that way, the three types of grief-affliction are destroyed. One went on seeing all the waves of the Ocean of God, that which can never be forgotten. Then the human sees Infinity – meaning: "all is Brahman" happens. -48

kabir raam rinjhaile, bikh amrit bil gay phuta
nag jo jodiye, sayihi sandh milaay -49

[Bengali:]

Kabir is saying: by appeasing Rama, poison becomes one with Ambrosia [upon being contacted] by Its qualities – meaning: [poison] becomes Ambrosia– like when something is broken into two pieces. By rejoining them both at those same places where the break happened, they become one. It is like that. -49

[Commentary:]

Kabir, take Atma-Rama [the Self] and make it one with the Paramatman [Supreme Self], separating poison and Ambrosia from each other. Because poison and Nectar are separate, there is "two." If poison merges with Ambrosia, then by the quality of Ambrosia, poison becomes Ambrosia. In that same way, mind's restlessness is like poison and Stillness is like Ambrosia. If this poison-like restlessness merges with the Ambrosia-like Stillness, then restlessness no longer remains. It is like this: a diamond is broken; when that diamond is put back together at the point where it was broken – meaning: all that which have become separate because of the division of the Supreme Atom – when all that is united with the Supreme Atom, then all is One. In that same way, if the restless mind is merged with the Atom of Stillness, they become One. -49

kabir raam jagat kusthi bhala, chnui chnui parta chaam
kanchan deha kehi kaam ki, ja mukh na hi raam -50

[Bengali:]

Kabir is saying: even having festering leprosy is fine, if the person does japa [repetition of mantra] of the Name of Rama. And the mouth from which the Name of Rama does not issue forth – even if those [people] are beautiful, they are useless. -50

[Commentary:]

Kabir, a Kriyavan, even if he has festering leprosy, is good. The non-Kriyavan [may be] beautiful [but] is useless. -50

**kabir raam jagat daalidri bhala, tuti ghar ki chaan
kanchan mandil jaan de, jnaha bhakti nahi jnaan -51**

[Bengali:]

Kabir is saying: even being a poor person is fine if one repeats the Name of Rama. A broken-down house is good with the repetition of the Name of Rama. But a place where there is no devotion or Knowledge – even if that place is a golden temple, it is nothing. -51

[Commentary:]

Kabir, being a Kriyavan is good even if one is poor – the one whose house's roof has broken off – meaning the par avastha of Kriya. Leave the house made of gold; Kriya and Kutastha are not there. -51

**kabir taat odike hari bhaje, taaka naam saput
maya eyari makhara, kete gaye kaput -52**

[Bengali:]

Kabir is saying: one who has [only] a cloth sack to put on his body yet meditates – that is the one who is "suputra" [worthy person]. And many "kuputra" [low personages] have fallen by being caught in maya and [living a life of] joking and kidding around. -52

[Commentary:]

Kabir, one who does Kriya is "suputra," even if he has [only] a cloth sack on his body. And the one who is caught in maya – meaning: they always [think] "mine, mine" - these persons falsely say, "I am your friend"; seeking to eat and possess, [they] speak a bunch of pretentious talk and just spend time [with others in this way]. "Makhara" - meaning: via joking and kidding around, they [superficially] please others, get their affection and try to gain benefit from that. So many hundreds of these types of "kuputras" leave [or: pass away] from this world [in this way]. -52

kabir sab jag nirdhana, dhanabant nahi koye
dhanabanta soi janiya, jaake raam dhan hoye -53

[Bengali:]

Kabir is saying: the entire world is actually without any wealth. Actually no one is wealthy. The only ones who can be recognized as wealthy are those who have the Name of Rama. -53

[Commentary:]

Kabir, because the world is in motion, everyone is actually wealth-less– meaning: the Stillness Substance is not in anything at all. The Stillness Substance is verily wealth. The one for whom [Stillness] has happened – verily it is he who is wealthy. -53

kabir jaaki gnaathi raam hay, taako hay sabsidh
karjore thari parei, aat sidh nao nidh -54

[Bengali:]

Kabir is saying: the one who has the Name of Rama is the one who also has all the "siddhis" [super-rational powers]. And, even the eight "siddhis" and the nine "nidhis" [treasures] are there with folded hands, present by him. -54

[Commentary:]

Kabir, the one who is always merged in Brahman – he has all "siddhis" because he is seeing world as Brahman. The eight "siddhis" and the nine "nidhis" are standing with folded hands in front of him.

Eight "siddhis" = anima [being atomically small], laghima [being nearly weightless], garima [being infinitely heavy], varima [being infinitely large], pratikamya [being able to realize any desire], pratishtha [presence or access to all things], ishitva [lordship] and vashitva [power to subjugate all]. The nine jewels = gold, silver, diamond, pearl, emerald, coral, ruby, sapphire, touchstone. With "karjor" [folded hands - palms in form of prayer or obeisance], these eight "siddhis" and nine "nidhis" are there – meaning: putting two hands together is "karjor" - when the yogi has become Brahman. In that State, by the Desire of no desire – that Desire from Brahman by which the world comes about – because of that Spiritual Desire – immediately upon that [Desire] arising in Subtle Form, that work [meaning: manifestation, act, happening] happens by the atomic movement of the atoms. In this way, "karjor" and in this way, the eight "siddhis" are always present. -54

kabir pargat raam kahu, chaane raam na gaaye phuske
dora doori karu, jo bahuri na lagaaye gaaye -55

[Bengali:]

Kabir is saying: there is no harm in uttering the Name of Rama outwardly, but there should be no obstacle within oneself for Rama. Cast away the rope of murmuring/whispering because it does not return and rejoin again – meaning: the Name of Rama by the mouth is of no use. -55

[Commentary:]

Kabir, you can say the Name of Rama with the mouth, but that Name of Rama should not cause an obstacle to the Kriya of the Inner Self. Cast away the rope of murmuring/whispering, because it will not return and rejoin – meaning: whispering "Rama, Rama" by the mouth – when one has to speak with another person, that whispering is broken. It does not rejoin again. But the "sticking" that is of the Inner Self [to Kutastha], does not break again. For this reason, let go of the Name of Rama uttered by the mouth. -55

kabir bahar knaha dekh laaiye, antar kahiye raam
kaho mahaula khalak so, para dhaneese kaam -56

[Bengali:]

Kabir is saying, say the Name of Rama within yourself. Why are you trying to look respectable outwardly? What is the use of being "big" here? The One without Whom there can be no one who is wealthy – it He Who is needed. -56

[Commentary:]

Kabir, who are you trying to show off to, by chanting the Name of Rama outwardly? Say the Name of Rama inwardly by the Inner Self. What is the need to pass the examination of the people of the world – meaning: the people of the world should give praise because there is work being done here for one to be a "dhanaban" [person of wealth]. "Dhanaban" = one who keeps wealth. The reason for keeping wealth is for the contentment of the Self. The satisfaction of mind is not possible in anything other than the par avastha of Kriya. Just as when there is money one is outwardly wealthy, similarly if one resides in the par avastha of Kriya one is inwardly wealthy. The work that has to be done here is for the sake of enjoying wealth [only]; there is no work here that is about leading people to saying good things about oneself. -56

kabir naam bisaro dehako, jeeo dasha sab jaaye
jabhi chore naam ko, tab hi laage dhaaye -57

[Bengali:]

Kabir is saying: all troubles of the jiva [individual] go away when the name of the body is forgotten. Then when one forgets the Name of Rama, then again all troubles come back and latch on. -57

[Commentary:]

Kabir, in the par avastha of Kriya the body itself is forgotten and all of the states of the restless mind go away. And when that State [par avastha] leaves – so take care and attend to that which brings about that State [par avastha]. -57

kabir raam naam nahi chorie, yeh parteeta dir
bnadhi kaal kalp vyape nahi, bhori naam ki sadhi -58

[Bengali:]

Kabir is saying: do not ever let go of the Name of Rama; tether to It very firmly, because [otherwise] you will not be able to avoid/escape the hand of "kaal" [time]. Meditate upon the rope of the Name. Then you will be able to get across [or: go beyond]. -58

[Commentary:]

Kabir, do not ever, ever let go of the par avastha of Kriya, and tether to This firmly with a faithful mind. "Kaal" [time] – that which passes – and, accompanying time, everything [also] passes away. It is like this: if upon the rising of the sun that state of the day remained [the same], there would not be the times of one period [of the day], a second period and so on. But because of the movement of the sun [figuratively speaking], all those times are happening – meaning: the concept "I will die." These two [time and death] are no longer pervading the body, because by becoming Still one has avoided/ escaped the hand of time, the hand of death, and this can be experienced, because the one who is to die – he himself has become Still. And one actually looks at whether the "rope" form of the par avastha of Kriya is properly there [or: happening] from the Muladhar to the head. -58

kabir raam hamare maat hay, raam hamare taat
raam hamare mitra hay, raam hamare bhrat -59

[Bengali:]

Kabir is saying: Rama is the One Who is my mother; Rama is the One Who is my father; Rama is the One Who is my friend; Rama is the One Who is my brother. -59

[Commentary:]

Kabir, Prakriti and Purusha have come forth from Atma-Rama [Self]. Atma-Rama is Friend and Brother, because there is no helper and friend comparable to It. -59

kabir raam hamare ashram, raam hamare varan
raam hamare jaati hay, rahihi raam ke sharan -60

[Bengali:]

Kabir is saying: Rama is the One Who is my ashram [or: shelter]; Rama is verily my [only] caste; Rama is truly my [only] race, and I am totally surrendered to Rama verily. -60

[Commentary:]

Kabir, it is verily Atma-Rama Who is one's Home. He is

the colorless Caste. He the Race of being One. For this reason, abide always and constantly in the remembrance of the Self – meaning: do Kriya. -60

kabir raam hamare mohanee, raam hamare shikh
raam hamare isht hay, raam hamare rikh -61

[Bengali:]

Kabir is saying: it is Rama Who is my enchantress, and it is Rama verily Who is my disciple. Rama is truly my god of worship; Rama is the One Who is my sage. -61

[Commentary:]

Kabir, Atma-Rama Guru is keeping one enchanted. It is verily Atma-Rama Itself Who has become the disciple. It is He Who is the "Ishta" [deity] – meaning: He is in the par avastha of Kriya. He is the Sage – meaning Brahman Itself. -61

kabir raam hamare mantra hay, raam hamare
tantr raam hamare aushadhi, raam hamare yantr -62

[Bengali:]

Kabir is saying: Rama is my true mantra; Rama is my true tantra; Rama is my true medicine; Rama is my true yantra [scientific mechanism]. -62

[Commentary:]

Kabir, it is verily Atma-Rama Guru Who goes to the par avastha of Kriya and gives salvation to the Heart/Mind via the Tantra of oneself – meaning jiva. He is Medicine – meaning: if one abides in Him, no illness happens. It is He Who is "Yantra" - meaning: residing in Brahman, there is the experience of all things and Bliss. -62

kabir raam hamare bhumiyan, raam hamare deo
raam hamare saadh hay, karhi tinhi ke seo -63

[Bengali:]

Kabir is saying: Rama is my true stable ground; Rama is the One Who is my god; sadhana is my Rama also; He is the One Whom I serve. -63

[Commentary:]

Kabir, it is verily Atma-Rama Who is the Muladhar; it is verily Him Who is Brahman; it is He Who is the One doing sadhana. Serve Him verily – meaning: do Kriya. -63

kabir teerath hamare raam hay, barat hamare raam
daan hamare raam hay, nahi aur se kam -64

[Bengali:]

Kabir is saying: Rama is my pilgrimage; Rama is my vow; Rama is my offering; I do not do any act [or: anything] without Rama. -64

[Commentary:]

Kabir, Atma-Rama [Self] is actually everything – the Muladhar [or: basis, root] of "teertha" [pilgrimage]; "brata" [vow] – meaning: "kriyas" [in this case: rites] and such are Atma-Rama; "daan" [offerings] – meaning: Rama is also the One Who gives Kriya. When everything is Rama, then there is no act at all without Rama – meaning: "all is Brahman." -64

kabir moti chuni raam hay, hari heera o laal roopa
sona raam hay, bhojan saajan maal -65

[Bengali:]

Kabir is saying: my Rama is pearl and ruby; God is diamond and "laal" ("laal" = very precious stone); silver, gold

– these are also my Rama; food, lover, joy – all is my Rama. - 65

[Commentary:]

Kabir, by becoming Still, it is Atma-Rama Himself that becomes Kutastha – the One Who is the Priceless Treasure, finding Whom one becomes Supremely Fulfilled, abiding in Whom one attains Supreme Bliss and the One Who is All. -65

kabir sona roopa kaal hay, kankar paathar heer ek naam mukta mani, taako japhi kabir -66

[Bengali:]

Kabir is saying: gold and silver are verily "kaal" [time or death]. The diamond is a pebble, a stone [only]. And the one Name is my only pearl and jewel. Kabir does japa [meditative repetition] of That only. -66

[Commentary:]

Kabir, greed is verily the reason for sorrow/suffering. The diamond is nothing but earth. The Jewel of Brahman – meaning the par avastha of Kriya – it is That that the Atma-Rama Guru is constantly doing. -66

kabir jab hi raam hriday aandhaar, bhaye paap ko naash manukh chinigi aagko, padi pudane ghaas -67

[Bengali:]

Kabir is saying: when Rama emerges in the heart, then all fear and sin are destroyed, like when just a little fire catches on old grass and burns it up. It is like that. -67

[Commentary:]

Kabir, when Atma-Rama Guru is revealed in the heart, then mind no longer goes in other directions, like when old grass becomes a flame upon a spark of fire falling on it. -67

**kabir raam jo raji ek hay, paap jo rati hazaar arash
raai ghat sanchare, jvaari kare sab chaar -68**

[Bengali:]

Kabir is saying: there is [only] one desire for Rama, and there are thousands of desires for sins. When Rama spreads in the "house" [or: "pot", "body"], then He burns all desires and casts them out. -68

[Commentary:]

Kabir, there is only one pleasure expressing Atma-Rama Guru – meaning: the Atom is naturally subtler than subtle – the par avastha of Kriya (Brahman). "Sin" - meaning: putting mind in other directions. That is in the thousands – meaning: the mind is constantly moving. That Brahman-Knowledge spreads in the body and burns everything to ashes – meaning: It made everything One Brahman. -68

**kabir pahile bura kamaaike, baandhe bikshi pat
koti karm kaate palak me, jab aaoe hari ot -69**

[Bengali:]

Kabir is saying: I have tied a bundle full of the poison of doing bad deeds in the past. But when God comes and keeps one in His guard, then even millions of "karmas" [fruits of past acts] will be cut away in a single instant. -69

[Commentary:]

Kabir, one has tied for oneself a bundle full of poison made from all the bad deeds of the past. A bundle of millions of poisonous things are ended in a single instant – meaning: when all became Still (abiding in Brahman) – when, upon abiding in the par avastha of Kriya, all things were destroyed –

meaning: all became Brahman, then God destroyed everything and came to the lips – meaning: there is no desire to speak. One becomes automatically mute. -69

kabir koti karma kaate palak me, jnao ranchak aaoe
nam anek janma jao puni kare, nahi naam bin thnao -70

[Bengali:]

Kabir is saying: even millions of karmas will be cut away when the Unmoving State of the Name will come. Even if you do virtuous works for many lifetimes, nothing will happen by that either. There is no other way other than the Name. -70

[Commentary:]

Kabir, upon becoming Still, in an instant, all fruits of karma are cut away – if one stays a bit in the Unmoving State. And if one does [good] karma for many lifetimes with the desire for outcomes – if this is so, then there is absolutely no other place [of recourse] other than the par avastha of Kriya, where one will get Deliverance – meaning the par avastha of Kriya. -70

kabir jinko jaysa hari janiya, tinko taysa labh
jose baasan bhajai, jab laagi dhase na jaao -71

[Bengali:]

Kabir is saying: in whichever way one knows the Lord – in that very same way one gets what one gets. Just as striking a vessel strongly breaks it, in that same way, if one meditates with great strength of devotion, God enters the body, breaks the body and bestows "videha" [bodiless] liberation. -71

[Commentary:]

Kabir, however it is that one has known the Lord – meaning: [the way that one] has done Kriya – so is his attainment. Like breaking a vessel – up to the point of not yet falling apart – meaning: cracking the vessel strongly, the vessel is broken. Similarly, if one meditates upon God a great deal, God enters the body and breaks the body – meaning: became bodiless. -71

kabir hari ko sumiri le, praan jaye ga chuti
gharke pachaare aadmi, chalat lahi ge luti -72

[Bengali:]

Kabir is saying: constantly do remembrance of the Lord. If this is not done, then life [or: life force [prana]] will go out [or: outside]. People are there right next to one's house. When going, one shall gather it up. -72

[Commentary:]

Kabir, constantly call the One Who extinguishes all – meaning: constantly remain in the par avastha of Kriya. If this is not done, life [or: life force [prana]] will leave. One shall grab and throw down all people. When moving, whatever is nearby, one shall gather it up. -72

kabir lut shake to lutle, raam naam hay luti
pheri paache pachtaoge, praan jahige chuti -73

[Bengali:]

Kabir is saying: the Name of Rama is lying about. Gather up as much as you can gather up, because when life [or: life force [prana]] goes out [or: outside], one will regret it in the end. -73

[Commentary:]

Kabir, gather up as much as you can gather up. "Lota" [getting/taking] – meaning: taking things from somewhere else and keeping it as one's own – meaning: however many days that you are alive, do as much Kriya as you can. The Name of Rama – meaning the par avastha of Kriya, that is verily the "loot."* If you do not stay in the par avastha of Kriya, when life [or: life force [prana]] goes, you will suffer. -73

[*Translator's note: The word "loot" has the same meaning in Hindi and Bengali as in the West - "cache," "found wealth" etc.]

kabir luti shake to lutle, raam naam hay luti
naam nagni ke gaho, naato jaysa chuti -74

[Bengali:]

Kabir is saying: the "loot" of the Name of Rama is lying all around. Grab as much of the "loot" as you can. Keep the Priceless Jewel with such care [like this:] who knows if it will be gone or not. -74

[Commentary:]

Kabir, if you can do it, stay in the par avastha of Kriya all the time. And hold on to that Priceless Treasure firmly [or: well]. If you do not hold on to It, It will go away. -74

kabir luti shake to lutile, raam naam bhandar
kaal kanth tab gahahige, roken dasho duar -75

[Bengali:]

Kabir is saying: the storehouse/treasury of the Name of Rama is there. Grab as much as you can. And, upon closing the ten doors, keep "kal" [time or death] Stilled in the throat. -75

[Commentary:]

Kabir, the one who will do Kriya – it is he who will have fulfillment in the par avastha of Kriya. This "loot" is lying about. One who can – please gather it up by doing Kriya. "Kal" - that which passes – keep this "kal" Stilled in the throat by closing the ten doors – meaning: when Stillness happened in the par avastha of Kriya, then the ten doors are also no longer open, because the one who is to go out through the ten doors – he himself has become Still, then who is there to go out? Because of this, whether the ten doors are open or not open – both are same. -75

kabir raam naam japi likhie, chori jiu ki bani
parishme biti gayi, soi aapu par jani -76

[Bengali:]

Kabir is saying: leave the talk of ordinary jivas [or: everyday life] and take up the "japa" [meditative repetition] of the Name of Rama. Time was wasted uselessly. Now I am here knowing the Self and the Supreme Intelligence. -76

[Commentary:]

Kabir, take up the doing of Kriya, and, while abiding in the par avastha of Kriya, whatever the jivas [or: people] have said – leave all that, because – time, which is being unused – you can easily do Kriya. You are uselessly wasting that very time by just talking. The Cause [or: Source] of that [or: any] speech [ability] is the Self and the Supreme Intelligence. -76

kabir raam naam nidhi lijiye, tyaji maya bikh boj
baar baar nahi paayie, maanukh janam ki moj -77

[Bengali:]

Kabir is saying: cast off the load of poison that is known as maya. Grab hold of the Treasure of the Name of Rama, because you will not be able to have the fun that is in this human birth again and again. -77

[Commentary:]

Kabir, abide in the par avastha of Kriya. The load of poison that is known as maya – that which has come about by putting mind in other directions – that will go away automatically. [Do Kriya] because you will not have this human birth again and again, and the Stillness in the par avastha of Kriya which is [known] in this human birth – you will not get that again as well. -77

kabir raam naam japi lijiye, jab lagi diya baati
tel ghaate baati bujhei, tab shogra din raati -78

[Bengali:]

Kabir is saying: take up the repetition of the Name of Rama, because the wick of the lamp is becoming dry. As soon as the oil finishes, the lamp will stop. Then every day will be like night. -78

[Commentary:]

Kabir, take up the doing of Kriya. As long as the Soul is in the body – this Kriya of the Soul is like the oil [of the lamp]. If it is let go, then the Soul will go out [like the flame going out], and will no longer remain. Then one will be lying down day and night [or: day and night will be lying down]. -78

kabir shuta kya kare, jaagi na japei muraree
ek din bhi chor na, lambe paao pasari -79

[Bengali:]

Kabir is saying: what are you doing lying around? One day you will have to lie down with your legs stretched out anyway; so wake up and practice the Name of the Lord. -79

[Commentary:]

Kabir, what are you doing lying around? Wake up and do

Kriya. The day of lying down with your legs stretched out will be there anyway. -79

kabir shuta kya kare, uthi keon na roye dukh
jaaka baasa gor me, so keon shoye sukh -80

[Bengali:]

Kabir is saying: what are you doing lying around? One whose home is the grave – what kind of pleasure is he getting from lying around? Why does he not get up and feel sorrow and cry? -80

[Commentary:]

Kabir, what are you doing by lying around? Cry a bit, why don't you, upon thinking about your suffering. How is one lying about happily if one's home is in the grave? How can there be peaceful sleep when there is the fear of death? -80

kabir shuta keyan kare, gun gobind ka gaao tere
shir par jam khara, kharach dei kya khaao -81

[Bengali:]

Kabir is saying: how is one lying around in contentment when the god of death is standing by his head? He should be singing the praises of the Lord. What did you eat with the expense allowance you received? -81

[Commentary:]

Kabir, what are you doing lying around? Look into Kutastha and do Kriya. The god of death is standing by your head. What did you eat with the expense allowance you received in the form of Kriya and the singing of the praises of the Lord – meaning: what did you do? -81

kabir shuta kya kare, shute hoy akaj
brahmako asan tiga, shoyat kaal ki laaj -82

[Bengali:]

Kabir is saying: what are you doing lying around? No work gets done if one is lying down. The seat of Brahmaa [the creator] even falls away. As soon as one lies down, "kal" [time or death] comes and swallows [one]. -82

[Commentary:]

Kabir, what are you doing lying around? No work gets done by lying down. The Seat of Brahmaa fell away. When even He lay down to sleep, then "kal" came and swallowed [one]. -82

kabir shuta kya kare, kaahe na dekhai jaagi
jaake sang so bichura, taahike sang laagi -83

[Bengali:]

Kabir is saying: what are you doing lying around? Wake up and see. The One Whom you were with, you let Him go. Stay enjoined with Him again. -83

[Commentary:]

What is Kabir doing lying down? Why do you not wake up and see Atma-Rama [Self] Guru? The One Whose company you had, you let go. If you lie down, then it is with Him/That that one should stay enjoined. -83

kabir nid nishani neech ki, uth kabira jaagi aur
rasayan chorke, tom raam rasaayan laagi -84

[Bengali:]

Kabir is saying: sleep is verily the sign of low types of persons. Kabir, wake up and rise, and instead of doing the "rasayan" [lit.: chemistry] of trivial things, do "rasayan" of Atma-Rama [Self]. -84

[Commentary:]

Kabir, sleep is the sign of the lower, because if one abides above upon rising there, sleep does not happen. In the waking state, rise above. "Rasayan" - meaning: bringing about the previous state via the use of another liquid [or: substance] is called "rasayan." Casting off the constant effort to have samsara according to one's desires – you are Brahman – abiding in the par avastha of Kriya via Kriya, stay enjoined with the "rasayan" of that. -84

kabir aapne pahare jaagiye, rahiye nahi shoye
na jaano chin ek mo, keska pahaara hoye -85

[Bengali:]

Kabir is saying: remain awake on the watch regarding the Self. Do not be asleep. Who knows if in an instant there will be keeping watch for who knows who [or: what]? -85

[Commentary:]

Kabir, stay awake on the watch regarding the Self – meaning: you have got the responsibility of keeping watch from birth until death. Now patrol the boundaries of your Self very thoroughly – meaning: abiding in the Awareness of the Self, do Kriya. Do not lie down on your watch. You do not know who will keep watch on whom in the realm of "kal" [time or death] in even one moment. -85

kabir shoya so niphal geya, jaage so phal lei
saaheb hak na raakhei, jab mange tab dei -86

[Bengali:]

Kabir is saying: it is by lying down that there is

fruitlessness, and it is by remaining awake that fruit is attained. The One Who is the Owner – He does not hold on to accounts of debt and collateral. If one asks, He immediately gives. -86

[Commentary:]

Kabir, there is no fruit if one lies down, because then unawareness is awake – meaning: it is when there is Awareness that fruit is attained. Atma-Rama Guru does not hold on to accounts of collateral and debt for anyone. When one does Kriya, He gives immediately at that time. -86

kabir keyso kahi kahi kuhukiye, shoiyena paao pasari raati dio sapha kuhu kana, kabuhu ke laage gohaari -87

[Bengali:]

Kabir is saying: to whom shall say again and again, "What are you doing? Do not lie around with your legs stretched out. Work day and night. It is not certain exactly when someone will call." -87

[Commentary:]i

Kabir, to whom shall I say that one should always "kuhu, kuhu" - meaning do Kriya? And do not lie around with your legs stretched out. If you do not do Kriya night and day, then when will you hear the call? -87

**kabir jayse man maya rame, tayse ram ramaye
tara mandal chorike, jahan ke so tahan jaaye -88**

[Bengali:]

Kabir is saying: if mind romances in the Self the way that it takes romances in maya, and renounces all "taramandal" – if that happens, then it will go back to the very place from which it came. ("Taramandal" - titles, manner of dress etc. - the false vanity of the individual. Leave these.) -88

[Commentary:]

Kabir, the way that mind romances in maya ("maya" [illusion] = me and mine – yet it is untrue; "satya" [truth] = I am nothing at all; nothing is mine) in that same way, the One Who is romancing within – meaning Atma-Rama – do romance in That. Just as because of romancing in maya all mayic events are being seen, if one romances in the Self, one can see all the incredible events of Brahman. Leave these "taramandal" [see Bengali explanation above] meaning: Taj Mahal, Junmamsjid, Vidyasagar, Nyaya-Panchanon etc. - cast off all these various "stars," because these will return where they came from – meaning: to Substance. And the Brahman Who is in this Substance – if you are able to reside in that Brahman, you will be able to know both Truth and illusion ["Satya" and "maya"]. -88

kabir jaagat shoyat raam kahu, pare, utane, raam
uthat baithat raam kahu, paot achoyat raam -89

[Bengali:]

Kabir is saying: in the waking state, in the state of sleep, when getting up, sitting down, when eating or washing up after eating – always say "Rama, Rama." -89

[Commentary:]

Kabir, this work absolutely must be done. If it can be dug and marked into the mind in this way one time, then no matter how busy the mind may be, that work will be reminded of because of that being inside, because even if mind becomes distracted while doing other activities, in the midst of being unmindful, as soon as that reminder of that work [of the first sentence of this paragraph] comes to mind, immediately that work emerges in the mind/heart. Just as when a mayic work is dug and marked into the mind, it automatically emerges in the mind, in the same way, if the Name of Rama is dug and marked into the mind, the mind will automatically abide in That on its own, without any volition/desire [provoking it to do so]. And, continuous abidance in this way and thus entering the Atom of Brahman, even though one is awake in the waking state, he is not awake [in the ordinary sense] – because the waking state and the Awakened State in the Atom of Brahman – even though one is awake, it is not the waking state [in the ordinary sense]. In this way, while lying, while being on one's belly, on one's back, getting up, sitting down – one is constantly in the Atom of Brahman – and while eating, because the Atom of Brahman is in the food substance – because of entering into that Atom, one does not eat even while eating. It is like this for washing up after eating as well. - 89

kabir khudha kaali kukuree, kare bhajan me bhang
wako tukura daarike, sumiran karo nihshank -90

[Bengali:]

Kabir is saying: "kal" [time or death] is the dog of hunger in the jiva [individual] – meaning: desires come and obstruct and break up sadhana. For this reason, give it something to eat and fearlessly do remembrance. -90

[Commentary:]

Kabir, "kal" is the hunger-dog. "Kal" = darkness – meaning: one cannot see. Yet there is the craving to eat again and again. That desire to stay in the world happens. This hunger is that which breaks up the doing of Kriya. Give it a bit of food (bread) to eat and fearlessly do Kriya. -90

kabir griheeka tukra apach hay, take lambe dnaat
bhajan kare to ubare, nai to phare anaat -91

[Bengali:]

Kabir is saying: the householder's food is indigestible; it is not digestible because it has long teeth – meaning: the householder person earns money by many sinful acts. He buys food and such by that money. It is because of this that that is not digested. If one does sadhana, then that comes up and out. Otherwise it cuts into the nadis [vital pathways or vital parts of the body]. -91

[Commentary:]

Kabir, the householder's food is not digestible because it has long teeth – meaning: the householder earns wealth via sinful acts, and because of buying food with that [type of] wealth, sin gathers in that food. At the time of eating, that food is host to sin. In that food are the long, long teeth of sin, eating which one is infused with many types of sins. If one does Kriya, those teeth come up and out. Otherwise, the one who eats – the vital parts in the belly are sliced and spill out – meaning: eating food with that sin, the poison of that sin burns up the whole body, including the vital parts in the belly. -91

kabir girihee keri madhukaree, khai rahe jo soi
kahe kabir sumiran bina, ant duheli hoi -92

[Bengali:]

Kabir is saying: like the honey-gathering bee, one wanders about eating begged food from householders. If he does not do remembrance within himself, then one milks dry to the end of that which is of the food-giver and the household – meaning: all benediction is forcibly taken. -92

[Commentary:]

Kabir, the honey-gathering bee of the householders (meaning: one who brings food by begging from householder's homes) – the one who eats that food – if that person is being without remembrance – meaning: if he his not remembering the Self – that person milks dry to the end of what the householder food-giver and the food-bearing house has to give – meaning: one milks dry all the benediction – meaning: one takes it forcibly. -92

kabir gobindke gun gaaote, kabhuna kijiye laaj
aab padabi aage mukti, ek panth dui kaaj -93

[Bengali:]

Kabir is saying: do not ever be ashamed [or: be unduly shy] about singing the praises of the Lord. First there will be good, and liberation will also happen. With one thing two things will be done. -93

[Commentary:]

Kabir, do not ever be ashamed about lifting the tongue and witnessing the Bindu. First, by becoming Still and attaining Bliss, everyone will say good things. And then, continuing to do this way, you will be merged in Brahman in the par avastha of Kriya. Doing Kriya brings about merging in Brahman, and everyone gives praise. -93

kabir gun gaaye gunha kaate, rate raam biyog
ahinishi hari dhyaoe nahi, mile na durlabh jog -94

[Bengali:]

Kabir is saying: if one sings the praises of the Lord, all of the bad qualities are eradicated, and the separation from Rama is no more seen, but if one does not meditate upon the Lord day and night, then from where will one find the Priceless Union? -94

[Commentary:]

Kabir, by doing Kriya itself, all wrongs go away. But one does not completely enjoin with Atma-Rama and do Kriya day and night. For this reason, one does not get that Priceless Union that is the par avastha of Kriya. -94

kabir kathinaai khari, jo sumrei hari naam
shooli upan khelna, girei to naahi thaam -95

[Bengali:]

Kabir is saying: one who does the remembrance of the Lord's Name has a particular difficulty, because if one is to play on top of a spike, one has to be alert. Otherwise, if one falls there is no rescue. -95

[Commentary:]

Kabir, it is difficult to do the True Kriya. It is like playing on top of a spike. If one falls, then there no place any more. -95

kabir lamba marg duri ghan, bikat panth bahu
bhaar kahe kabir kneo paiye, durlabh hari didaar -96

[Bengali:]

Kabir is saying: it is one thing that the road is long, and more than that, the home is also far away. There are many fears on the road as well and there is a heavy load too. Kabir is saying, "How can one find the Merciful Precious Lord in this situation?" -96

[Commentary:]

Kabir, the road is of course long and the home is very far away – meaning: the par avastha of Kriya upon continuously doing Kriya. There are many fears on the road as well – meaning: there are extreme obstacles and fearful things in doing Kriya – meaning: one can see all terrifying forms and there is a feeling of heaviness in the head. Atma-Rama Guru [Self] is saying, "How can one, in the midst of sorrow, find the Precious Lord" – meaning the Kutastha Eye. -96

kabir harike milan ki, baat shuni ham doye ki
kachu harika naamle, ke kar ucha hoye -97

[Bengali:]

Kabir is saying: I have heard two statements about Union with the Lord. Among these, one is that one can get it by doing the Name of the Lord; the other is that it happens by staying above. -97

[Commentary:]

Kabir, we hear two statements about Union. One: via Kriya one can get the Lord; and the other one: one can get Him by abiding in the par avastha of Kriya. -97

kabir ankhriya jhnaipari, panth nihaari nihaari
jibhri anchala pare, raam pukari pukari -98

[Bengali:]

Kabir is saying: continuously looking at the road, the eyes have become bewildered – meaning: I am not able to see anything well, and from continuously loudly yelling "Rama, Rama" foam gathered on the tongue. -98

[Commentary:]

Kabir, I cannot see anymore with the eye [or: in the Eye]. Continuously looking at the road and saying "Rama, Rama" [constantly], the tongue has become blistered. -98

kabir nayanhune jhari laia, rahat vahe nishi shaam
papiha jneo piya piya kare, kab re milenge raam -99

[Bengali:]

Kabir is saying: papiya (a special bird) – like the way papiyas cry day and night, "Piya, piya" - meaning: "O Beloved! When will I find you?!" In this way, one is crying day and night, tears falling from the eyes. The call is this kind of call. -99

[Commentary:]

Kabir, day and night tears are falling from the eyes, [crying] like the papiya, "O Piya [beloved]!" - meaning: O Beloved Rama! When will I find You?! -99

**kabir chinta chingi uriya, chaudish laagi laiye hari
sumiran hathe ghara, beghi lahu bujhaye -100**

[Bengali:]

Kabir is saying: thoughts are like sparks of fire, inflamed and flying all around one. Taking the full pot of water in the form of the remembrance of the Name of the Lord, put out the fire-like thoughts. -100

[Commentary:]

Kabir, thoughts, like sparks of fire, are inflamed and flying all around one. The full pot of water in the form of the Name of the Lord – meaning in the form of Kriya – is in the hand. By that, put out all the fire-like sparks of thought – meaning: if Kriya is done, no thoughts remain. -100

**kabir chinta to hari naam ki, aur na chitoe daas jo
kuch chitoe naam binu, soi kaal ki phnaas -101**

[Bengali:]

Kabir is saying: the thought of the Name of the Lord is the [true] thought. All other thoughts are of no use. Whatever one thinks about without the Name, those are all of the death-noose of "kal" [time or death]. -101

[Commentary:]

Kabir, abiding in the par avastha of Kriya is verily the only True Contemplation. All other thoughts are not [true] thoughts. All contemplation other than the par avastha of Kriya are all the death-noose of "kal" - meaning: the cause of dying – rope around the throat. -101

kabir svapneme bar baraike, jore kahega raam
waake pag ki paitari, mere tanko chaam -102

[Bengali:]

Kabir is saying: the one who, in a dream and loudly, says "Rama, Rama" - know that the skin of my body is the sole of his foot. -102

[Commentary:]

Kabir, the one who does "catch it, catch it" in dream – meaning: does Kriya powerfully in a nearly unseen way – his shoes are of the skin of my body – meaning: I am his most humble servant. -102

kabir nimikhi nimiranu kijiye, ur antar so raam
kahahi kabir raam kahu, sakal saoare kaam -103

[Bengali:]

Kabir is saying: end blinking, and see Rama within and without. Kabir is saying, "If you do like this, He will fulfill all your desires." -103

[Commentary:]

Kabir, end blinking and see Rama within and without. It is only when mind goes from one thing to another thing that the eyes blink. When one saw One in all places, then, because of mind not going to other things, the eyes did not blink. Kabir is saying: teach Kriya to others. Verily all of your acts will be made successful by Atma-Rama. -103

kabir bhajan kareta bhaje sabhe, gun indri chit chor
sar pantha chandan parihari, jab chari bole mor -104

[Bengali:]

Kabir is saying: everyone does meditation and they do get in the meditative state, but the gunas and senses have stolen the chitta [heart]. For this reason, the Lord as Consciousness is not able to be seen. It can be seen through "work". Just like a snake, when it takes shelter by a sandalwood tree, it does not move from it, yet when a peacock comes and crows, then the snake leaves the sandalwood tree and flees – in this way, when the Peacock in the form of the Lord comes, the gunas and senses all flee. -104

[Commentary:]

Kabir, "bhajan" [meditation] – meaning: upon doing Kriya everyone flees – meaning: everyone becomes entranced/paralyzed. Among these, the primary qualities [gunas], senses and the chitta have stolen Kutastha – meaning: because of Kutastha being in the very body itself, It is not being seen. Only because He is hidden by the covering done by the gunas and the senses is the reason He is not being seen. The snake, upon smelling the scent of sandalwood, is perched on the sandalwood. When the peacock spread its plume and crowed, immediately, the snake left the sandalwood and fled – meaning: in Yonimudra, like the spreading of the plume of the peacock, Kutastha revealed Himself. Then all gunas and senses did not remain. -104

**kabir shvas suphal soi janiye, hari sumiran laaye aur
shvas ehu gaya, kari kari bahut upaaye -105**

[Bengali:]

Kabir is saying: know that only that breath is fruitful, that
breath which enjoins with the remembrance of the Lord. And
regardless of many other possibilities, all other breaths were
useless. -105

[Commentary:]

Kabir, know that only that breath is fruitful, the one which
has merged with Brahman in the par avastha of Kriya upon
doing Kriya. All other breaths were useless, taking other
possibilities – meaning: putting mind in other directions. -105

**kabir baaki pnuji shvas hay, chin aaoe chin jaaye
taako aysa chaahiye, rahe raam lolaaye -106**

[Bengali:]

Kabir is saying: those persons, the entirety of whose
possessions consist of breath only, those who have no other
fund at all, those for whom breath is the only capital on which
can be relied upon – and that even is not Still for even a
moment – it goes out one time and comes back – people in this
situation should always be absorbed in Atma-Rama [Self]. -
106

[Commentary:]

Kabir, there is no store of funds on the Earth, because
nothing remains. Whatever there is, is only for a few days
only. It is being seen that the only capital is breath, verily. But
that breath is not Still for even one moment. It comes one time
and goes out again. Those for whom the only store of funds is
only this breath – they should constantly remain absorbed in

Atma-Rama. If one remains in this way, one will get Supreme Bliss in the par avastha of Kriya. -106

kabir kahan bharosa dehko, binashee jaye sin maahi
shvas shvas sumiran kare, aur upaaye kachu nahi -107

[Bengali:]

Kabir is saying: how can one rely on the body? It is destroyed in an instant. I am not seeing any other way; the one and only way to save this is to do remembrance with every breath after breath. -107

[Commentary:]

Kabir, there is absolutely nothing reliable with the body; it is destroyed in an instant. The way to save this body – there is no other way than by doing remembrance with every breath. -107

kabir ajapa sumran ghat beeche, din ho shirishiri
janihaar taahi so man laaile, kahahin kabir bichaar -108

[Bengali:]

Kabir is saying: "ajapa" (the jiva is always doing the "japa" [repetition] of this mantra) – keep the mind in its remembrance. By doing that, an unspeakable State will come about. That itself is Brahman. Kabir Saheb is saying this upon knowing so. -108

[Commentary:]

Kabir, upon doing Kriya, abiding in the par avastha of Kriya is itself Brahman. Keep mind in That itself. Kabir Saheb is saying this upon knowing so. -108

kabir ajapa sumiran hothay, kaho shant kohi thaur
kar jihba sumiran kare, eh sab manki daur -109

[Bengali:]

Kabir is saying: "ajapa" [automatic japa] remembrance is the only place [way] for sadhus. And doing japa with mala or repeating sacred names with the tongue – these are the running of the mind only; nothing comes of it at all. -109

[Commentary:]

Kabir, Kriya is verily the place of those who are of peace. Doing mala japa and saying "Rama, Rama" with the mouth – these are the running of the mind only – meaning: like the way mind runs to eat sweets, in the same way it runs to do mala japa and [repeating] the [physical] name of Rama. Like the way one suffers when one has no money in hand yet goes to eat from a sweet shop but cannot have the sweets to eat, in the same way, because of not attaining anything from the repetition of the name of Rama by the mouth or doing japa with mala with the hand, there is suffering for the heart. -109

kabir ajapa sumiran hothaya, shunya mandal asthaan
kar jihba tahan na chale, man pangul tahan jaan -110

[Bengali:]

Kabir is saying: by ajapa remembrance, one is established in the Realm of the Void. Rosary and tongue cannot go there. Mind, like a lame person, also cannot go there. -110

[Commentary:]

Kabir, ajapa japa happens in the par avastha of Kriya. Rosary, tongue and mind do not go there. -110

kabir mala kaatki, bahut jan kari pher mala
pher shvas ki, jaame ganthi nahi sumer -111

[Bengali:]

Kabir is saying: do not turn the mala [rosary] made of

wood; turn the mala of the breath, which does not have a knot at the end [like a physical mala]. -111

[Commentary:]

Kabir, do not turn the mala made of wood so much; turn the mala of breath, which does not have a knot at the end. -111

kabir man mala satguru dei, paon surtite poye binu
haate nishidin phire, brahm jap tahan hoye -112

[Bengali:]

Kabir is saying: satguru has taught one the mala of the mind. Keep that mala threaded by the breath. Turn it day and night without the use of hands. After that it will be the japa of Brahman. -112

[Commentary:]

Kabir, satguru has taught one: keep the mala threaded with breath. Turn it day and night without the use of hands. After that is the japa of Brahman in the par avastha of Kriya. -112

kabir mala jap na kar jap, mukhte kah na raam
man mera sumiran kare, maay paaye bishraam -113

[Bengali:]

Kabir is saying: do not do japa either with mala [rosary] or the hand; do not say "Rama" with the mouth either. My mind is automatically doing remembrance. I have got rest. -113

[Commentary:]

Kabir, do not do japa with mala or the hand, and do not say "Rama" with the mouth either. Mind is doing the remembrance of my Self. Then I got rest – meaning: if there is no mind, there is no separate "me" - meaning: the par avastha of Kriya. -113

kabir malato karme phire, jihba phire mukh maahi
manuya to chaudish phire, ye to sumiran naahi -114

[Bengali:]

Kabir is saying: the mala is turning by the hand; the tongue is also "turning" in the mouth. The mind is also turning about in all directions. Remembrance cannot be done by these. -114

[Commentary:]

Kabir, the thing with which you are doing remembrance of by the hand that mala is only turning and turning. The tongue by which you are saying the name of Rama – that tongue is also "turning" about. The mind by which you are doing these two acts – that mind is running around in all directions. How is this the doing of remembrance? Because - "smaran" [remembrance] meaning: contemplation of some object from "before" – this is called "smaran." "Before" [or: in the beginning] there was the One Brahman only the par avastha of Kriya – Brahman. Without that State, mind does not become Still. When mind is running, then even if you do thousands of japa with mala, if the mind is not Still, nothing will happen. -114

kabir raam naam ka sumiran, hansi kare bhau
khijh ulta sulta nipje, jayse khet ka bij -115

[Bengali:]

Kabir is saying: one who is always in the remembrance of the Name of Rama – people of the world express irritation at him, and laugh and joke about him. But these do not harm him. Although such things can push him back a bit [emotionally], but no harm comes of that as it is like seeds on a farm, whether they are scattered upside down or right side up, the sprouts will go upward anyway and the roots will go down into the earth anyway – meaning: [it] will remain as is. -115

[Commentary:]

Kabir, in the remembrance of the Name of Rama – meaning one who is constantly in the par avastha of Kriya – people become irritated with him and laugh at him, because everybody talks with others, and one who resides in the par avastha of Kriya does not even feel like or want to talk at all. Of course, people become irritated by this and laugh and joke, [saying sarcastically,] "He is a yogi!" etc. Upon hearing all these things, even if he [sadhak] is pushed back a bit [emotionally], that [spiritual] State does not go away. It is like when seeds are thrown into farming soil, not all seeds' "mouths" are towards the ground. But no matter which way the seeds are, it is absolutely certain that sprouts will go up and the roots will go into the earth. In that same way, no matter how much [the sadhak] is taken aback [by derision], [the State] will nevertheless be the same again. -115

kabir sumiran maha laagi de, surti aapni shoye kahahi
kabir samsara gun, tujhe na byape keye -116

[Bengali:]

Kabir is saying: enjoin mind to remembrance. If this happens, mind will not go in other directions and be lying down by itself – meaning: will be Still. Kabir is saying, "If this happens, the attributes of samsara cannot permeate you any more." -116

[Commentary:]

Kabir, no matter what anyone says, keep mind glued to the par avastha of Kriya. If mind is enjoined There, then instead of going in other directions it will remain lying down – meaning

"I"-ness. Kabir Saheb is saying that samsara, which is passing away, and its attributes which are passing away – these two cannot permeate you – meaning: [samsara] cannot attach itself to you. -116

kabir sumiran surti so, hot rahat hay mor ahut
mukh sumiran kare, ahinishi kai karor -117

[Bengali:]

Kabir is saying: remembrance is profoundly happening for me all the time verily – meaning: mind is always enjoined, and one is doing many millions of remembrance by screaming with the mouth. -117

[Commentary:]

Kabir, Atma-Rama Guru [Self] is abiding with the mind enjoined in the par avastha of Kriya, like when the peacock spreads its plume and keeps mind on that. Then the lips and mouth do millions of remembrance day and night – meaning: to pronounce with the mouth takes time, and if mind is enjoined, there is no need for time. It is always glued [to the par avastha]. It is when this happens that "ajapa" [automatic japa] happens, because that which is bound to time has count [or: numeration], and that which is not bound by time – japa of that cannot be done [manually]; it is happening all the time on its own. -117

kabir ragrag bole raamji, rom rom ra rankar
sahajei dhuni lagi rahe, kahahi kabir bichaar -118

[Bengali:]

Kabir is saying: in every "nadi" [meridians in the body], "Rama" is being spoken, and in every hair of the body, Rama is sounding "ONNNG" [OM]. That Sound is happening by Itself. Kabir Saheb is saying this from observation. -118

[Commentary:]

Kabir, that Atma-Rama is speaking in every nerve, and He is speaking in every hair of the body. All senses are experienced in the head. Because of this, the Word of the Atma-Rama - "ONNNG" [OM] – is constantly happening in every nerve and hair on the body. That Sound is happening on Its own. Kabir Saheb is saying this from observation. -118

kabir sahaj hi dhuni laagi rahe, setoyeh ghat maahi
hirde hari hari hot hay, mukh ki haajti naahi -119

[Bengali:]

Kabir is saying: the Natural Sound is verily united to this body. "Hari, Hari" [God, God] is going on all the time in the heart. What need of it [repetition] is there in the mouth? -119

[Commentary:]

Kabir, that Omkar Sound is united to this very body – meaning: It is the body. And then, in the heart – (the par avastha of Kriya has taken mind from all directions and brought it). When there is this State, then what is the need to say "Hari, Hari" with the mouth? -119

kabir panch sakhi piu piu kare, chata sumir man
aai surti kabir ki, paaya raam ratan -120

[Bengali:]

Kabir is saying: the five senses are crying "Piu! Piu!" "Piu" [beloved] – meaning: Swami [Lord - Self]. The five senses [are] the five "sakhi[s]" [lovers or friends] – meaning: Prakriti [Manifestation]. The One who is Mind is remembering. In this kind of State, Kabir got the Precious Treasure Who is Rama. -120

[Commentary:]

Kabir, "sakhi" - meaning Prakriti – the five senses in this body – they are crying "Piu! Piu!" - meaning: they are crying "Self, Self." Whatever That Self is making me do, it is only that that I am doing. And the "sixth one" is the Self, Who takes mind – meaning: in order to do remembrance of Brahman, one first does it rightly in the mind and then does it [remembrance]. Continuously doing remembrance of Brahman, Kabir's Self got the Rama-Jewel in the par avastha of Kriya. "Ra[a]ma" = ("r[a]" = sound [relating to] the fire-seed Kutastha; "aa" = sound [relating to] a lengthy period of time; "m[a]" = sound [relating to] being Still from the "Manibandha" [the jewel hold] to the heart) – this State is "Treasure" - meaning Priceless. That which is similar to something else is not priceless, because there is a thing that is like it, and That Which has no equal is of course Priceless. Kabir got this Rama-Jewel. -120

kabir mera man sumire raam ko, mera man raamhi aahi apne raam hi hoye, shish noyayon kaahi -121

[Bengali:]

Kabir is saying, "My mind is doing remembrance of Rama. My mind has become Rama and my self has also become Rama. Now who should one bow one's head to?" -121

[Commentary:]

Kabir, my mind is doing remembrance of Rama. Now mind is doing remembrance of Brahman. As long as it is doing remembrance, for that long has the mind verily become Rama, upon doing this continuous remembrance of Brahman. When I have become Rama, then to whom shall I do pranam [bow]? - 121

kabir tu tu karte tu bhaya, mujhme rahi nahu
waron tere naam par, jit dekhti ta tu -122

[Bengali:]

Kabir is saying: by doing "You, You," one became You. Then "I" no longer remained. Glory to His Name! In whichever direction one looks, You are there verily – meaning: "two" is not. Everything has become One. There is no one even there to say "One." -122

[Commentary:]

Kabir, the self, upon continuously telling God, "You are Lord. You are Savior, Master. You keep me in happiness etc." - meaning: upon continuously doing Kriya – became "You" in the par avastha of Kriya. No more "I-ness" remained in the Self. The Name which is the par avastha of Kriya – I express my gratitude to Him. Wherever I look, You are there verily – meaning: everything has become Brahman. -122

kabir tu tu karte tu bhaya, tujhme rahe samaay
tomhi maahi mil raha, ab man anat na jaay -123

[Bengali:]

Kabir is saying, "When, upon doing 'You, You' I have become You Yourself and I am staying in You, and I am staying merged in You, then mind does not go to other places any more. -123

[Commentary:]

Kabir, by doing "You, You" to God, I became "You." When I became You, then I entered You and remained there. It is like a thorn which pricked the foot. The thorn entered the foot but then again the thorn came out. But like the times when the thorn stays inside and eventually becomes the flesh itself, like that I become dissolved in You. Then mind no longer goes to other places – meaning: there is no separate mind. So who will go? -123

kabir sumiran chorike, pal jo bahar jaaye kahe
kabir sumiran bina, kaho kahan taharaaye -124

[Bengali:]

Kabir is saying: leaving remembrance, if mind goes in other directions even for one instant – Kabir is saying that there is no place to Rest [become Still] without remembrance. Where will one stand [Rest]? Except for remembrance, all else is in motion. -124

[Commentary:]

Kabir, if mind leaves the par avastha of Kriya for even one instant and goes in other directions – Kabir Saheb is saying, "Tell me where will you stand [Rest] except for in the par avastha of Kriya?" This is because apart from the par avastha of Kriya all else is in motion. -124

kabir kaheta jaat ho, shunta hay sab koye raam
kahe kal hoyega, nahi to bhala naa hoye -125

[Bengali:]

Kabir is saying: everyone has said and everyone is hearing that there will be good if the Name of Rama is practiced. If it is not done, evil will happen– good will not happen [or: it will not be good]. -125

[Commentary:]

Kabir, Atma-Rama Guru is telling everyone and everyone is hearing that it is upon doing Kriya that there will be Stillness in the par avastha of Kriya. If this is not done, it will not be good [or: good will not happen]. -125

**kabir bhali bhneyi hari bichreye, shirki gayi baalaai
ham jayse tayse rahe, ab kuch kahi na jaaye -126**

[Bengali:]

Kabir is saying: it is good that now I have forgotten to
say "Hari" [God]. The evil weight on the head has fallen off.
Now whatever I was, I am remaining as That. What this
State is – that I have no ability to say. -126

[Commentary:]

Kabir, now it seems I have forgotten about doing Kriya,
and the troublesome weight that was on my head – that is no
more there. However I am, I am remaining as that. What this
State is now – that I am unable to say. -126

**kabir jan kabir bandan kare, kis bidhi kishie seo
waar paarki gami nahi, tu man man manij deo -127**

[Bengali:]

Kabir is saying: devotees are singing praises and saying,
"By which set of rules should we serve?" The thing that has
no boundaries – its shore has no address. Therefore, do the
offering with mind to Mind Itself via the mind. This is what
is known as service. Otherwise who will do service for/to
whom? -127

[Commentary:]

Kabir – devotees of Kabir are singing the praises of
Kabir Saheb. Seeing this, Kabir Saheb is saying that
everyone is singing my praises, but no one at all knows how
to serve. There is no address for the shore of this worldly
ocean – meaning: the one who goes to the shore across
samsara – that one no longer sings praises nor does he do

service, because – Kabir Saheb's Self is saying to himself that you are the Mind of mind – its Mind – meaning Brahman. When you yourself will become God, then to whom will you do service after that? -127

LIKHTE AAKIL KO ANG

Elucidation on the Matter of Buddhi [intelligence, intellect]

**kabir aakil arashte utri, bidhi na dinho baanti ek
abhaga rahi gaya, ekanha liya sughaati -1**

[Bengali:]

Kabir is saying: the buddhi [intelligence] that has come
down from Para Brahman – God has equally distributed that to
everyone. I have taken a beautiful bank [like riverbank] and it
is I who has become "abhaagya." "Abhaagya" [without luck,
or without fate, or without share, or without division] –
meaning: one who has no "bhaagya" [luck, or fate, or share, or
division] ("na" + "bhaagya" = "abhaagya") - meaning: one has
become "bhaagyatit" [beyond "bhaagya"]. -1

[Commentary:]

Kabir, Atma-Rama Guru [Self] is saying that buddhi has
come down from Para Brahman – meaning: buddhi is the
activity of the Still Self – "this is my duty," "this is not my
duty" etc. And this buddhi has come from Kutastha Brahman –
meaning: when the self is totally Still, [it is] Kutastha, and
when in it is a little bit still, it is buddhi – this is good, this is
bad – this kind of buddhi. He [Lord] has distributed "bidhi"
[correct knowing] equally in the heads of everyone. "Bidhi" =
"bi" = verity, "dhi" = buddhi – meaning: the buddhi which has
no end – meaning Brahman. Only Kabir Saheb has become an

"abhaagya" [see previous paragraph]. "Bhaagya" = experiencing the fruits of acts performed in a past life. The one who does not have that – he is "abhaaga"[meaning in this case: "without fate"; colloquial meaning: "without luck"]. Yet upon becoming "abhaaga," I am seeing that not one person is at the beautiful bank [like riverbank]. "Sughaat" - meaning: "sundar ghaat" [beautiful bank]. "Beautiful" is that which captures the mind. With the singular exception of Brahman, nothing captures the mind at all. "Ghaat" [bank] = descending which, one can take a thorough bath – meaning: the bank on which no one says anything. If there is "two" [there is] speaking, talking. When it becomes "all is Brahman," then there is the beautiful bank. Otherwise there is no possibility of that happening. -1

kabir jas panchi bandhan para, suya ke buddhi naahi
aakil bihuna maanoa, eo banha jag maahi -2

[Bengali:]

Kabir is saying: the bird that has fallen into bondage – it has no buddhi. Man too, bereft of buddhi, has fallen into the bondage of life and death in this world. -2

[Commentary:]

Kabir, the mind that has no buddhi – the mind which has fallen into bondage - "aakil" [buddhi] – meaning: the human being bereft of the par avastha of Kriya, and the bird without buddhi – both are verily representing the bondage of the coming and going in the world – fallen into the bondage of birth and death. -2

kabir bina osil chaakri, bina aakil ki deh
bina gyanka jogiya, phir lagaaye kheh -3

[Bengali:]

Kabir is saying: a job with no income – meaning: one does

not receive a salary yet continues to work at the job, and a body with no buddhi – meaning: there is no steady understanding of any subject; there is no knowledge of right and wrong [or: good and evil], yet one has taken on a body – and a yogi without Knowledge – meaning: one [who] has not attained Brahman-Knowledge yet has taken on the title of "yogi" - it is these types of persons who are like ferries – meaning: like ferry trips they are just coming and going [meaninglessly]. -3

[Commentary:]

Kabir, a job with no remuneration – meaning: there is no revenue yet one is going to every "darbar" [wealthy household; door [as in "door to door"]; place of business] – and a body without the Infinite Happiness of the par avastha of Kriya; the life of one who has no samadhi is futile; and the yogi without Knowledge – meaning: one [who] does not know what Brahman is, yet is representing himself as a "yogi" by having matted hair and putting on ashes on the body. These people are only like riding a ferry – meaning: [endlessly] on the ferry trip of birth and death. -3

kabir jal paroane michri, ghat paroane buddhi
jaako jaysa guru mila, taako taysa shuddhi -4

[Bengali:]

Kabir is saying: whatever kind of guru one has got, his purifying is of that kind – meaning: one's knowledge is of that type. Just as the kind of water indicates the kind of fish – in deep water there is the possibility of finding big fishes, and in shallow [or: little] water there is mainly the possibility of finding small fishes, and the kind of body that one has got – his buddhi is also in that way - "ghat" = body – meaning: there are many different types of bodies – like idiots, who also have bodies – however one's "aadhaar" [container] is, so is that one's buddhi. -4

[Commentary:]

Kabir, the water indicates the type of fish – meaning: the way that one does Kriya will determine the way that the restless fish-like mind will become settled. And the way that one sits in steadiness after doing Kriya – his buddhi – meaning the Stillness – will be in that way. In the way that one has got Atma-Rama Guru, he will be purified – meaning immaculate – in that way. There is nothing Pure at all other than Brahman only. -4

LIKHTE UPADESH KO ANG

Elucidation on the Matter of Upadesh [teachings, initiation]

kabir hariji ehi bichaariya, saakhi kahe kabir
bhaosaagarme jeeb hay, shuni kai laage teer -1

[Bengali:]

Kabir – upon knowing Bhagavan Hari [Divine Lord], Kabir Saheb is speaking as "saakhshi" [witness]. "Saakshi" = "sa" + "akshi" = ("sa" = "with" or "by" + "akshi = "eye") = the Eye. The Eye that satguru reveals – it is He Who is the One Eternal Witness Himself. Kabir Saheb is speaking on the matter about Him, because upon seeing jivas fallen in the world-ocean, it feels like arrows are attacking his [Kabir Saheb's] body. [For souls] to be freed from this, the Witness is speaking. -1

[Commentary:]

Kabir, "Hari" = the One Who destroys the three types of afflictions – meaning [the One Who is] Brahman. "Vichaar" ["bichaar" in the doha] = ("vi" = "vigata" [passed], "chaar" = to do "charan" [surrender]) – meaning: when on is able to surrender in all, then it is "vichar" - meaning: "all is Brahman" happened.

139

"saakshi" [witness] = ("sa" = "with" + "akshi" = "eye")
"Kabir" = "kaya" - "Kabir" means body "bhaosaagar" [world-ocean] = birth, death

Brahman, upon entering all things, discerned this: that Kutastha Brahman Who is within the body as the Eye Itself – it is He Who is Truth. Kabir Saheb is saying, "Upon seeing jivas fallen in the world-ocean, it is feeling like arrows are attacking my body, because "jiva" [individual], itself is actually "Shiva" [Lord], and being jiva, it can end desire and be freed from the hands of death." Because of not ending desire, [the jiva] is caught in the bondage of birth and death. -1

kabir kal kal tatkal hay, bura na kahiye koye
an bowe so daahino, bowe so lunta hoye -2

[Bengali:]

Kabir is saying: "kal" [time] is itself that Brahman. No one speaks of Him badly. The seed is sown and one reaps its fruit, meaning: one falls into the hands of birth and death, and one who does not sow – meaning: one who does not speak good and bad – it is he who becomes liberated. -2

[Commentary:]

Kabir, "kal" = that which passes away. And so it is such, and it is the movement of that which is still, because that which moves – its nature is to move; and that which is still – when that moves, one can know "oh there it moves" - but the movement of that which is still – there is nothing at all other than Brahman which has Stillness, and so it is that the mobile and immobile are both verily Brahman. This "Kal" of "kal" is "Tatkal" - meaning: when both mobile and immobile are Brahman, then you cannot say that someone [or: something] is "bad." One who does not sow – his south side ["dakshin dik" - also means: right side] – meaning: one discerns: this is good;

this is bad. To discern/discriminate is called "bona." One who does not sow this discernment – meaning: one [who] does not accept good and bad and knows all as Brahman – that one broke through both sin and virtue. And one who sows it, in order to reap its fruits, falls and remains in the hands of birth and death. This is indebtedness. -2

kabir jo toko knata boye, taako boro tu phul
toko phulka phul hay, woko hay trishul -3

[Bengali:]

Kabir is saying that the person that – like a thorn in one's body – stops one from doing beneficent work – calm him down with sweet words like flowers and bring him to do beneficent work. Your flower-like words are of real worth, and that person's words are like a trident. He will die from the wrongness of his own words – meaning: one who tries to stop holy work from taking place – he himself ends up with death. - 3

[Commentary:]

Kabir, the person who puts a thorn in you when you try to do remembrance of Atma-Rama [Self] – meaning: stops you – that which feels like painful thorns to Kriyavans. The Kriyavan will give flowers to that person – meaning: he will say with a very sweet voice, "Please do Kriya once and see how much happiness and joy there is in this." By this, the Kriyavan gets flowers from flowers – meaning: like the way mind is happy from flowers, in that same way, not only is one experiencing Bliss upon doing Kriya himself, seeing that [another is doing Kriya], more Bliss comes to the heart of [the Kriyavan], and there is a trident for the one who does not listen to the words of the Kriyavan – meaning: "ida," "pingala" and "sushumna" - these three breaths kill that person. -3

kabir kahete ko kahi jaan de, unhaki budh mat-i lehu
shaakt aao puni shoyan ko, pheri jabab mat-i dehu -4

[Bengali:]

Kabir is saying: do not take in the ideas of those who only talk. Let them say whatever they are saying; there is no need to listen to them. It is like a dog whose nature it is to go "woof, woof." Let them bark, do not respond to them any more. -4

[Commentary:]

Kabir, those for whom the habit is to only talk – meaning: a person is seeing that one has put oil on oneself and is going to take a bath [a typical practice in India], but still, because of being bound by habit, that person says, "So sir! You are on your way to take a bath!" Let these types of people blabber on. Do not take in their ideas, because the talkers have become certain that: "I will definitely die. For the days that I am alive – let me indulge and enjoy by dancing and singing." A "shaakta" [one type of Tantrik practitioner] is drinking liquor and blabbering on and on, and a dog is barking upon seeing a shadow move. Do not respond to these people, because if you speak to a drunk person, he will say a thousand things, and if the shadow moves a lot, the dog will bark even more. "Drunk person" - meaning: a person who is intoxicated with the matters [of the world]. If he sees someone doing beneficent work, he immediately starts to blabber. Like a dog, as soon as he sees one doing Kriya, he immediately starts to bark that the end result of doing yoga will be the emergence of "roga" [infirmity], and where there even could be a few more days to live [indulge], one did not live even that. Do not respond to these types. -4

kabir hasti charaye gyanke, sahaj dolecha daari
shoyanroop samsar hay, bhukan de jhakmaari -5

[Bengali:]

Kabir is saying: put the natural carpet [seat] on the elephant and seat Knowledge on top of that, but most of this world is dog-like, they will meaninglessly bark. There is no harm in that. Let them bellow. -5

[Commentary:]

Kabir, sit on the natural seat on top of the Elephant of Knowledge. The world is dog-like. Let them bark. Like the way an elephant becomes clean [from bathing], gets up from the water and again gets dust on the body, in the same way, while staying in the par avastha of Kriya the entrancements of the dust of the world gather about, and, staying in that State – the "natural carpet [seat]" - meaning: the five-colored cloth – meaning: it goes element by element in that State; it continues going in that State automatically. "Samsara" [world] = that which passes on – upon seeing Stillness, this dog-like samsara is going on barking. Let them bellow. -5

kabir gaarite sabh upje, kaal kasht aaru mich
haari chale so saadhu hay, laagi mare so neech -6

[Bengali:]

Kabir is saying: all kinds of things can arise from insult and derision; eventually even violence can come about. Even if nothing like that happens, there can be emotional suffering. The reason for this is because this is not wanted [by the world]. The sages accept defeat [in words] to those who insult them, and go away. And those who are of low type – they end up bickering and fighting. -6

[Commentary:]

Kabir, all kinds of things arise from [someone's] insulting and derision– meaning: from one insult, he ended up giving another thousand insults, and with this, time was wasted. Kriya did not happen. And perhaps, from refuting, violence came about. If not that, then there is the great emotional suffering. And saying just one thing causes all such things to take place in the mind and one ends up disgusted with oneself. The sage accepts defeat [in words] to those insult him, and goes away. And the one who is of a low type– he protests. -6

**kabir kahe may kya kahon, thaake brahmaa mahesh
raam naam to tu saar hay, sabh kaahu upadesh -7**

[Bengali:]

Kabir is saying, "What can I say about that State where even Brahmaa and Mahesh [aspects of the Hindu Trinity] stayed put – meaning: They could not speak about It – know that the Name of Rama verily is the Essence [of everything]. There is no other possible way. There is no route other than Atma-Rama [Self]. It is this that is the Teaching of/for all." -7

[Commentary:]

Kabir, Atma-Rama Guru [Self] is saying, "What can I say, because, upon mind merging in Brahman in the par avastha of Kriya, no desire even remains. When neither mind nor desire are there, then who will speak? And the State about which Brahmaa and Maheshvar [aspects of the Hindu Trinity] have quit speaking – meaning: They have given up – meaning: They are unable to speak any more. "Brahmaa" = desire, at the Muladhar; "Mahesh" = at the navel as "Rudra," at the heart = in the Form of "Ishvara," at the throat = in the Form of "Sadashiva" – all of Them became Still upon the One Self being Still. When They became Still then naturally They stopped and stayed put. And it is so that the Name of Rama, which is the par avastha of Kriya – from Which all substances have been created – that State is the Essence of all substances, and It is the Teaching of/for all – meaning: it is the duty of everyone to abide in that State." -7

kabir jinha jaysa hari jaaniya, tinhako taysa laabh
jayse pyaas na bhajaai, jab laagi dhase na aar -8

[Bengali:]

Kabir is saying: in whichever way it is that one has known the Lord, his attainment is according to that. It is like: however much water you drink will determine how much of thirst is quenched. When at once you will drink a good deal of water, then the thirst will be completely gone. -8

[Commentary:]

Kabir, in whichever way one knows the Lord - "Hari" [Lord] = the One Who takes away [the illusion] – meaning: in whichever way whomever knows the par avastha of Kriya – his attainment is according to that – meaning: as much as one stays in the par avastha of Kriya, so much will be his [attainment] – three types of suffering are taken away. Thirst does not get quenched as long as water does not enter the body – meaning: one who remains in the par avastha of Kriya for only a short while – his thirst in the form of sorrow/pain does not get quenched, and one whose mind has entered the par avastha of Kriya – his thirst goes away. -8

kabir raamnaam ki lut hay, luti shake so lut
pheri paache pachtaahuge, jab tan jaaiye chut -9

[Bengali:]

Kabir is saying: the "loot" [meaning is same as in English] of the Name of Rama is there. If you want to grab It up, then grab It up. Otherwise there will be great regret at the time of leaving the body. -9

[Commentary:]

Kabir, the loot of the par avastha of Kriya is lying about. It is a Thing which is meant to be grabbed up – Wealth – because as soon as Wealth is got, there is satisfaction. The par avastha of Kriya is lying about, whoever wants, do Kriya and grab It up, lest there is suffering again and again. When I leave this body I will be saying, "Alas! Alas! If I did Kriya all the time then I would not have ever had to die." -9

kabir is duniyame aaikye, chori deo tom aayet
lena hoye so leile, uthi jaatu hay paayet -10

[Bengali:]

Kabir is saying: you have come to this world for a moment. Do not be proud. And if you want to take, then take now, because your life-force is diminishing day by day. -10

[Commentary:]

Kabir, having come to this Earth, do not be proud. And if you want to take, then take now, because breath is going away by day. -10

kabir kuru bande to bandegi, jo paaoe paak didaar
aosar maanukh janma kaa, hoye na baarambar -11

[Bengali:]

Kabir is saying: if you have received Kutastha Brahman, then give praise, because this human life will not happen again and again this way! -11

[Commentary:]

Kabir, Atma-Rama Guru is saying: O Glorious One!! Give praise! Praise "I AM" - because from the Praised – meaning: from Brahman – the Self [Atman] has come. Self, make YourSelf Your Own – meaning: do Kriya. If you have received the Pure Eye – meaning Kutastha Brahman – you have got just this little bit of a break [relief], because you have traveled 8,400,000 wombs and got this human birth. And it is not so that you will definitely get another human body after death – meaning: however one sins, so will be the birth that one gets, and again [at some point] one will get another human birth. -11

kabir johi marg sai mile, taahi chalo kari hos pheri
paache pachtaayega, kahe na maanasee rosh -12

[Bengali:]

Kabir is saying: walk carefully on the road on which you find Brahman, because if you do not do so then you will regret it later. And if you do not listen to my words then there will be anger in the mind. -12

[Commentary:]

Kabir, walk with alertness on the road on which Brahman is found, otherwise you will suffer later. If you do not listen to my words, then you will be angry inside – because when one falls down from becoming unconscious from the intoxication in the par avastha of Kriya and cracks his head, one thinks, "Oh what a good technique I've received. Now my head is broken." -12

kabir baar baar to so kahun, shunre manua neech
banijaraake bayel bneo, pyayre maahi mich -13

[Bengali:]

Kabir is saying, "Hey lowlife mind! I'm telling you again and again! You aren't listening! You are like the oxen of "bolde[s]" ("bolde[s]" = those who put goods on top of oxen and sell their wares at the market or bazaar. These people are called "bolde[s]"); scraping the ground, you are uselessly walking around in the market and bazaar." -13

[Commentary:]

Kabir, Atma-Rama Guru is saying, "Hey lowlife! I'm telling you again and again and still you're not listening!" The mind that does without telling it to do so is excellent. The one that does upon telling it to do so is of the mediocre nature, and the one that does not do even when told to do so is. "Like the oxen of "balde[s]," you are uselessly scraping the ground and going on ("balde[s]" = those who put goods on top of oxen and do trade that way; these people have goods of small value; they travel far for little profit) – you are that way, you lowlife! A mind who is a carrier of the load of traders who carry cheap goods! You are uselessly roaming!" An enterprise of little worth – "there will be beneficence; I will go to Indra-loka [heaven] etc." - the mind that carries a load of this type is low. -13

banijare ke bayel jeo, tanda utra aay ek nahake
duna bhaayi, ek chale mool gnoaye -14

[Bengali:]

Kabir is saying: the load on the boldes' [see "Bengali" section of doha 13 above] oxen – when the load on both sides is taken down, the oxen are freed. Emancipation is the real profit. With one base capital, two things happened. Some spent eternity with that one base capital! Some even spent the base capital itself. -14

[Commentary:]

Kabir, it is like: the baldes' [see "Commentary" section of doha 13 above] oxen are freed when the load from both sides is taken down. And some baldes have double profit, and for some even the base fund/capital is taken away. "Balde" [trader with oxen] = Kutastha; "balad" [ox] = self/Self. The self has a load on two sides – when it has passed ida and pingala and is going in sushumna, then the Self is emancipated. And for some Kutasthas there is double profit – meaning: the 3 are moving only on the outside; when the tongue goes up, outside and inside are both [same]. And some Kutasthas, after flinging off the intoxication of matter, very quickly cast off the body. -14

kabir banijake bayel jeo, bharmat phire chaudesh
khnar lahe bhoosh khatu hay, bin satguru upadesh -15

[Bengali:]

Kabir is saying: one is just like the bolde's oxen which travel about in every direction with "gur" [molasses, date sugar] loaded on their backs, but because of not having initiation/teaching from satguru, they eat chaff instead of the "gur" that is sitting on their backs. -15

[Commentary:]

Kabir, the baldes' oxen are roaming about in every direction and carrying a load of "gur" [see Bengali section above]. They are eating chaff – meaning: mind, who is under the Lordship of Kutastha, is going around in every direction, all the while carrying Kutastha, but because of not having teaching/ initiation from satguru, it is eating chaff. -15

kabir harika naan le, tyaji maaya bikh boj
baarbar nahi paai ho, manukh janam ki moj -16

[Bengali:]

Kabir is saying: abandon the poison that is maya, and grab hold of the Name of the Lord. You will not get the fun of this human birth again and again. -16

[Commentary:]

Kabir, Atma-Rama Guru is saying that you should take up the doing of Kriya and abandon the poison that is maya. "Bish" [poison] = the body burns terribly from ingesting poison – in that same way, the craving for money and women [sexual lust] do not end. When craving is not satisfied, there is agonizing pain, and if one falls into the current of the fun of maya, there is no rescue. For this reason, cast off maya, because you will not get a human birth or its own fun again and again either. The fun of human birth is only one: the par avastha of Kriya. -16

kabir jora aaye jor kiya, piya aapnaa pahichaan lena hoi so leile, uthat hay kharihaan -17

[Bengali:]

Kabir is saying: when power came to the body, then vayu also became strong, then one automatically came to know Swami [Lord]. Now, whatever you wish to get, ask Him and get it from Him. It is only when the time of harvesting grain arrives that grain is put into "khamaar" ("khamaar" = the place where harvested crops are kept). -17

[Commentary:]

Kabir, because doing Kriya with power and forcefully going into sushumna as if injected from a syringe, then vayu became strong. Immediately upon that force coming about, one's Swami-Self, the One Who is the Supreme Person, became present. Recognize it. The time for harvesting for "khamaar" [threshing floor, farmyard] has come. When harvesting time for "khamaar" arrives, everyone gets busy and puts grain in the silo. When the silos are full, the lord of the house is happy. In the same way, the Supreme Person has arrived and is here. Whatever you desire, ask and take it, because after that state, no desire remains – when there is no space left in the silo [or: it is completely full]. -17

kabir jauban jaaji deha tyaji, chale nishaan bajaay
shir par shvet saraaycha, diya budhapa aay -18

[Bengali:]

Kabir is saying: when youth leaves the body, then a flag flies as a sign – meaning: gray hair and the state of old age show up. -18

[Commentary:]

Kabir, youth is going away, flying the sign of a white flag on the head. Then the state of old age will come. For this reason, whatever you can do, do it while you are in your youth. -18

kabir jora aaye jot kiya joani dinha pit aankhan upar ke
chuli, bikh bhar khaaye meeth -19

[Bengali:]

Kabir is saying: youth has gone and the state of old age has come. Now there is no ability to do sadhana with power. The body has become lax; the eyes have developed cataracts; the body is now restless from the agony of the poisonous things that one ingested in the past, thinking that they are sweets, and "kal" [death] is also near. -19

[Commentary:]

Kabir, "kal" [time, death] has come and is imposing its power – meaning: the body has become lax in the state of old age; cataracts have developed in the eyes; all the poison-filled things that one ate thinking that they are sweets – now one is completely restless from agony [of having had those things] – meaning: death has come. -19

**kabir kananha laagi bol kahe, man nehi maane haari
raaj beraaji hot hay, shaake to raam sambhari -20**

[Bengali:]

Kabir is saying: talking has to be done close to the ear because the ears cannot hear [very well]; the mind does not obey; it is irritated about everything; it agrees with one thing and is disagrees another; there is no satisfaction in anything at all. The only emancipation from this condition is only Atma-Rama [Self]. When one has Ramachandra [Lord Rama], one does not suffer any more. -20

[Commentary:]

Kabir, in the state of old age, because of the ears being able to hear only a little, one brings the ears close to the speaker's mouth and [still] not being able to hear, one asks again and again, and what does it matter that the ears cannot hear, the mind itself is not accepting of anything. If it finds something that it desired, only then is it agreeable, otherwise it is obstinate. Only the One Rama can rescue one from this pain of the state of old age – meaning: if one does Kriya, that suffering does not happen. -20

**kabir uncha dishei dhau rahara, madhi chitaoe
shol ek harike naam binu, jam paarega rol -21**

[Bengali:]

Kabir is saying: in the state of old age, [doing] sadhana and meditation feels very difficult, very lofty and far away, and on top of that, maya has surrounded one from every direction. In this kind of condition, there is no way out except the Name of the Lord, otherwise one day there will be the Lord of Death, and you will weep. -21

[Commentary:]

Kabir, because meditation feels very lofty and far away in the state of old age, meditation feels very difficult, and one is ever increasing his attachment towards those who are in the house, and one is calling upon one's grandchildren and relatives with affection. Without the one Name of the Lord (Kriya), one day the Lord of Death will bring weeping and crying! -21

kabir tyaji chuta saharme, kasbe pari pukaar
daroaja diya raha, nikli gayaa asoaar -22

[Bengali:]

Kabir is saying: because the mind-Self has left the place, the people of the neighborhood are screaming. The doors are all closed, but the One Who was there – He is not there. -22

[Commentary:]

Kabir, in the city of the body, the mind-horse is running off, and everyone is screaming in the little neighborhoods of the body, that "cataracts have developed in the eyes" etc. All the doors are there – meaning: eyes, ears, arms, legs – they are as they were. But Kutastha Brahman, the rider of the mind-horse – He is going away. -22

LIKHTE BHAKTI KI ANG

Elucidation on the Subject of Devotion

bhakti dilaol upaji, lyaye ramanand pargat
kiya kabirjee, saat dvip nao khand -1

[Bengali:]

Ramananda* brought and bestowed the seed of devotion, and there was Kabir ji's revelation of the seven islands and nine divisions. -1

[*Translator's note: Traditionally, Kabir Saheb's guru is thought to be Ramananda Maharaj, a Vaishnav saint who was one of the few known saints at the time to completely disregard caste and religion when it came to accepting disciples. (Kabir Saheb is thought to have been born a Hindu but raised by Muslims.) Sri Ramananda is also thought to have initiated several other well-known saints of the time.]

[Commentary:]

"Bhakti" [devotion] = belief in the teachings of guru. Continuing to have faith in the teachings of guru, there was emergence in the heart, like the way the sprout is within the seed. It is not sprouting because there is no field. If there was the proper kind of earth, it would certainly sprout. In the same way, Brahman and Brahman's Supernatural Powers are everywhere. Upon sowing the Seed of Brahman in the earth of

155

devotion by Kabir Saheb, all Supernatural Powers took birth in the heart. This Seed was brought by Ramananda, and Kabir ji's Revelation happened – meaning: Kabir Saheb – the seven islands – meaning: there was Revelation in the body of seven nadis and the nine doors. -1

kabir bhakti nishenee mukti ki, chare sant sabh dhaaye binha praanee aalas kiya, janma gaye jahadaye -2

[Bengali:]

Kabir is saying: devotion itself is the sign of liberation. The sages and saints are going onward by riding on top of that. The being that is lazy about that – his life went fruitlessly. -2

[Commentary:]

The only sign of liberation is faith in the teachings of guru, the faith on top of which all saints are riding and going onward by that. "Sant" [saint] = one who is constantly in the par avastha of Kriya. The sage who is lazy about staying in that State – his life itself fell in the cracks – meaning: that which was needed to happen did not happen. -2

kabir kaaj chare nahi bhaktibin, laak kathay jao kaye shabd sanehi hoye rahe, gharko pahunchey shohye -3

[Bengali:]

Kabir is saying: without devotion and belief no work is accomplished. Nothing will happen with millions of words. The one for whom affection for the Omkar Sound has taken birth, and the one who has reached the House of that Omkar Sound – only for him can it happen. -3

[Commentary:]

Kabir, without belief no work attains excellence. Blabbering millions of words is murderous. One talks a lot from the shastras [scriptures], but because there is no faith, it does not work. One for whom affection comes about for the Word – meaning: one for whom there is affection for the Omkar Sound – he reaches the House – meaning: as long as one listens to the Omkar Sound, vayu remains still. With vayu continuously remaining still, the par avastha of Kriya is attained. -3

kabir khet bigaare kharthua, sabha bigaare kur bhakti bigaare laalchee, jeon keshareeme dhur -4

[Bengali:]

Kabir is saying: just as weeds destroy a field/farm, and as a congregation is ruined by one leper – meaning: it is like – if there is a leprosy-afflicted person in the congregation – everyone feels repulsion upon seeing him and instead of sitting in that congregation, they break up the gathering – in the same ways [as the two examples above], greed also destroys devotion – like what happens when there is saffron that is full of dirt. -4

[Commentary:]

Like a farm is ruined by kusha [tough grass] and reeds – meaning: if reeds grow on a rice field, rice does not grow on that field. A leper ruins a congregation. If there is a leper in a congregation, it is an unpleasant sight to see and the people of the group feel repulsed as well. Devotion is ruined by greed – meaning: "I have a desire to listen to the Omkar Sound." As long as one did not hear the Omkar Sound, so long did one not believe in the teachings of guru. Without belief, devotion did not come about. Without devotion, nothing was accomplished. Like dirt on saffron – meaning: if one eats saffron, there is a pleasing scent, but if there is dirt in that, it crunches in the teeth and causes problems, and because mind stayed on what is happening with the teeth, one did not smell the scent – in that same way, because of mind not being on the Omkar Sound – alas! "Can I hear the Omkar Sound in this or not" - upon this kind of thing rising in the mind, devotion did not come about. Because of not having devotion, no fruit came from Kriya. Thus, it is by doing Kriya without desire and with faith in the teachings of guru that there is fruit. -4

kabir timiri gai rabi dekhte, kumti gai gurugyan
satya gai ek lobhte, bhakti gai abhimaan -5

[Bengali:]

Kabir is saying: ("rabi") upon seeing the sun, ("timir") darkness is destroyed; with the Knowledge of satguru, wrongful ideas are destroyed. The One Who is Truth – He is lost with just one bit of greed. And as well, devotion is destroyed by vanity. -5

[Commentary:]

Kabir, upon witnessing the Sun of Kutastha, darkness was cast away. By knowing Atma-Rama Guru [Self], wrongful ideas were cast away – meaning: if mind is constantly on the Self, wrongful ideas no longer remain. Truth left with just one bit of greed. Truth = Brahman – because of mind being under the power of greed, and thus going in other directions, mind became separated from Brahman. Because of vanity, devotion went – meaning: because I don't know, I went to guru. I should just listen to what guru says, because I should not speak about matters about which I do not know. [But] I did not do that and I began to argue about supernatural matters. Because I did not understand, faith did not come about in guru's teachings. I should remain in the Self, because outside of the Self I have no ability to know, but because of vanity I am outside the Self. Why did Brahman create this? -5

kabir bhakti bhaao baado nadee, sabhe chale ghaharaaye salitaa soi saraaiye, jo jeth maas thaharaaye -6

[Bengali:]

Kabir is saying: devotion is like the river in the month of Bhadra [mid-August to mid-September], whoever falls in the current is taken away. [But] one who can go even after knowing the parched conditions like the month of Jaishtha [mid-May to mid-June] – it is he who is excellent. -6

[Commentary:]

Kabir, having faith in the teachings of guru and being in the par avastha of Kriya – which is like the river in the month of Bhadra – meaning: like the way the rivers in the month of Bhadra are full of tremendous currents, in the same way, there is [tremendous] intoxication in the par avastha of Kriya. And just as a river in the month of Bhadra pulls everything away with its current, in the same way, the desires goes away in the par avastha of Kriya. Every river is full of torrent in the month of Bhadra, but the river that is truly strong is the one that is full of torrent in the month of Jaishtha. In that same way, there is intoxication for everyone in the par avastha of Kriya, but the one for whom that State does not go away even in the periods of intense suffering, like the sun in the month of Jaishtha – it is he who is excellent. -6

kabir kahe pukaari kai, kyaa pandit kyaa shekh bhakti hetu shabde gahe, bahuri na kaachai bhekh -7

[Bengali:]

Kabir is loudly telling pandits [Hindu scholars] and shekhs [Muslim scholars], "In order to have devotion, become engaged in the Omkar Sound. If that happens, then there will be no more need to dress up with dot [religious symbol on the forehead] and loincloth." -7

[Commentary:]

Kabir Saheb is loudly telling pandits and shekhs that in order to have faith, become absorbed in the Omkar Sound. It is then that you will understand and faith will come about. This was in Me verily, yet I did not know. When faith happens, there is no more need to dress up with tilak, dot [both religious symbols on the forehead] and loincloth. -7

kabir kaamee krodhee laalchee, inhate bhakti naa hoye
bhakti kare kai sooreeyan, tan man lajjaa khoye -8

[Bengali:]

Kabir is saying: devotion does not happen for those who are lustful, full of anger or greedy. Not regarding body, mind and prestige, some hero/warrior [types of people] are able to have devotion. -8

[Commentary:]

Kabir, "kaamee" [lustful person] = one who has desires related to the body; "krodha" = anger — which is of the mind; "laalchee" = greedy — devotion does not happen for these three types of people, because mind is in the direction of obtaining fruits/results. And the person who is a hero/warrior [type], devotion is for him only, because he — with the body — meaning: if someone jokes about him because of being in yoga asana, he does not care; he does not find fulfillment of the mind in anything but the Self; if someone says derogatory things about him, he does not feel shame; and, feeling that everyone's talk is of no value, he does Kriya. -8

kabir bhakti doar hay sankraa, rahi dashaye bhaay
man airaot hoye rahaa, kis bidhi paytaa jaay -9

[Bengali:]

Kabir is saying: the door of devotion is extremely subtle —

that which is being known in subtle form through the ten doors. Mind – he is verily like an elephant ("Airavat" [god of elephants]). How will he enter that [subtle door]? -9

[Commentary:]

Kabir, the door of faith is very subtle, which is being experienced in subtle form via the ten doors. By the Atom of Brahman – meaning: the Star in the Kutastha, the Omkar Sound in the ear, smelling scents from far away with the nose, nectar on the tongue, touch on the skin – in this way, two noses, two eyes, [two ears,] one mouth, one sex organ, one anus, one holder of hairs [skin] – are experienced in their subtle forms/functions via the Atom of Brahman. How will the elephant-like mind ("Airavat") enter that Subtle Brahman – the Atom of Brahman? -9

kabir gyan na bedhiya, heerdaya nahin judaaye dekhaa dekhi bhakti kare, ranga nahin thaaharaaye -10

[Bengali:]

Kabir is saying: if one is unable to penetrate Knowledge, the heart does not become calm. And those who practice devotion by looking about – they do not get True Peace. -10

[Commentary:]

Kabir, if one is unable to penetrate Knowledge – meaning: if one does not enter the par avastha of Kriya and stay there, the heart is not fulfilled. One who practices devotion by looking about – meaning: he practices because of seeing that it has done good for others – his enchantment does not remain – meaning: the par avastha of Kriya [does not remain]. -10

kabir chema khet bhal jotiye, sumiran beej jamaaye khanda brahmanda shukhaa parai, bhakti beej nahi jaaye -11

[Bengali:]

Kabir is saying: plough well the field of forgiveness; in it, sow the seed of remembrance. The Universe and all its pieces can dry up, but the seed of devotion never fails. -11

[Commentary:]

Kabir, plough the field of forgiveness and farm it well, and sow the seed of remembrance – meaning: plant it. The Universe and all its pieces dry up, but not the seed of devotion.

"Khetra" [field] = that in which harvest happens – the harvest of the field of forgiveness goes to the one who says it – meaning: one who insults a yogi – the yogi sows those words in the field of forgiveness, and the fruit of that comes about for the one who speaks the harshness. Farm the field of forgiveness well. There are two oxen on the field – ida and pingala, and the ploughshare [ploughed groove in the field] is sushumna – meaning: firmly stay in sushumna at all times. Sow the seed of "sumiran" [remembrance] (the par avastha of Kriya) – meaning: remain always in samadhi. "Khanda" = piece – meaning: staying once in the Atom of Brahman and again coming to this side – it dries up in this way. And the Infinite Universe – meaning: staying constantly in the Atom of Kutastha, there is the coming together/congealing.

The seed of devotion does not go away – meaning: even if Perfection/ Realization is not attained, faith remains for one in the next life. -11

jneo jal pyaro machri, lobhee pyaro daam maat hi pyaro baalaka, bhakti piyaar raam -12

[Bengali:]

He is saying: just as the fish loves to be in water and loses its life when it is out of the water, the greedy man similarly does not want anything other than money. Just as the child cannot bear to be without mother, in the same way devotion cannot be without Rama. -12

[Commentary:]

It is like the fish which loves water. The fish stays always in the water. If the fish is without water even for moments, it thrashes and writhes about. The greedy person wants nothing at all except money. The child loves nothing other than mother. In that same way, the devotee does not want anything except Atma-Rama [Self]. When mind leaves the Self and goes elsewhere, it immediately begins to thrash about and writhe like the fish. -12

kabir bhakti bhekh bada antaraa, jaiche dharanee akaash bhakta jo sumirai raam ko, bhekh jagat ki aash -13

[Bengali:]

Kabir is saying: there is a huge difference between "bhakti" [devotion] and "bhek" [outward appearance], like sky and Earth. It is the devotee that does remembrance of Rama, and the one who puts up an outward show actually keeps his hope with the world. -13

[Commentary:]

Kabir, "bhakti" [devotion] = upon having faith in the teachings of guru, the Settledness in the par avastha of Kriya; "bhekh" [outward appearance] = fake [or: imitated] devotion.

There is a massive difference between "bhakti" and "bhekh," like Earth and sky. Just as everyone is walking about on top of the Earth and doing all kinds of things, in the same way, if someone insults or does wrongful deeds, the yogi does not say anything about that and remains calm and steady like the Earth. And the sky is nothing at all, only moving. One who is a devotee does Self-Kriya and remains in Atma-Rama in the state of samadhi. And the one who is fake is like the moving sky; he keeps hope with the world – meaning: he does not get the Stillness. -13

kabir par naa taate hot hai, mante kijai bhaao
paramaarth parateet me, yeh tan rahe ki jaao -14

[Bengali:]

Kabir is saying: you are experiencing yourself in the "other" (the body of sense-organs), and whatever feeling is coming to the mind, it is doing just that. When you come to know the Supreme Wealth/Knowledge, then whether this body stays or goes will not make a difference. -14

[Commentary:]

Kabir, who are you? Brahman. It is only that you have made a relationship with the "other," which is the body, and you have become "you" and performing all actions [in this way]. The Mind by which you are doing all actions, make romance with that Mind. When romance is there, you will become One and reside beyond the three gunas. Afterwards, "shreshthartha" [greatest wealth] – meaning: That Wealth, like Which there is no other of such value – there will be faith in that Wealth – meaning: you will become That Itself, regardless of whether this body stays or goes. -14

kabir jab tab bhakti sakaamata, tab tak nihphal seo
kahe kabir ohon kno-o mile, nihangkamee nij deo -15

[Bengali:]

Kabir is saying: as long as you have desire-oriented devotion, for that long will it be fruitless. Kabir is saying: by practicing desireless devotion, one gets the God of one's Self – meaning: as long as there is wanting, for that long will one not get Him. -15

[Commentary:]

Kabir, up to the point that you do Kriya with desire-oriented devotion, for that long will that Kriya be fruitless. Kabir Saheb is saying, "How will you get It?!! Because the One Who is your God – Kutastha Brahman – He is without desire. When you will become That Itself, then no desire will remain for you, because as long as there is desire, for so long were you not able to be Brahman." -15

LIKHTE PREM KO ANG

Elucidation on the Matter of Love

eha to ghar hai premkaa, khaala kaa ghar naahi
shish utaare bhnui dhare, so paite ghar maahi -1

[Bengali:]

Kabir is saying: this is verily the house of Love. This is certainly not the house of someone else. One who brings his head down and holds it on the earth – he will enter the house. -1

[Commentary:]

This is the house of Love, not the house of "maasi" [maternal aunt]. One who will cut his head off and hold it on the ground is the one who will enter the house. "Prem" [love] = the thing from which mind does not stray elsewhere. "Maasi" = the mother of mind; the outer phenomena. "Maasi" is this body. One goes to maasi's house, spends a few days enjoying oneself and then comes back home again. [Thinking] that one will be able to stay [conjugate] with these sense-organs of this body and still go to the house of Love – meaning: to Brahman – this is not possible. Bring the head down and hold it on the earth – meaning: when, from [or: in] the earth-like body, you will abide in the head, and after which when you will abide in the Muladhar, then you will enter the house – meaning: you will enter the Atom of Brahman. -1

167

kabir shish utaare bhnui dhare, upar raakhe
pnaao daas kabira eyon kahe, aysaa hoye to aao -2

[Bengali:]

Kabir is saying: putting head in the ground and the legs above, Servant Kabir is saying, "If you can do this, then come." -2

[Commentary:]

Kabir, by vayu becoming Still in the head, and thus the Kulakundalini awakening and becoming "samaan" [same] from Muladhar to Sahasrar, the head is on the ground – meaning: it is held in the Muladhar and the legs are above (these two [are] Kriya). Servant Kabir is saying, "If you can be like this, then come into the house!" (When you can be this type of Kriyavan, then come into the house.) -2

kabiryeh ghar to prem kaa, maarag agam agaadh
shish kaat paalra dhare, laage prem samaadh -3

[Bengali:]

Kabir is saying: this is verily the house of Love, and this is also the path for other Inaccessible/Unknowable Areas. If one cuts one's head off and balances the scale on both sides – when that happens, then the samadhi of Love has happened. -3

[Commentary:]

Kabir, so the house of Love is right here! The path to the house of Love is "agamya" [inaccessible/unknowable] (meaning: only that which is moving is able to be accessed/known, and That which is Still – That has no coming and going; it is automatically inaccessible/unknown), and "agaadh" [unfathomable] – meaning: no matter how much one stays in the par avastha of Kriya, one cannot find Its end. When one cuts of the head and balances it on the scale, then the Love-samadhi happens. Head = sushumna; scales = ida and pingala. By cutting off the place of the scale-holder that is above, the two scales fall down and lie there and the scale-holder is on top of them. That ida and pingala became Still and the sushumna went on. Then the scales were no more. Then those two gunas [primal attributes] became Still and became One, and sushumna went on above into the Substance. -3

kabir prem bhakti kaa gharaa, uncha bahutak maath
shish kaat pagutar dhare, tab pahunchegaa haat -4

[Bengali:]

Kabir is saying: the pot of Love is higher than even the head. One cannot reach it with the hands. When one cuts off the head and holds it below the

feet, then one can have it in hand [meaning: one can have the pot of Love in hand]. -4

[Commentary:]

Kabir, "prem" [love] = that thing, when absent, that it is no problem to give up one's life. The pot of devotion and Love is higher than the head; it cannot be had in the hand. One got it after cutting off the head and holding it under the feet – meaning: do Kriya with Love and devotion. But no matter how much Kriya you do, it is very difficult to go to the head. When one gets the Stillness Substance and there is power from the head to the feet – meaning: with the power of vayu, it can rise to space [or: in the air] – then one can get it in the hand – meaning: if one becomes Still, one can grab hold of It. -4

kabir prem na baari upaje, prem na haat bikaay
binaa premkaa manoa, baddhaa jampur jaay -5

[Bengali:]

Kabir is saying: Love does not come from water [like other living things]; Love is not sold [found] in the marketplace either. The human being that is without love – he goes to the city of death tied and bound. -5

[Commentary:]

Kabir, "prem" [love] – meaning: being One in all ways – meaning: the par avastha of Kriya – meaning: being merged in Brahman – meaning: "all is Brahman." This Love does not arise from water and It does not arise from earth – meaning: by destroying the body and doing by sucking the blood out does not allow Love to happen. And Love does not happen in woman [lust] and liquor either, because in both there is their own selfish desire for pleasure. If by filling the woman's stomach the man did not again have to eat, then it could be said that Love has happened. And if one was not taken by liquor – and if at all times of the day and night the intoxication remained always and the same, then it could be called Love. And It is not sold in the marketplace either, because as long as the desire remains for buying, selling and profit, for that long Love does not happen. Now, the human being that does not have Love – he is taken tied and bound to the city of death – meaning: there is death in order to take a birth again. -5

kabir sheesh utaran na kaaha, dinho bhaao bataay
tino lok ka sheesh hay, jore utaaraa jaay -6

[Bengali:]

Kabir is saying: it is not that I have been talking about [actually] cutting of the head. I have spoken about a state of "bhaav" [feeling-being-experiencing]. The three worlds themselves have heads, which can be brought down with force. -6

[Commentary:]

Kabir, before I had spoken about cutting off the head – it is not [actually] so. I have spoken about "bhaav" [see paragraph above] – meaning: the par avastha of Kriya. This "sheesh" [head] is in each of the three worlds – meaning: head (heaven), heart (Earth), legs/feet (underworld). One can bring them down via intense Kriya. -6

kabir prem piyaalaa so piye, jo sheesh dacchina dey
lobhee sheesh na de sake, naam premkaa ley -7

[Bengali:]

Kabir is saying: the one who gives his head as a "dakshinaa" [religious offering] to guru – verily it is he that fills the cup of the Nectar of Love and drinks it. And the greedy person cannot offer it [the head]; he has love by name only; he did not get Love in actuality. -7

[Commentary:]

Kabir, the one who gives his own head as the "dakshinaa" [see above paragraph] is the one who can drink from the cup of Love. The one who is greedy cannot offer his head; he only carries the name of "love." When there is no "me," then there is no head – meaning: in the state of samadhi, there is no "me." The abode of "buddhi" [intellect, mind] is the head; for this reason the head has been recognized as prime. "Lobhee" [greedy] = those who are always trying for profit – they do not want to do Kriya, because of: "will anything happen or not by doing that?" The greedy persons want the fruit first. They just speak with their mouths. If Liberation happens, then there is Release; otherwise there is the fulfilling of karma again and again. -7

kabir sheesh kaat pashangaa kiyaa, jeeu surahee bharileen jehi bhaave so aaile, prem aami kahi deen -8

[Bengali:]

Kabir is saying: having cut off the head, and having balanced the scales, the jiva [individual] filled up the pot of the body. The persons who want to fill up – come, fill up. This is verily the Inaccessible/Unseen Love. The lowly Kabir has said this. -8

[Commentary:]

Kabir, cut off the head and balance the scales. The containers of the scale are heavy on one side and light on the other side. Among these two containers, one is rajah guna and tamah guna, and the other is sattva guna. "Sattva guna" - worship of the Divine, recitation of scriptures etc. In rajoguna and tamoguna are worldly things and woman [lust]. Sattva guna is in the head. The head is heavy. And whatever there is, all happens from the head. If there is no head, there is no body. For this reason the head is heavy. Upon continuously doing Kriya and thus becoming Still in the head, all of the misbehavior that was there – all went away. When this Stillness is brought to the Muladhar, all three gunas become "samaan" [same; equilibrium; merged; one]. And the wine-pot has no head – meaning: from the throat to the Muladhar is one pulled straight state. The persons who want to fill this wine-pot, come and fill it up. The Love that is [here] is the Unseen/Inaccessible. Kabir Saheb thus said so – meaning: where there is motion, there is coming and going, and where there is Stillness, there is no movement [or: path of movement] for going there. -8

kabir prem piyaala bhari piyaa, raachi rahaa gurugyan diyaa naagraa shabd kaa, laal khaare maydaan -9

[Bengali:]

Kabir is saying: drink up from the bowl filled with the Nectar of Love. When that happens – that is when you will be able to know all of the expounding from guru. You will be able to hear the Omkar Sound like the "naagra" [a type of kettle drum] when "laal" [precious one] (special, priceless Jewel) is stood erect on the open field of Brahman. -9

[Commentary:]

Kabir, "prem" [love] = One – meaning: the par avastha of Kriya. Fill the bowl of Love and drink. "The bowl of Love" = head. From the well of the body, fill up the bowl of Love – meaning: do Kriya. Then you will be able to know all that Atma-Rama Guru [Self] is speaking about – meaning: you will see all kinds of wonderful, beautiful, extraordinary happenings, and at that time you will hear the Omkar Sound like the sound of "naagra" [see above paragraph], and "laal" [precious one] in the Form of Priceless Kutastha Brahman – He revealed Himself in the open field (meaning: where there is no one at all). -9

kabir cchin pare cchin utarne, so to prem na
hoye aat pahar laagaa rahe, prem kahaaoe soe -10

[Bengali:]

Kabir is saying: once rises, once falls – that is surely not Love. The one who is connected at all times of the day and night – it is his Love that is truly Love. -10

[Commentary:]

Kabir, there is intoxication for a little while, and there is no intoxication for a little while – when it happens like this – that is not called "Love." The one whose intoxication remains, and remains the same, at all times of the day and night – it can be said that Love has happened for him. -10

kabir aayaa prem kahaan gayaa, dekhaaya sab
koy pal roye pal mo hnaase, soto prem naa hoy -11

[Bengali:]

Kabir is saying: so Love had come, and then where did It go? But everyone saw this: one is laughing one moment and crying another moment. That was also not Love. -11

[Commentary:]

Kabir, Love had come, and then where did It go? Everyone had seen: one cries for a moment and laughs for a moment. That is certainly not Love– meaning: being a Kriyavan itself there is intoxication for a short while, and then where did it go? When the intoxication was there, at that time there was Bliss, and not it is not there then there is no joy. This type of intoxication cannot be called Love. The one for whom intoxication is there at all times of the day and night – for him, Love is. -11

prem prem sab hin kahe, prem na chinhe koy jnohi
ghat prem pinjar base, prem kahaaoe soy -12

[Bengali:]

Kabir is saying: so everyone is saying "love, love," but no one at all knows Love. The one for whom Love has settled into the rib cage [or: bones] of the body – it is his Love that radiates beautifully, verily. -12

[Commentary:]

So everyone says "love, love," but no one at all knows what Love actually is. The body in which Love settles in the rib cage [or: bones] – that is called Love – meaning: everyone has said that if there is no love for God, everything is useless/meaningless, but they do not know what the par avastha of Kriya is. The head in which the cage of Love has set – meaning: the strips [of metal or bamboo] and the bars of the cage, and the bird of Prana [meaning in this case: the life-force, not one of the several prana-vayus] – the one in whose head this cage with Prana is set – meaning: becomes Still – it is for him that Love has happened. -12

kabir prem na chinhiya, chaakhi na kinho soadeya
shune gharka paahuna, jneo aaoe tneo jaay -13

[Bengali:]

Kabir is saying: so I did not get to know [or: recognize] Love, and I did not get the taste of Love either. Like a guest in an empty house – meaning: as it came, so it went – I did not get to know anything at all. -13

[Commentary:]

Kabir, so I did not get to know [or: recognize] Love. That which can be seen – that can be recognized. In the par avastha of Kriya, even oneself is not there; so who is there to recognize? And I did not get to lick Love and I did not get its taste. I am a guest in an empty house – meaning: in the par avastha of Kriya, as I am going, I am coming back the same. -13

kabir prem piyaare laal so, man mo kinho bhaao
satguruke prataapte, bhaalaa banaa haay dneo -14

[Bengali:]

Kabir is saying: having drunk the Nectar of Love, the "laal" [precious] ("laal" = special priceless Jewel) jewel of the heart is in "bhaav" [loving feeling] in Brahman – meaning: is always stuck to It. It is by satguru's power that I have received this type of opportunity. -14

[Commentary:]

Kabir, "piyaare" [loved one] – the one who is always wanted. "Laal" [precious] = priceless. I am staying in Brahman in the par avastha of Kriya at all times of the day and night. And I have made "bhaav" [loving feeling] in the heart – meaning: I have become beyond the three gunas [primal attributes]. By the power of Atma-Rama Guru [Self], I have now got a very good opportunity. -14

kabiryeh tan jvaron masi karon, likho raam ko naam likhnee karo kark ke, likhi likhi pathaao raam -15

[Bengali:]

Kabir is saying: burn this body and make "black" [ink] out of it, and in that "black" write the Name of Rama. And make a pen out of the pain of the mind/heart, write the Name of Rama and send it. -15

[Commentary:]

Burn this body and make "black" [ink]. And write the Name of Rama with that ink. "Karak" = meaning: making a pen out of your suffering, write the Name of Rama again and again and send it – meaning: burn this body and make "black" [ink]. If it is burned there are ashes and there is no form. In the par avastha of Kriya, even the mind becomes ash – meaning: nothing at all remains. "Kalee" - black – in the par avastha of Kriya – which can be said to be a kind of "black" - write the Name of Rama – meaning: abide in the par avastha of Kriya. The little pain [trying effort] in doing Kriya – that is the pain – meaning Kriya. Continuously doing Kriya, send the self to the par avastha of Kriya. -15

BIRAHA KO ANG

On Profound Longing
["Biraha" - Pain of Separation]

kabir peer peerani birha ki, aur naa kachu so haaye
jaysi peer hay birha ki, rahi kaleje chaaye -1

[Bengali:]

Kabir is saying: nothing at all is feeling good because of the pain of longing. Like this, the pain of longing has completely taken over the heart. -1

[Commentary:]

Kabir, in longing there is only Beloved and Lover; nothing at all feels good in the pain of longing. This kind of affliction of longing is happening; that affliction has completely taken over the heart. Not being able to see the one to whom love is being sent – that is called "biraha" [profound longing]. Staying in something else other than Brahman – the "biraha" for Brahman – in the pain of that longing, nothing at all feels good (except Brahman). This kind of affliction is happening. Longing has completely taken over the heart. -1

kabir chot santaaoe birha ki, sab tan jhanjhara hoye
maar nihaara jaanchi, ki bis kaa laagi hoye -2

[Bengali:]

Kabir is saying: from having to withstand the blows of the

pain of longing, the whole body has become full of holes, like a strainer. The one who has taken the beatings of longing and then known, and the one has been hit by such – it is he who has known. -2

[Commentary:]

Kabir, the one who is longing is withstanding the blows of longing. And his body has become full of holes, like a strainer. It is like when water is put into a water-pot full of holes – like how all the water leaks out – in that same way, the sadhu to whom the longing for the Supreme Being has come about nothing at all holds to his body – meaning: no pleasant or unpleasant things nothing at all holds the mind/heart. And there is this body full of holes like a strainer. The one who has taken the beatings of longing and then known, and the one who has been hit by such – it is he who knows. -2

kabir biraha bhujangam tan dacheo, mantra na laage koy raam biyogee naa jniye, jniye to bayur hoy -3

[Bengali:]

Kabir is saying: longing is like a snake biting/stinging the body. Not a single mantra is being able to be an antidote to the poison of that snake of longing. The person who has cut out Rama cannot go on living. If somehow he lives, then he lives in madness. -3

[Commentary:]

Kabir, the snake of longing is biting/stinging the body – meaning: thoughts/things, because not abiding in the par avastha of Kriya causes mind to be stuck to thoughts/things. And because of having no relief from the thirst of thoughts/things, mind is constantly crying, "Alas, alas!" The mantra of Kriya is noticed, kind of held to – meaning: mind does not hold to it. "Raam biyogee" [one who has left Rama] – meaning: one whose Self has left the body, how can he live? Another meaning is: if he lives then he becomes like "bayura" [wind-like] – meaning: like a mad person – [mind] in worldly thoughts/things at one time, [mind] with his children at another time – wandering about like a mad person. -3

kabir birha bhujangam paithike, kiya kaleje jaao
binhinee ang na mori, jo bhaoe to khaao -4

[Bengali:]

Kabir is saying: the snake of longing has sat in the heart and made wounds in the heart, but the one who is longing – he is going on withstanding it. He does not even turn to the side – meaning: he stays as he is. Now eat what you like. -4

[Commentary:]

Kabir, the longing for God – meaning: in the Substance – the snake of mind has sat in the heart and made wounds in it – meaning: one is writhing with pain, crying, "Alas, alas!" But the one who is longing is not closing up the body – meaning: is not turning to the side – meaning: is not putting mind in the thoughts/things. Now eat whichever of the two mentioned above that you wish to have. -5

kabir ragrag baje rabaab tan, biraha santaaye
nit aur na koi shunsi, sai shune ke chit -5

[Bengali:]

Kabir is saying: in every nerve the "rabaab" [lute] (Omkar Sound) is playing, but because longing is constantly causing grief, it is not allowing one to hear the aforementioned Sound. Only God Kutastha Brahman is listening. -5

[Commentary:]

In every nerve the Omkar Sound is manifesting, but the hero of mind is in another direction and is constantly causing grief – meaning: because of mind being pulled into thoughts/things, it is not allowing one to hear the Omkar Sound. The worldly matters cause great suffering because hopes are not completely fulfilled. Other than the Self and Kutastha, no one else at all can hear the Omkar Sound. -5

kabir biraha jo aayo darash ko, kaduaa laagaa kaam
kaaya laagi kaal hoye, mithaa laaga raam -6

[Bengali:]

Kabir is saying: when longing saw that this body of mine is itself "kal" [time, death], then all kinds of cravings and wrongful experiences went on happening. Only the Name of Rama went on feeling sweet, and everything else was felt as false. -6

[Commentary:]

When, while in the longing of the Lord, the one who is longing witnessed the Supreme Person, then his desires went on feeling bitter, and he began to feel that my body itself is "kal" [death, transiency], because if the was not there, he would be That Form. And only the Self felt sweet, because, the kind of satisfaction that one gets from sweetness, in that same way, the sweetness from abiding in the Self – nothing else feels sweet; everything else feels false. -6

kabir iha tan ko deeyalaa karo, baati melo jeeu
lohu sicho tel kari, tab mukh dekh piu -7

[Bengali:]

Kabir is saying: make this body the lamp, and make the jiva [ego] the wick, and make the blood of the body the oil [of the lamp]. If this happens, then you will be able to see the Face of the Beloved Lord. -7

[Commentary:]

Kabir, make this body the lamp – meaning: like the way a limp gives light, in the same way, constantly see Light in this body. Keep the jiva [ego] as the wick, and make blood the oil and soak [the wick]. Then you will come to see Face of the Beloved Who is "Narayana" [God-Person] – meaning: you will come to see the Face of Kutastha Supreme Person. -7

kabir biraha binaa tan shunya hay, biraha hay sultaan
jaa ghat biraha na sanchaare, so ghat jaanu mashaan -8

[Bengali:]

Kabir is saying: without longing, the body has almost become nothing [or: empty]. And that longing is happening for the "sultaan" [emperor] only ("sultaan" = the one who is the king of all the kings; he is called "sultaan"). Here, it is the mind which is the king of all the senses. Longing is happening to the mind itself. And the body in which that longing does not enter – know that that body is a burial/cremation ground. -8

[Commentary:]

Kabir, without longing, the body has become empty – meaning: longing is only there when Love has happened. The body that does not have the longing from the Love-affair with God, there is nothing in that body. And the one who is full of longing for "Narayana" [God-Person] – he is "sultaan" [emperor] – meaning: he is the king of all the kings – meaning: mind amidst the senses – this mind, by whose command things are going on. The one in whose body longing has not completely taken over – meaning: the body that is not on fire from the longing from the Love-affair with God – know that body to be "mashaan" [burial/cremation ground] – meaning: completely a dead body – meaning: it has no power to do anything. -8

kabir biraha raam pathaiya, saadhunke parmodh
jaa ghat taala meli hay, taako lay kari sodh -9

[Bengali:]

Kabir is saying: the aforementioned longing was actually sent by Atma-Rama [Self; Lord] Himself, so that there can be Joy for sadhus [sages]. And the "ghat" [container] in which – meaning: the body in which the lock is open – it is for that person that pure samadhi has happened. -9

[Commentary:]

Kabir, Atma-Rama Guru [Self; Lord] has sent longing for the sake of the true manifestation of Bliss for sadhus [sages] – meaning: upon separation verily, Love grows more. The body in which the lock is open – meaning: samadhi happens instantly upon just giving attention only – know that [beingness] to be Pure – meaning Brahman. -9

kabir ankhriya prem ki chuyia, jin jaane dukhriya
raam sanehi kaarane, roye roye ratariya -10

[Bengali:]

Kabir is saying: for the sake of Love, one is standing straight up, waiting expectantly with eyes full of tears. The one who has got the suffering of longing is spending all nights crying to unite with Rama. -10

[Commentary:]

Kabir, the needle of Love is standing straight up. The one who knows the suffering of longing is the one who is witnessing – meaning: one is unmoving inside the spine, yet there is no entrance to Brahman. The one for whom this kind of state has come about – it is only he who knows that kind of needle of Love, standing straight up and still in that way. Rama is the reason for Love's affection. One has become that way and is crying and crying every night, "Oh, oh! When will the needle enter Brahman?" -10

kabir soi aahe su svajana, soi aahe lokriya jao
lochan lohu chue, tabhi janiho tariya -11

[Bengali:]

Kabir is saying: know that that is the beautiful person – the one from whose eyes tears fall, and from whose eyes blood comes out – meaning: the eyes are always bloodshot. Know that samadhi is imminent for him. -11

[Commentary:]

Kabir, that is the person who is beautiful and good, and that is the person who is the person amongst people – the one for whom the needle of the Love for God has stood straight up. When his eyes have become red, like blood, then know it for certain that that is the person for whom samadhi will come about – meaning: there will be "samabuddhi" [one-mind-ness]. -11

kabir hangsa naadri karu, ro-o-na so karu chit
binaa roye ko paaiya, prem piyare mit -12

[Bengali:]

Kabir is saying: make the jiva [individual-ness] into sound. Do it in such a way – like the heart of those who cry [tears]. Who has ever got his beloved, lover or friend without having cried [tears]? -12

[Commentary:]

Kabir, make the "hamsa" form of jiva into sound and do [sadhana]. As the "hamsa" japa [repetitive chanting] is going on day and night for the jiva, make that into sound and do [sadhana] – meaning Kriya. Like the kind of one-pointedness that happens in the heart when one is tearfully crying out, make the heart like that. Without crying [tears], who has ever got Love, the Beloved or Friend?

"Prem" [love] = being One. "Priyaa" [beloved] = the one because of whom tears come if one does not see him/her. "Mitra" [friend] = one whose happiness and sorrow causes one's own self to have happiness and sorrow. -12

kabir soto duhkha na bisare, rowat balghati jaaye
man hi maah bisur na, jo kaathi ghun khaaye -13

[Bengali:]

Kabir is saying: he cannot forget the pain in his heart, and after crying and crying [tears], the strength of the body has also gone down; whatever was in his mind, he has forgotten all of it, all just because of lacking one thing. Like when wood becomes infested with "ghun" [wood-beetles], the beetles have eaten everything inside and made the wood a fragile shell – only the wood on the outer part is somehow hanging on. -13

[Commentary:]

Kabir, I am not able to forget that pain from not seeing the Supreme Person. I cannot even cry, because crying makes the strength of the body dissipate. The only way is to forget in the mind. Like a wood-beetle-eaten piece of wood – meaning: the piece of wood looks fine but the wood-beetles have emptied the inside of it – the mind will be like that – nothing but a shell because of not seeing the Lord. -13

**kabir knire kaath jo khaaiya, khayaa kinhu na
dith so ti ughaari jo dekhiye, bhitar jaama chith -14**

[Bengali:]

Kabir is saying: when wood-beetles eat a piece of wood, no one can see it happening, but one who picks up that piece of wood comes to know that there is nothing at all left inside [the wood]; there are only wood-dust [sawdust] left. -14

[Commentary:]

Kabir, the wood that has been eaten by insects – when the insects are eating, no one was able to see it, but one who takes off the outer peel of that piece of wood sees that there is only "chitaa" [sticky stuff] - meaning: wood-dust stuck together with insect saliva – inside. -14

**kabir chith jo jamaa chun ka, birha baura khay
bisari gayaa jo svajana, bedan kaahu na lay -15**

[Bengali:]

Kabir is saying: the body has been ground down, chewed through and ground into dust. The one who is mad with longing – he eats that dust. And the suffering from the Beloved having left – no one at all helps [or: supports] with that. -15

[Commentary:]

Kabir, like the way insects chew wood, and bore it down into a flour-like condition, powder congealed with saliva – in that same way, because of the longing for the Lord, the body has become a shell with stuck-together powder as the inside material. The one who is mad with longing – he is the one who eats that powder. The pain from the Beloved having left – no one takes this – meaning: with the suffering of separation, there is nothing else in the mind. -15

kabir hnaase piya nahi paaiye, binha paayaa tinha roy hnaasi khel jo piyaa mile, to kaun dohaaginee hoy -16

[Bengali:]

Kabir is saying: you will not get Him while laughing and joking. Whoever has got [Him] has cried [tears]. If the Beloved was able to be had by laughing and joking, then who would be "dohaaginee" [longing lover]? -16

[Commentary:]

Kabir, when the laughing mouth is closed, the laughter does not come out. At the time of laughing, first the mind opens, then the mouth opens. If mind is tied to the Lord, then laughter does not happen. One will not get the Supreme Person Beloved by going about laughing, because the one who has got [Him] has got [Him] by crying [tears] – meaning: when mind has gone in other directions, it is then only that one has cried [tears] from the longing for the Lord, then done Kriya again and again and got [Him]. If the Lord could be had by laughing and playing, then who would be "dohaginee" [longing lover]? "Sohaginee" [consort, wife] – one on whose head there is the vermilion dot [sign of marriage] – meaning Kutastha – that soul is married – and the one in whose forehead Kutastha is not [or: unknown] – that person is "dohaginee" - meaning widow. -16

kabir hnaasi khel jo piyaa mile, to kaun sahe khursaan kaam krodh trishnaa tyaje, taahi mile bhagoan -17

[Bengali:]

Kabir is saying: if the Beloved could be had by laughing and playing, then who would do sadhana like [being on] the razor's edge? Renouncing lust, anger and greed – [only] then can God be had. -17

[Commentary:]

"Khel" [playing; sport] = useless acts
"Kaam" [want; lust] = desire
"Krodh" [anger; rage] = anger, which causes heat
"Trishnaa" [thirst] = excessive desire on something of intense interest

If the Lord could be had by laughing and playing around ["khel"], then no one would be able to withstand the edge of the razor. Like [being on] the edge of a razor, yogis stay in the subtle sushumna. Just as when one is just a little unmindful with a razor, there can be a cut, in the same way, for yogis, if the mind goes just a little to other directions, the mind is cut from the Lord. By renouncing "kaam," "krodh" and "trishnaa" [see above], one can get God. As long as "I" am there, if "I" renounce, will they [the afflictions] leave? When "I" am not there, then "kaam," "krodh," "trishnaa" - they are automatically not there. -17

kabir haaus kare hari milan ki, aao sukh chaahe ang peedsane binu paduminee, putan let uchang -18

[Bengali:]

Kabir is saying: there is a desire to have the Lord God, yet there is also the desire for pleasures of the body, just as a woman does not want to bear the pain of menstruation, yet wants to have [or: give birth to] a child to hold in her bosom; it is like that. -18

[Commentary:]

Kabir, there is the desire to unite with the Lord, yet there is the desire for the pleasures of the body – meaning: by meditating upon the Lord, the body comes to equilibrium and becomes still, the mind is kept at the Feet of the Lord, and one becomes One [with the Lord]. There is no desire to bear the pain of this effort, yet there is the desire to unite with the Lord, like "padmini" - meaning: pampered woman – does not want to bear the pain of menstruation, yet wants to have [or: give birth to] a child to hold in her bosom; it is like the fact that this cannot happen. In the same way, without being able to bear the pain of the effort of meditation upon the Lord, one cannot merge with the Lord. -18

**kabir dekhat dekhat din ggayaa, nishbhi dekhat jaahi
birahinee piyaa paaoa nahi, jeeoyat rase man maahi -19**

[Bengali:]

Kabir is saying: so the day passed in front of one's eyes; the night will also go like that. Not having her beloved, the longing lover's heart was full of deep sorrow. -19

[Commentary:]

Kabir, the day passed in front of one's eyes; the night also passed in front of one's eyes; the longing lover did not get her beloved. The self is constantly in the pain of the longing for the Lord. This means: because of laziness, one is not doing Kriya and thus passing the days and nights, and because of not being able to see That Supreme Person, one is pining like a pampered woman. -19

**kabir ki birahineeko meechde, ki aapuhi dekhlaaye
aat prahar ka daajh naa, mote saahaa na jaaye -20**

[Bengali:]

Kabir is saying: make the longing lover understand. If this happens, then she herself will see. One cannot withstand the pain of longing, day and night, any more. -20

[Commentary:]

Kabir, "birahinee" [longing lover] is the one for whom longing is happening – meaning: the self's longing. Take Kabir's longing self and disgorge/expel it into Brahman; then it will be seen directly by oneself. One cannot withstand the pain of longing, day and night, any more. -20

kabir birahinee thee to kya bhaya, jvarin piya ko laar bahure mughudh gahe lari, biraha laajo maar -21

[Bengali:]

Kabir is saying: the longing lover was there, and what happened because of that! She was not able to become one with the beloved and burn and die as one. So – foolish lover who longs, you are going on the road of wrongfulness. You have no shame. So die in this shameless way. -21

[Commentary:]

Kabir, the self who is the longing lover who was there longing for the Lord – what happened to Kabir because of that? As it turned out, she could not become One with the Supreme Person and burn and die as One. Oh stupid longing self! You are going into an alley of wrongfulness. And since you could not die in longing, then go ahead, go on with having no shame. -21

kabir ho-o jo biraha ki lakri, samujhi samujhi ghughuyaay duhkha so tabahi bnachi ho, jab sakalo jvari jaay -22

[Bengali:]

Kabir is saying: the wood of longing burns in periods. When you know that everything has burned away, you will be relieved from suffering. -22

[Commentary:]

Kabir, the wood of the longing of not being One with the Lord lights up in periods. When from time to time one understands – meaning: mind goes in other directions and one can see, "all this time my mind was in other directions," right then does the wood of longing light up. When everything burns up, that is when you will be saved from this pain – meaning: then, in the par avastha of Kriya, all burns up and there is no pain. -22

kabir biraha agini tan mo laagi, gaye nayan jal
shukhi aabhute bujhe nahi, doy haat kar kuki -23

[Bengali:]

Kabir is saying: the fire of longing has caught the body and the tears in the eyes have dried up. Even if one uses both hands to pour water to put that fire out, far from being extinguished, the fire actually spreads. -23

[Commentary:]

Kabir, upon the fire of longing for the Lord catching the body, the tears in the eyes have dried up. Even if you use both hands to pour a big container of water to cool down that fire, far from the fire going out, it actually spreads. -23

kabir tanman e jvala, biraha agini shogee
mritak peedan jaanai, jaane giyo aagi -24

[Bengali:]

Kabir is saying: longing burned up the grieving person's body and mind, but the person was unaware of it. It is like when there is death, no suffering and affliction remain any more. -24

[Commentary:]

Kabir, the person who is grieving with the longing of the Lord, burned up his body with his mind – meaning: upon not seeing the Lord, he has stopped eating and sleeping, and saying "Alas! Alas!" he is burning up the body, but the fire knows the burning. When death comes to a person, he does not experience suffering and afflictions in the burning of the crem? crematory fire, but the fire knows that. -24

kabir prem binaa dheeraj nahi, biraha bina bairaag
naam bina jaaoe nahi, man man saako daag -25

[Bengali:]

Kabir is saying: without Love, patience does not take hold. Without longing there is no non-attachment [vairagya]. The scars of the mind are not healed by anything else except the Name. -25

[Commentary:]

Kabir, without Love, patience does not happen. "Prem" [love] = that which is impossible to live without – let everything else go if it must, but please do not let the Love for the Lord go away. One mind stays in one direction, it remains settled. Without longing, one cannot be "vairaagi" [in non-attached state], because other than getting that for which there is longing, nothing else at all feels good. Thus there is no desire [for anything else]. These desires do not go away with anything else except the par avastha of Kriya – meaning without that State, scars remain latent in the mind – meaning: even without thinking, things that were done at some time in the past – those things come up in the mind. -25

kabir biraha kayondal bhari liya, bairaagee doye nayan
paayaa darash madhukaree, chaki rahe rasana vayan -26

[Bengali:]

Kabir is saying: the "kamandalu" [ascetic's water-pot] of longing was filled and then "vairagya" [non-attachment] rose in the two eyes and desire ended. In this State, one witnessed the Source of Nectar, and the tongue and mouth became filled with Blissful Nectar. -26

[Commentary:]

Kabir, upon filling the "kamandalu" [see above] of the eyes of longing, desires ended. There was no Beloved Lord-Water in the "kamandalu" eyes and thus there was longing for Water. After that, when one saw Brahman wherever one looked, the longing for Brahman no longer remained, and desires ended. This is because there is desire only when there is some new object. When there is One everywhere, then automatically there is no desire. When the eyes witnessed the Nectar-Source – meaning: the One Who makes Nectar – meaning the witnessing of Brahman – one became desireless, and the tongue and mouth became full with Nectar; one went on drinking it – meaning: the Nectar dripping from the Sahasrar came to the tip of the tongue and filled up my mouth. -26

kabir nayan hamaare baaore, chin chin lote tujh naa tu mile na mai sukhee, ayse bedan mujh -27

[Bengali:]

Kabir is saying: my eyes are insane. From moment to moment it is wandering about here and there. One is not happy when one does not get something, yet one is also not able to be forbearing. I am not happy with anything. Such pain – yet I am not able to let it go either. -27

[Commentary:]

Kabir, my eyes are insane – meaning: just like a mad person does not understand good and bad, yet does things – it is like that. The stomach is full, but the eyes go towards sweets. Even though if one eats at that time there will be illness, one forgets about that and tries to eat the sweets. It is like this in every situation. Even if somehow, by holding and tying myself to It, I somehow got Kutastha, immediately the next moment my mind is on wanting a ripe mango. In this way, one is coming [back] to objects from moment to moment. O Lord! I am not able to unite ["mil"] with You ("milan" [intimate meeting; union] – meaning: becoming absolutely One). Thus one is not happy. This kind of pain has got me, yet I am not able to let it go either. -27

kabir phaari patoraa dhvajaa karon, kaam lari pahiraaye johi johi bhek piyaa mile, soi soi bhek banaaye -28

[Bengali:]

Kabir is saying: tear off your clothes and make a flag in the head, and put on a blanket. The manner of dress that will make it possible to have the beloved, put that on – meaning: within yourself, put on those types of clothes. -28

[Commentary:]

Kabir, tear off your clothes and make a flag – meaning: one was walking about wearing an outfit made of silk, and at this time one person asked about these nice clothes. Hearing this, one immediately began to proudly go into all kinds of detail about the clothes. (One has become an animal because of not having the Lord, yet there is such pride about an insignificant and trifling piece of cloth!) Tear up this ego and make a flag in the head – meaning: if one is abiding in the head, there is no "ahankaar" [ego]. Thus, after tearing this ego and making into a flag, will I stay as a naked person? No. Put on a blanket, like those simple ones used by lowly people – meaning: see yourself as small/humble. What is the need for casting off ego and being small/humble? Answer – the manner of dress that will enable one to get God – put on those types of clothes – not outside, but inside. -28

kabir parbat parbat mei phira, nayan gaonwaye roye
so butee paaoe nahin, jaate sadjeevan hoye -29

[Bengali:]

Kabir is saying: I have roamed about from mountain to mountain. I have cried and cried [tears] and ruined my eyes too. Still I did not get the essential herb, that by which death can be conquered. I did not get that. -29

[Commentary:]

Kabir, I traveled mountains after mountains, and I ruined my eyes by crying and crying [tears], but I did not get that herb – that by which death can be conquered – meaning: I thought, "This is a sadhu; that is a sadhu," and I went going about to all these people, and with the tears brought about from the fear of death, I became like a blind man, but I could not find that essential herb by which death can be conquered. -29

biraha tej tan mor rahaay, angsabhe akulaay ghatshoono
jeeuo piu omo, maut dhnuri phir jaay -30

/Bengali:/

Kabir is saying: only the fire of longing is left in body, and all the other parts have all [but] collapsed. An almost empty body is sitting about. There is a jiva [soul] in that body, but because the soul remained within the Beloved Lord, when death came to the body, it could not find that soul. -30

[Commentary:]

Kabir, the fire of longing for the Lord – that is all that my body is now – meaning: upon seeing the Supreme Person, that "me," this body, are both nothing at all; so is this body here or not? Answer – it is there. All the parts of the body are in an extremely desperate state – meaning: all the parts of the body are unkempt, because mind is not there. This vessel/container-like body is lying around emptily, because the jiva [soul] is staying in the Lord, the One Who is the Beloved. And death comes to the body, yet goes back without being able to find the soul, because one is in the body, yet is without the body. That Supreme Person – because of the soul residing in It, this body no longer remains – the sign of "videha" [bodilessness]. -30

kabir beyaa paay sarapka, bhaosaagar ke maahi jao
chore tao buri maro, gnaho to dache bnaahi -31

[Bengali:]

Kabir is saying: in the world-ocean I have found a snake as a vessel/boat. If I let it go, then I drown and die, and if I catch it then it bites/stings my arms. -31

[Commentary:]

Kabir, "bhavasamudra" [world-ocean] = that which is emerging – meaning: when this bubble-like body is destroyed, another little bubble is again and again emerging. In this emergence-oriented ocean, I have received the body of a snake – meaning: I have found a snake within this body, which is always "roaring" [sounding]. If I let this snake go into the hole which is this body, then it drowns [sinks in] – meaning: again there is the taking of birth. And if I catch it, then it bites/stings the arms – meaning: when there is Stillness after doing Kriya, "I" no longer exist. It is the sign of "jivan mukta" [liberated while still in the body]. -31

kabir nayan hamaare bichoheeya, rahore shankha ma jhur deoal deoal may phiro, deoch ugaa nahi sur -32

[Bengali:]

Kabir is saying: my eyes are in longing only. What they once saw – not seeing that again, they are just empty. And I went around to lots of gods and more gods. I could not see that gradually in an unseen way, there was even no more daylight. The sun even was not seen. -32

[Commentary:]

Kabir, my eyes are in longing – meaning: one time, one saw the Supreme Person with full vision, and is not able to see Him any more. Now, [you] just stay empty. And I went around from this god to that god, but gradually, in an unseen way, the day did not dawn. And I could not even see the sun – meaning: upon seeing the Supreme Person within the Sun of Kutastha only one time, I am not able to see Kutastha in that kind of Light and the Supreme Person within It, and I am only seeing darkness. -32

kabir galo tumhaare naam par, jno aate me lon aysaa birahaa meli ho, nit duhk paaoe kaun -33

[Bengali:]

Kabir is saying: mind melts into Your Name, like salt merges with flour. If, after longing, one merges like this, then how can there be any more of that unending suffering? -33

[Commentary:]

Kabir, mind melts into Your Name. "Naam" [name] = the par avastha of Kriya. The mind of that State melts and merges into Brahman, like salt merges with flour and dough. After this kind of painful longing, I will totally become One, because who can withstand day after day of suffering? -33

kabir sukheeyaa sab sangsaar hay, khaaoe showe nit
duhkeeya daas kabir hay, jaage sumire chit -34

[Bengali:]

Kabir is saying: I see that in this samsara [world] everyone is pretty much happy, as everyone – with endless pleasure – is eating, sleeping – always engaged in these things. But servant Kabir is saying that only I am the sufferer, because I am always staying awake and doing remembrance of God, just in case I forget. -34

[Commentary:]

Kabir, everyone in samsara [world] is happy, constantly with the desire of: "I will always eat well and sleep well." Kabir is saying that only I am the sufferer, because I am always staying awake and meditating on Consciousness that is Kutastha, just in case I forget. -34

kabir biraha jvaalaai may jvalo, jvalti jvalhar jaayo
mahi dekhat jvalhar jvare, soto knahan bujhaayo -35

[Bengali:]

Kabir is saying: I have completely burned up in the burning of longing. Now my "me" is no more. The One Who was giving me this burning has also burned up – meaning: Oneness has happened. Now the burning has also gone somewhere and become extinguished. It cannot be found in any location any more – meaning: there is no person there to see whether it is there or not. -35

[Commentary:]

Kabir is saying: because of the fire of longing burning me, I have completely burned up. Upon my burning up, the One Who was burning me – meaning Kutastha – He is also no longer there. And seeing me, Kutastha also burned up –

meaning: Oneness happened. And the burning of longing went somewhere and became extinguished. Nothing about it is ascertainable any more – meaning: when I am not, then who is there to witness where one was freed from the burning? -35

kabir biraha jvalaai may jvalo, mujhe biraha ka duhkha chaahan baythat darapati, mati jvari jaaoe rukh -36

[Bengali:]

Kabir is saying: because of the burning of longing, I have completely burned up. The pain of longing is making me sorrowful. I find no happiness anywhere. I am even afraid to sit in the shade, in case the shade also burns up because of me. There is longing, because there is no happiness in anything at all. -36

[Commentary:]

Kabir, I am burning to death in the fire of longing, because I cannot see Kutastha all the time. Because of this, I am full of the sorrow of longing. If I go to sit in the shade of some tree, I have fear there too, in case the tree itself burns up from the fire of longing – meaning: even being in the shade there is no happiness. -36

kabir birahinee jvalti dekh kay, saai aaye jaay prem bund te sichi kay, tan me layi milaay -37

[Bengali:]

Kabir is saying: seeing that the longing lover is burning up, God came running, because the longing lover could die by the burning of longing. He came and watered [the fire] with the droplet of Love and cooled off [the fire], and He took [the lover] and merged [the lover] in His own Body. Thus there was no sign of the body of the longing lover left any more. -37

[Commentary:]

Kabir, Kutastha saw the longing lover who was dying from longing. He then came running – and [quenched the fire with] Love – because mind does not like anything else any more – Kutastha watered with the Bindu [drop] Form – meaning: upon seeing [Kutastha], mind was cooled, and the body merged in Him veirly – meaning: because of mind mixing into It as One, there was no sign of the body left. -37

**kabir may birahinee ke peed me, daagan diyaa jaay
maas gali gali chnui padaa, may jo rahi gale laay -38**

[Bengali:]

Kabir is saying: upon seeing the affliction of the longing lover, he became saddened. The flesh from the body of the longing lover is melting and falling off. There is no place where there is any sign [of the body left] – in this kind of state, what else can happen? Let me remain embraced with her. -38

[Commentary:]

Kabir, one became saddened by seeing the afflictions of the body of the longing lover, but that there could be any sign of the body left from longing that could be seen – there is no possibility of that, because the flesh of the body is melting and melting, and falling off. Kutastha is saying, "I will now remain embraced [with her]." -38

**kabir chaari paaoke palang sho, choli laayo aaagi
jaa kaaran ye taattaakiyaa, soi naa gale laagi -39**

[Bengali:]

Kabir is saying: I lay down on a bed with four legs, but fire had caught at that time. I could not remain embraced with the One for Whom I suffered so much – meaning: I could not become One. -39

[Commentary:]

Kabir, I lay down on a bed with four legs, and at that time fire has caught on the body. The One for Whom I suffered so much – still He did not stay embraced – meaning: the four Vedas became Still, a skeletal Form of the Lord came out in the back; in that, the Lord also went on revealing Himself in a shaking way. The Lord for Whom I have put all pleasures in the garbage – still I was not able to become One with that Beloved One. -39

kabir koye kar kattoriya, muthi kar gahi haad jich
pinjare birahaa base, maasu knahaare daad -40

[Bengali:]

Kabir is saying: I took the well and kept it in my hand like a bowl, because it is difficult to draw water from the well. The body is weak; the bones have come out; the reason for making it easy and drink from the bowl is because of being in this state. There is no flesh but only bones in the body in which longing resides. -40

[Commentary:]

Kabir has made the well into a bowl – meaning: upon continuously doing Kriya, the well became a bowl – meaning: it is at hand. It takes a long time to draw water from the well and drink, and it does not take a long time to drink from the bowl. And because of doing Kriya, there are nothing but bones for the body. If one puts a hand there, one cannot find any flesh, only bones. The cage in which the longing resides – meaning: the cause of the longing – meaning: the place where Kutastha is residing – there is no bone or flesh, nothing at all that I can think even about any such thing. -40

kabir raktamaasu sab bhachi gaye, neku na kin ho
kaan ab biraha kukur bhaye, laage haad chaban -41

[Bengali:]

Kabir is saying: all the blood and flesh have gone from the body; the ears have also gone; I cannot hear anyone calling. Now the longing has taken the form of a dog and is chewing and eating the bones. -41

[Commentary:]

Kabir, upon continuously having mind on the Lord, neither blood nor flesh, nothing at all remained. All was eaten up by the Lord. And although the longing lover is calling so much, no one is hearing that at all. Now, the Lord has become a dog and is chewing on the bones – meaning: He entered the bones. -41

kabir birhaa bhayaa bichaaona, odhan bipati biyog
duhkha shir haane paonte, kaun banaa sangjog -42

[Bengali:]

Kabir is saying: the longing itself has become the bed, and I have taken the absence of the Beloved as my blanket and am lying with my body covered with that blanket of separation. From head to feet I am being attacked by sorrow. I am seeing nothing but absence [separation]; where is the Union? -42

[Commentary:]

Kabir, the longing for the Lord has become the bed – meaning: the bed of feeling "Oh Beloved! Oh Beloved!" day and night, because I am actually finding pleasure [like lying in bed] in that longing itself. Here I am with the blanket made of the separation from my Beloved, and sorrow is making me suffer from head to feet. So, it looks like there is nothing but absence [separation] – that is all I'm seeing anyway! So, where is the Union? -42

kabir kaun jagaaoe brahmako, kaun jagaaoe
jiu kaun jagaaoe surati ko, kaun milaoe piu -43

[Bengali:]

Kabir is saying: who will awaken Brahman? And who will then bring awakenedness to jiva [individual soul]? Who will awaken the beautiful endeavor? And who will bring about the Union with the Beloved? -43

[Commentary:]

"Jaagaa" [waking] = meaning: abiding with mind kept stuck on something. When mind is not on anything then it is lying down, because sleep comes [when mind is not stuck on something/one thing].

Who will awaken Brahman? The Self. Who will awaken jiva? Prakriti; because jiva is actually Shiva. If Prakriti is not there, how can Purusha be there? Who will awaken "surat"? "Su rati" = the beautiful endeavor – meaning: keeping mind on Kutastha – [meaning] Kriya. And Brahman, Which is the par avastha of Kriya – who will bring about Union with Him? Kriya. -43

kabir biraha jagaaoe brahmako, brahma jagaaoe
jiu jiu jagaaoe surati ko, surati milaoe piu -44

[Bengali:]

Kabir is saying: the longing itself will awaken Brahman. Brahman will awaken jiva, and jiva will awaken the beautiful endeavor. And the beautiful endeavor will itself bring about Union with the Beloved. -44

[Commentary:]

Kabir, the longing is bringing one to awaken to Brahman. Whose is the longing? The self's. It is self that is constantly crying "Alas! Alas!" because of not being with Brahman, and when it is merged in Brahman it is happy. Upon getting Brahman again and again, when He [Self] finally stayed fixed on [Brahman], then He [Self] awakened Brahman – meaning: the Power of Brahman is now in Atman. Brahman is awakening jiva because although Mind-Brahman is in Prakriti, because of going into the Supreme Person, Shiva has awakened. If there is no Prakriti, then where can mind be? Thus, it is Prakriti Herself making the awakening. If the Supreme Person does not desire it, then mind has no ability/power at all. By going into the par avastha of Kriya a little bit at a time, mind gets that State. If one does not do Kriya, there is no way to get the par avastha of Kriya. -44

kabir may tomko dhnurte phiron, tom kaahe naa miliyaa raam hirdaya maahi uthi milo, yeh sakal tomaaro kaam - 45

[Bengali:]

Kabir is saying: I am searching around trying to find You; why don't You stay one with Atma-Rama? Why don't You rise into the heart and stay United? All this is actually Your doing. -45

[Commentary:]

Kabir, I am searching and searching around for You – meaning: I am doing Kriya, thinking about how, when and where I will find the Supreme Person Lord. You are supposed to be Rama, the Lord of Loving Delight. Why aren't You Uniting with me and making Loving Delight here? O Beloved Lord! Emerge in my heart and become One with me, because all of this is only Your doing. When woman and man unite, the duty of the man is to rise in the heart – and in this case I am the Devoted Wife and You are the Beloved Husband. -45

kabir biraha jagaaiya, pari dhadhnore chaar
may koi koyala ubre, jvaaro duji baar -46

[Bengali:]

Kabir is saying: longing awakened and the kettle-drum of the prayer-call of longing began sounding loudly. Then everything was burned to ashes in the fire of longing. The charcoal of "I" remained. Now burn that again. -46

[Commentary:]

Kabir became awakened by longing – meaning: the Supreme Person suddenly revealed Himself and again hid. Then the kettle-drum of longing began to sound, and the fire of longing burned everything to ashes. Well, everything did burn to ashes but the charcoal of the "I" thought, which kept on being there, because: "I" saw the Supreme Person. In that case, the Supreme Person and "I" are two. Oneness has not happened. Kabir is saying, "Burn it ["I"] again." -46

kabir tan man jauban jvaarike, bhasam jo kariya deha
kahahi kabir yeh birahinee, uthike tato hay kheha -47

[Bengali:]

Kabir is saying: body, mind, youth have been burned to ashes. Kabir is saying: this longing lover is saying, "The One by Whom this state has happened – where is there any sign of Him?" -47

[Commentary:]

Kabir, all substance, mind, youth and body have been cindered. It is in such a state that the longing lover is up and rambling on and on, saying that there is no sign of that [Thing] because of which this condition has come about – meaning: because of the Still vayu entering in every nerve of the body, some places in the body are doing "kan, kan, jhan, jhan" [ringing, buzzing]. Mind is not interested in tasting anything other than Brahman and does not go in any other direction. "Jauban" [youth; vitality] = at the time of youth, all senses become full of force, but all of the senses of the longing lover are without fire. When there is no work for them in the midst of all this, then they are ashen. The One Who has burned all that and the One Who has burned the body to ashes – the longing lover is up and rambling on and on, saying that the cause of this condition – that Brahman – where is there any sign of Him? This is because space is from Brahman; from space is vayu etc. -47

kabir biraha soto hati rahe, manua meraa sujaan
haadmaas nakh khat hay, jiyate kare mashaan -48

[Bengali:]

Kabir is saying: longing is eating up bones, flesh, nails – all these. It has made a good mind/heart and the jiva itself like a cremation ground. -48

[Commentary:]

Kabir, because of not being able to withstand the pain of longing, the grieving heart came to this: "I will not look again at the face of the Black Moon [Sri Krishna – Lord], but my good mind/heart does not go to anything else other than that Krishnachandra [Beloved Krishna]." And bones, flesh, nails are all eaten up – meaning: the vayu that was going in the bones, the vayu that was going in the flesh – they became Still. And the nails were also eaten eup – meaning: there is no power to move the hands; there is no movement in the flesh; and there is no force [of movement] in the nails; all of these have gone. Although I am alive, but I am like the cremation ground – meaning: as in the cremation ground there are bodies but they have no ability, in that same way, everything is there but there is no force [to move]. It is this that is known as "jivan mukta" [liberated while alive in the body]. -48

kabir so din kaysaa hoyegaa, raam gahahige bnaahi
aapnaa kari baithaaosi, charan knaol ki chaahi -49

[Bengali:]

Kabir is saying: when will that day come for me, that day when Rama will come, hold my hand, make me His own, and have me sit in the shade of His Lotus Feet? -49

[Commentary:]

Kabir, how will that day come about for me, that day when Rama will take my arm and sit me down as His own in the shade of His Lotus Feet? "Rama" = Atman [Self]. "Baahudvaya" [two arms] = ida, pingala – when they are Still, that is the "holding." "Aapna kari" [make [something or someone] one's own] = upon continuously seeing the Supreme Person in this body, the experience comes that I also am the Supreme Person. "Charan" [feet; or: the act of moving] = one who leaves this body and goes into another body. "Kamal" [lotus] = the lotuses of the six chakras. "Chaahi" [shade] = in the shade; the kind of contentment that comes about when on gets out of the sun and sits in the shade – in that same way, when Atman is Still in the heart, there is the experience of coolness. -49

kabir ankbhari bhari bhetiyaa, man nahi baadhe dheer
kahe kabir te ko mile, jab lagi hoye shareer -50

[Bengali:]

Kabir is saying: I want to have Him fully be in my lap and look at Him, but the mind just does not stay still. Kabir is saying: the one who has stuck the body and the mind [to the Lord] – it is he who gets [the Supreme]. -50

[Commentary:]

Kabir, there was no happiness in that type of satisfaction. I want to fill my lap up with the Beloved Lord, but mind did not stay in the Stillness Substance – meaning: mind went towards bathing, eating etc. Kabir Saheb is saying that it is he who gets the Beloved Lord – the one who has melded his body with [the mind/heart] into That – meaning the par avastha of Kriya. -50

kabir jiu bilambaa piucho, alakh lakh nahi jaay gobinda mile na jhalbujhai, rahe bujhaay bujhaay -51

[Bengali:]

Kabir is saying: jiva went and merged into Brahman; then he was [the] Unseen. He cannot be seen any more. Oneself is not even there; so who will see? Thus, the Unseen cannot be seen. It is when one gets Govinda [name of Sri Krishna; or: Lord] that the fire [of separation] is extinguished. Until one gets [Him] – up until then there is no freedom from the burning. One has to make the mind gently understand again and again. -51

[Commentary:]

Kabir, jiva went into Beloved Brahman and merged – meaning the par avastha of Kriya. No one can see the Unseen, because at that time oneself is himself not there. Mind wants to have Govinda, but that fire which is the "not getting" - there is no freedom from it without having Govinda. Then let me gently make the mind understand again and again – meaning: let me do Kriya again, in case I get that State. -51

kabir lakri jari koylaa bheyi, mo man ajahu
aagi biraha ki yodi lakri jarai, sulaagi sulaagi -52

[Bengali:]

Kabir is saying: the wood of mind has burned up and become charcoal. But the fire of longing is still on my mind. Because of the wood of longing being wet, the pieces are burning slowly. -52

[Commentary:]

Kabir, the wood of mind has burned up with longing and has become charcoal. But the fire of longing for the Lord is still there on that burned up mind. The sad thing is that [my] mind's wood of longing is wet – meaning: it is not pure and clear (it is in maya). Because of this, the wood is burning in stops and starts – meaning: going on abiding in maya, suddenly it [sadhana] comes to mind. -52

kabir nishu din daajhai birahinee, antar gat ke laaye
daas kabiraa ko bujhai, satguru gaye lagaaye -53

[Bengali:]

Kabir is saying: the longing lover is dying from the burning of longing going on day and night. The One that she is crying for – well, He has gone far away. Servant Kabir is saying: what is happening to her – how can others understand it? The one whose pain it is – it is she who knows. Satguru has lit this fire of longing. -53

[Commentary:]

Kabir, that Beloved Lord Supreme Person Who has traveled far away – fixated on Him, the longing lover is dying from the constant burning. Kabir is saying, "Who can understand that this kind of thing has happened to me? And this fire of longing has been lit by satguru." -53

kabir shushat bara rukhraa, may jan latriya
tere naam bilaamiyaa, jnyo jal machriya -54

[Bengali:]

Kabir is saying: longing is extremely dry. But even though it is dry, I am wrapped around Your Name like a vine, or like the way a fish is in water. -54

[Commentary:]

Kabir, in the pain of longing the tree [the mind] has dried up. But I am wrapped like a vine around Your Name – meaning: because of the par avastha of Kriya – like fish in water. -54

kabir jo jan birahee naamke, jhine pajar taasu
nayan na aaoe nidari, anagan jaamai maasu -55

[Bengali:]

Kabir is saying: the one who is constantly suffering from longing – that person's ribs are sticking out. And thinking on and on, "when will I have Him?" there is no sleep in the eyes. And flesh does not gather on the body – meaning: one does not become fat. -55

[Commentary:]

Kabir, the one who is longing for the par avastha of Kriya – contemplating and contemplating, that person's ribs have begun to stick out. And thinking on and on, "when will get my Beloved Lord?" sleep does not come to that person's eyes and flesh does not gather on the bones – meaning: that person does not become fat. -55

**kabir jo jan birahee naam ke, tinha ki gati bhayieha
dehee so udim kare, sumiran kare videha -56**

[Bengali:]

Kabir is saying: what is the way for the one who is longs for the Name of the Lord? The one who is embodied does his work with vigor. And by remembrance one gets the attainment of bodiless liberation. -56

[Commentary:]

Kabir, the one for whom the par avastha of Kriya is not happening – that longing person's way is this – meaning: the work that is there for the embodied person – he does that with vigor, and the bodiless one does remembrance of the Lord. -56

**kabir jo jan birahee naam ke, sada magan man mnaaha
jyo darpan ki sundaree, kaahu na pakari bnaaha -57**

[Bengali:]

Kabir is saying: the one who longs for the Name – that one is ever and always absorbed in his mind, and is thinking that way, and from time to time is trying to desperately catch [the Lord]. But one is not getting [the Lord]; like the reflection in a mirror can be seen but not had; it is like that. -57

[Commentary:]

Kabir, the one who longs for the Lord – because of not being able to be One, that person is ever absorbed in the mind. In what way is the Lord? Just like there is the reflection of a beautiful woman in a mirror, yet there is no way to hold her, in that same way, the Lord is in Kutastha, yet no one at all has the power to catch Him. -57

SAAKSHI GYAAN
BIRAHA KO ANG

[Witness/Direct Experience] Elucidation on Spiritual Knowledge and Longing

**kabir chin-gi aag ki, mo tan pari uraay tan j
vari ke dhartee jvari, aur jvare ban raay -1**

[Bengali:]

Kabir is saying: because of a little spark of fire flying around and falling on my body, my body has caught fire even down to the ground. And the forest that is the greatest among forests – that has also burned up. -1

[Commentary:]

Kabir, a spark of fire has fallen on my body. It has lit my body and even the ground that is holding me has caught fire. And the forest that is greatest among forests has also been burned down – meaning: upon seeing many types of Light in Yonimudra and at other times – wanting to see that [vision of Light] until the end – doing pranayam night and day – the body is weak. And the coming and going to Muladhar – that has also burned up, and that which is the root of all suffering, desire, has also burned up. But I did not get the Supreme Person. -1

kabir deepak paaoak aaniyaa, tel bhariyaa
aasang tino mili ke joia, udi udi pare patang -2

[Bengali:]

Kabir is saying: the lamp is alight because of oil and fire, and because of these three things working together, the lamp is burning. But because of other addictions, the moth-like mind is flying into [the fire], burning and dying. -2

[Commentary:]

"Pradeep" [lamp] = Kutastha. "Paaoak" = Light. "Tel" [oil] = jiva [individual soul]. Because of oil bringing fire, the lamp is alight. And it is burning because of these three working together. And in that, the moth – which is mind going in other directions – is burning – meaning: mind is not going in other directions. All this is done only so that one can have the Supreme Person. -2

kabir hirdayaa bhitar dvo baare, dhnuaa na pargat
hoy jaaki laai so lakhe ki jinha naai sangjoy -3

[Bengali:]

Kabir is saying: "two" are burning in the heart – meaning: two flames are burning. But the smoke from them cannot be seen. I cannot see the One Whom I was looking to see. -3

[Commentary:]

Kabir, "two" are burning in the heart, but the smoke from them cannot be seen, and the One Who is the Substance Equally in everything – I cannot see Him – meaning: ida and pingala are both aflame. There is no thing that becomes inflamed without burning. In this, one of them is being inflamed by matters of the world, and the other is being inflamed by women [lust] and such, yet no smoke is seen. If one sees smoke, one can become careful that there will be a fire – meaning: if [the danger] can be known before the wrongful deed takes place, then it is possible to not have to face it. But those two come in such a subtle way that it cannot be known. After the deed is done, it comes to mind that the act was wrongful. And that Beloved Lord who is the Substance Equally in everything – I cannot see Him. -3

kabir maara hay so mari gyaa, brahma agni ki bhaal
murakh koi jaane nahi, chatur lakkhe sab khayaal -4

[Bengali:]

Kabir is saying: the one who was struck with the Spear of Brahman-Fire – well, he is dead. Those who are fools cannot understand anything at all. The clever person is observing all experiences/feelings. -4

[Commentary:]

Kabir, the person whom I struck with the Spear of Brahman-Fire has died. One who is a fool does not know anything at all, and one who is clever – it is coming to his mind. This means: by striking the self with the Self, the self has died – meaning: one has become Still because of the Fire-Spear of sushumna. One who is a fool does not know anything at all about these things, and the clever person sees that it is by doing Kriya only that the self has become Still. -4

kabir maaraa hai mari jaayegaa, binaa saang ki bhaal
paraa pukaarai, birich tar, aaju mare ki kaal -5

[Bengali:]

Kabir is saying: the one who was struck – oh he will surely die. You see, he was struck with a spear without a blade. He has fallen under a tree and is screaming. He will die either today or tomorrow. -5

[Commentary:]

Kabir, the one whom I struck with the blade-less spear has basically died, but he has not died completely; there is still a pulse beating. Now he has fallen under a tree and is screaming, but he will die either today or tomorrow. This means: via the Self-Kriya, upon continuously making the self settled, the self became Still but not completely. And in that state, the self is in the Wish-fulfilling Tree of Kutastha and feeling, "When will there be Stillness?" This is because if there is Stillness then there will at once be Oneness. And at that time if feels like there will be Stillness either today or tomorrow. -5

kabir chot santaaoe biraha ki, sab tan jhnajhar
hoy maarani haraa jaanchi, jhi jis lagaaye hoy -6

[Bengali:]

Kabir is saying: the longing lover is suffering quite a lot. The entire body has become like a sieve [or: shattered]. The One Who gives the blows is the One Who really knows, and the One because of Whom this pain is happening – well, He is lying down. -6

[Commentary:]

Kabir, there is so much pain because of being struck by longing. And because of these blows the entire body has become like a sieve [or: shattered]. The One Who is striking is the One Who really knows, and the One because of whom this type of suffering is happening – well, He is lying down. Because of not being One with the Supreme Person and from the blows of [the feeling of] not having Him, there is suffering. And at that time it is being experienced that vayu is moving through the entire body. The Self Who is striking is the One Who actually is knowing the pain. But the reason for this suffering, which is to have that Brahman – meaning the par avastha of Kriya – well, He has become Still. -6

**kabir jhal uthi sakalo jvaraa, khapar phuta sanjut
hamsaa jogee ramee gayaa, aasan rahi bibhut -7**

[Bengali:]

Kabir is saying: because of the Flash-fire of Brahman, everything has burned up; even the skull cap has cracked and burned up. The "Hangsa" yogi was having delight in the Self. He went away. The asana [seat; seated position] and miraculous powers remained lying around. -7

[Commentary:]

Kabir, in the par avastha of Kriya, everything has burned up by the flame of the Brahman-Fire – meaning: at that time desires and such – none of such things remain, and oneself is also not there. And at that time it feels like the skull cap has flown off yet is still attached. The "Hangsa" yogi who was having delight went away. Only the eight siddhis [miraculous powered] remained on the asana. -7

**kabir aagi laageeni rame, knaado jvariya jhaari utar
dakhin ka panditaa, mare bichaari bichaari -8**

[Bengali:]

Kabir is saying: because of fire catching on water, water has also burned up; mud has also burned up. Those who are argumentation oriented pundits are dying from talking and discussing about north and south and such. -8

[Commentary:]

Kabir, water has caught on fire – meaning: the self has burned up. Because of water catching on fire, mud has burned up with it – meaning: all the senses have burned up. And all those pundits who collect "dakshina" [financial offerings for spiritual services] are dying from doing nothing but discussing a lot. -8

**kabir dvou laagi saayer jvaraa, macchi jvariaa aay
daadhe jeeb na ubare, satguru gaye lagaaye -9**

[Bengali:]

Kabir is saying: because of "two," the water has burned. The fish-like mind that was in it has also burned up. Satguru has stuck initiation on the person, and [thus] the burning person is here. -9

[Commentary:]

Kabir, "two" - meaning ida and pingala, having entered the sushumna, the deer-mind has burned up. And the moon-mind (fish) – meaning the still mind – has also burned up. But jiva [individual soul] has not been able to go beyond – meaning: "all is Brahman" has not happened. This is pain. Satguru has stuck [the sadhu] to this by giving him initiation. -9

**kabir guru dagdhaa chela jvalaa, biraha jagaayi
aag tinukaa baapuraa ubraa, guru pure ki laag -10**

[Bengali:]

Kabir is saying: the guru is burning and the disciple has also burned up. And the fire of longing has stayed awake. When satguru stuck it [to the sadhu], then all three got up and started to do. -10

[Commentary:]

Kabir, the self is burning up – meaning: has merged in Brahman. Then the disciple, which is ego, has also burned up. After that, the fire which is the "not knowing" of "what is the par avastha of Kriya after all" is being awakened. Amongst the things that have been gained because this happening, something like a "spot" has been gained – meaning: [Kutastha] is being seen at all times everywhere. The full satguru has stuck it [to the sadhu] – meaning: the way that guru has instructed – doing it that way, this has come about. -10

kabir aahari sang laagiya, mrigaa pukaarai roy
jehi ban ham kreeda kiyaa, daavat hay ban soy -11

[Bengali:]

Kabir is saying: because of meeting with the hunter, the deer is crying loudly, because the forest in which I used to play – alas! that forest is burning! -11

[Commentary:]

Kabir, deer-liquor = the ruler of mind is the hunter and he is dying with the jiva – meaning: because of taking mind into the Settledness Substance by doing Kriya, mind is dying. Then it is screaming, "The forest in which I used to play – that very forest is now burning up" - meaning: the forest of many desires is no more. -11

kabir mai ghar jvaraa aapnaa, liyaa lukaayaa haath
ar ghar jvaaro taahika, jo lagai hamaare saath -12

[Bengali:]

Kabir is saying: I have held the torch with my own hand and I myself have lit my own house, and I will burn the houses of others too, whoever wants to be with me. -12

[Commentary:]

Kabir, I myself have burned down my own house, but one Torch is still in hand – meaning: the Torch of Kutastha. Now if someone wants to be with me, I will light fire to his/her house too – meaning: he/she will also attain Kutastha. -12

**kabir pattan shaaree jvar gaya, dhaagaa ek na daadh
gar siri, pagree kashaa, paraa kutum baadh -13**

[Bengali:]

Kabir is saying: whatever clothes there were to wear – well, they have all burned up; not even a thread of those clothes remained. I will climb the stairs that are within the house, and I will bind a turban tightly, to prevent the relatives from coming. -13

[Commentary:]

Kabir, all of the clothes have burned up – meaning: the clothes of thought in the head are no longer there (the par avastha of Kriya). The clothes of thought have burned away. Not even a little of the thread of those clothes is seen where the clothes were before. And the pain of burning up is also not there, because when one is under the sheet of cloth there is intense thought, and when one is above the sheet of cloth – meaning: there is not even an iota of thought in the par avastha of Kriya. The cloth on top of my head has now burned up. Now what do I do? Let me put up the ladder of the six chakras in the body, climb it and tie a tight turban – Kutastha. All the sense-organs are now prevented from coming – meaning: it was no longer necessary to do all the work of the sense-organs by engaging the mind. -13

**kabir ghar jvaare ghar ubre, ghar raakhe ghar
jaay ek aachamva dekhiyaa, muyaa ko khaay -14**

[Bengali:]

If the house is burned, that is actually when the house becomes more beautiful, and when the house is preserved [or:

kept], that is actually when the house is lost. And I saw a wonder – that a dead man ate up "kal" [time; death]. -14

[Commentary:]

Kabir, if the house is burned, the house stays. And if the house is preserved [or: kept], then the house is lost. I saw a wonder: the person who has died – he eats "kal" [see above] – meaning: the one who burned up the body by the fire of Kriya – he went to sahasrar and got Brahman in the par avastha of Kriya. And the one who remained in the body – he had destruction happen to him. I saw a wonder that – the vayu that has died – meaning: has become Still – that eats "kal" - meaning: that ate up the passing time – meaning: coming and going became Still. -14

kabir sorthaa samundar laagi aagi, nadeeyaa jvaari kaylaa bhayi dekh kabira jaagi, macchi tarivar chori gayi -15

[Bengali:]

Kabir is saying: the ocean is on fire, and the river has burned up and become charcoal. The fish climbed to the top of the tree. Seeing this, Kabir awakened. -15

[Commentary:]

Kabir, the ocean is on fire. The river has burned up and become charcoal. Kabir Saheb awakened and saw that the fish has climbed up on top of the tree. This means: because of the world-ocean (desire) becoming desireless via Kriya, all of the acts that are taking place via the sense-organs due to desire – they have all burned up and become charcoal – meaning: the senses have not completely gone – yes it is true that they are all still there, but they are all experiencing One Brahman. Then Kabir Saheb became filled with wonder at seeing that all of this was actually already there within MySelf, but I somehow did not see it for all these days. And at that time the Bindu is on top of the tree of the body – meaning: It has gone up in the head. -15

kabir aage aage dvou baare, paache hariyaraa hoy
balihaari wo brich ki, jaa jari kaate phal hoy -16

[Bengali:]

Kabir is saying: there are "two" burning in the front [or: "two" burning at first]. There is a green color afterwards [or: behind; following]. Glory to this kind of tree which gives fruit when the root is cut out. -16

[Commentary:]

Kabir, there are "two" burning in the front [or: "two" burning at first]. After that the green color happens. Glory to that tree which gives fruit after cutting out the root ("jari" [see doha]). This means: like the way that one Kutastha is being seen now, later two Kutasthas will be seen in front of the Eye [or: eyes]. Those two Kutasthas are burning in the front [or: burning at first]. After that, this Kutastha will become green-colored. Glory to that Tree (Self), cutting Whose root – meaning: becoming Still – brings forth this Fruit of the Kutastha. -16

kabir biraha kulhari tan bahai, jaao na baadhai roha
marne ki shangsai nahi, chutee gayaa bharam moha -17

[Bengali:]

Kabir is saying: the pick-ax of longing is cutting throughout the body – meaning: it is striking. There is no problem with having to die. All delusion and attachment have gone away. -17

[Commentary:]

Kabir, the pick-ax of longing is cutting through the whole body. Those strikes are upon the self. There is no thought of death – meaning: there is no fear that I will die, because delusion and attachment have gone. This means: because of not Uniting with the Beloved Lord, longing is cutting some days in the hands, some days in the legs – in this way throughout the whole body – meaning: the blows of vayu are causing pain, like the strikes of a pick-ax. But those blows are not hurting the self/Self because the self/Self is in Brahman. And I have no fear of death [or: because of death], because delusion and attachment have run away. -17

kabir svapnaa rainka, paraa kae ye chek jab
shoyo tab dui janaa, jab jaage tab ek -18

[Bengali:]

Kabir is saying: there was a dream that was seen at night; it came to the heart. When one was asleep [or: lying down] there were two beings; when [the person] awakened, there was one. -18

[Commentary:]

Kabir, when one is sleeping and seeing a dream in one's heart – at that time, there are two beings when lying down. And when there is no dream being seen, then there is one. In that same way, when there is the witnessing and experiencing of Kutastha in the heart, at that time it is [the sense of] "two" lying down in the heart. And in the par avastha of Kriya there is One. Then there is no seeing, hearing – nothing at all is there. -18

kabir paani maahi par jvali, bhayi aparbal aagi
saritaa bahati rahi gayi, meen rahe jal tyagi -19

[Bengali:]

Kabir is saying: the fish is in the water. Its fins are burned up. There is no more power in the fire. The river flowed and flowed and then became Still. And the fish left the water and stayed [was living]. -19

[Commentary:]

Kabir, the fire was so heavy that the two fins of the fish in the water burned up. And that in which the fish was – that is flowing on. And the fish is staying [living] after leaving the water. This means: in the river of "kaaran" [cause] – meaning: because of the fish merging in Brahman, the mind-fish let go of the fins of ida and pingala and went on moving in sushumna. The mind, which was in such intense Brahman-fire and vayu-water – that [the vayu-water] continues moving in substance to substance – and mind has left the vayu-waters and is staying in Brahman. -19

kabir brahma agni tan mo laagi, laagi rahaa
tat jiu ki jaane oh birahini, ki jaane o piu -20

[Bengali:]

Kabir is saying: the Brahman-fire caught on the body, and the jiva [being] remained connected to that. Maybe he himself is the longing-lover or maybe he himself is the Beloved. -20

[Commentary:]

Kabir, the Brahman-fire has caught on the body. And the one who is jiva is enjoined with Brahman. And leaving that State – whether he himself is the longing-lover or Beloved – only He is experiencing that. In the par avastha of Kriya, the self could no longer stay in the body and has merged in Brahman. He is experiencing both the pain of leaving samadhi and being Kutastha. -20

**kabir pawok roopee raam hay, sab ghat rahaa samaay
chit chakmak chin hataay nahi, dhnuaa hoy hoy jaay -21**

[Bengali:]

Kabir is saying: the One Who is Rama is in the Form of Fire in all bodies, and the one who is the flashing flint of chitta [individual mind] – he disappears like smoke. -21

[Commentary:]

Kabir, the Atma-Rama [Self] Kutastha which is in the Form of Fire – He is in all bodies verily. The chitta [individual mind] flashes and glitters but does not stay. It goes away little by little, like smoke. -21

**kabir kar kaaya chakmak kiyaa, jhaaraa baarambaar
tin baar dhnuaa bhayaa, chauthe paraa angaar -22**

[Bengali:]

Kabir is saying: I have made the body into flint and have struck it again and again. Three times there was smoke. It has become cinder on the fourth time [attempt]. -22

[Commentary:]

Kabir, upon making the body and the hands into flint, and striking again and again, three times there was smoke – meaning: first: there is nothing at all that can be seen – darkness; second: it is like smoke in Kutastha; third: "vigyaan pada" [knowing the science of it; or: Supreme Knowing]; and fourth: there was Revelation [or: there was Light] like burning cinder. -22

**kabir pahile prem na chaakhiyaa, mujhe niraashee aay
paache tan man haat lay, gaye chamkaa laay -23**

[Bengali:]

Kabir is saying: when I could not get the taste of Love at first, I became full of disappointment. Later, by working the body and mind skillfully, I saw a wondrous sight. -23

[Commentary:]

Kabir, when at first I could not taste Love, I became full of disappointment. After that, upon taking the body and mind in hand [or: taking up the body and mind] and doing Kriya, a wonder struck upon me. Having taken Kriya, I do nothing but Kriya. Even by doing so, because of not seeing anything real and thus becoming full of disappointment, it felt that I will not do Kriya anymore with no reward. Because I have received it [Kriya], I took up the body and mind and anyway went on doing Kriya, and continuing with it, I suddenly saw a wondrous sight and was startled – that all this time the movement was outside; now I see that the movement is going on inside. -23

kabir birahaa mmujh so eo kahe, gaadaa paakro mohi charan kamal ke mojme, lai baythayo tohi -24

[Bengali:]

Kabir is saying: longing has told me this also: "Hold me properly. If this happens, I will take you and sit you down in the fun of the Lotus Feet. -24

[Commentary:]

Kabir, longing is saying this: "Hold me properly. I will sit you down in intoxication of the Lotus Feet." The separation from the Beloved Lord is saying, "Hold me properly" - meaning: "the mind going in other directions is the pain of separation [longing - "biraha"]; do not let the mind go in other directions." "In the intoxication of the Lotus Feet" – meaning:

"upon always doing Kriya, I will take you into the par avastha of Kriya and sit you down [in It]" - meaning: upon always doing Kriya, the par avastha of Kriya will automatically stay stuck [to oneself]. -24

kabir aaguanee to aaiya, gyaan vichaar vivek
paache hari bhi aayiaa, sagari saaj samet -25

[Bengali:]

Kabir, those who come first have arrived – knowledge, discernment and discrimination [or: correct perception]. After that, the Lord too came, all dressed up in full regalia. - 25

[Commentary:]

Kabir, those who come first have arrived – meaning: "gyaan" [knowledge] = knowing; "vichaar" [discernment] = is what I am seeing true or not; "vivek" [discrimination; or: correct perception] = becoming One (beyond doubt/conflict). After that, the experience of the Lord went on happening in the heart – meaning: because of being Still in the heart, the experience of Kutastha went on happening. He arrived dressed in full regalia – meaning: there was the witnessing of Kutastha accompanied by all the perfections [or: all the perfected ones]. -25

LIKHTE PARICHAY
KI ANG

On Getting to Know [or: On Certain Characteristic Attributes]

kabir tej anant kaa, jaysaa suraj shayan pati
sang jaagi sundaree, kautuk dekhat nayan -1

[Bengali:]

Kabir is saying: what is the fire/energy of Infinite Brahman like? It is like when the sun "lies down" - meaning: after it sets, there is neither visible fire nor darkness, only the light remains; it is like that. The beautiful wife stays up for the sake of her husband's company – the eyes look with loving wonderment – meaning: because of the presence of her husband, the wife experiences joy. At that time, the eyes also keep on looking at the vision of the husband only. It happens like this for the sadhak. -1

[Commentary:]

Kabir, the fire/energy of Infinite Brahman is like the time after the sun sets. Neither light nor dark – the State is like that. When, to this Prakritiwife – meaning: when in this body "Purusha" = (Beloved Lord) comes and is present, then, upon seeing the Beloved Lord, a great Bliss is experienced in the body, and the Eye [or: eyes] look on with loving wonderment. -1

227

**kabir paarbrahmke tej kaa, kaysaa hay anumaan
kyaa woki shobhaa kahon, dekhan ki parmaan -2**

[Bengali:]

Kabir is saying: how can one imagine how the Power of ParaBrahman is? What description of Its Beautiful Glory can I give? If It is not seen directly, one cannot understand. -2

[Commentary:]

Kabir, how can I comprehend the Power of ParaBrahman? And how should I describe Its Beautiful Glory?! The one who has seen knows the proof of it – meaning: Kutastha in the Bejeweled Throne and all Perfected Beings seated in front – it is not possible to convey an idea about the Power of that kind, because there is nothing else like That. And what can I speak of the Beautiful Glory? The one who sees – it is he who knows. What can others know? -2

**kabir agam agochar gami nahi, tnahaa jhalke jyoti
tnahaa kabiraa bandogi, paap punya nahi dvoti -3**

[Bengali:]

Kabir is saying: it is not possible to go there. It is hidden to all of the senses. The intellect cannot reach there. Light is Ever-Effulgent there. It is there that Kabir went and did full prostration. There is no dual experience – such as sin and virtue – in that Place. -3

[Commentary:]

Kabir, there are flashes of Light from a Place which is inaccessible and hidden, and totally absent of thought. Kabir Saheb is saying, "My salutations are in that Place, where there is neither sin nor virtue." -3

kabir man madhukar bhayaa, kiyaa nirantar baas
knaol jo phulaa nirbich, woi nirakhe nij daas -4

[Bengali:]

Kabir is saying: the one who is mind has become a honey-bee. And he is residing in the Place with no end. There all substances are blossoming like lotuses. That is seen by one who is the servant of himself – meaning: the one who is the servant of Atman [Self] – it is only he who sees [this]. -4

[Commentary:]

Kabir, mind has become a honey-bee. And it is ever residing in the place where lotuses bloom without water. The one who is the servant of himself is the one who is seeing that. Mind has taken on the characteristic of the honey-bee – meaning: like the way the honey-bee brings back honey from all the flowers and gathers up the honey, in that same way, mind goes from here and there and comes to stay in the Self-Brahman. And he is residing in Brahman constantly and always. Then all the lotuses of all the substances [or: elements] blossomed. This means: all of the qualities of the five elements became revealed. The one who is the servant of himself – meaning: the one who constantly serves the Atman [Self] – it is only he who sees [this]. -4

kabir chhip nahi saagar nahi, svaati bund bhi
naahi kabir mati nipje, shunya shikhar gad maahi -5

[Bengali:]

Kabir is saying: there is no sea; neither are there sea-shells; there are no water-droplet-like "bindus" [spots] of astronomical/astrological stars. Yet, a Bindu-like Pearl is being seen in the Orb of the Void. -5

[Commentary:]

Kabir, there are no sea-shells; there is no ocean; there are no bindus of astronomical/astrological stars. Yet, in the peak of the Mountain of the Void, a Pearl is being seen. There is no sea-shell, no ocean, no bindus of astronomical/ astrological stars, yet a Bindu is being seen in the Void – meaning: in the light and darkness – a Bindu is being seeing in front of oneself at all times. -5

kabir ghatme aoghat paaiyaa, aoghatyo hi ghaat
kahe kabir parche bhaya, guru dekhaai baat -6

[Bengali:]

Kabir is saying: I have found an "aghat" [non-body; non-happening] within the "ghat" [body]. Now I have come to know the "aghat" as the "ghaat" [riverbank]. "But," says Kabir, "I came to know all when guru showed me the path." -6

[Commentary:]

Kabir, within the "ghat" I found an "aghat." And I am seeing that the "aghat" itself is "ghaat." Kabir Saheb is saying, "Now I have come to know. Guru has shown the path." Within this body is the constructed "ghaat" [riverbank] of in-breath and out-breath. And the "aghaat" [non-riverbank] is the par avastha of Kriya. I got That. Kabir Saheb then came to know all. And guru showed the path to get to this "aghaat" [non-riverbank]. -6

kabir jnahaa matihu ki jhaalree, heerhu ko pargaash
chaand surya ki gami nahi, tnahaa darshan paaoe daas -7

[Bengali:]

Kabir is saying: the Place where there are tassels of pearls, and a diamond-like Light is effulgent – neither moon nor sun can go to that Land. There is only one way to go to this kind of

Land. One who can take up the feeling of being a servant –
meaning: see oneself as small – it is only he who receives
"Darshan" [beatific vision]. An egotistical person does not get
"Darshan." -7

[Commentary:]

Kabir, the Place where there are tassels of pearls and the
Light of diamonds – moon and sun have no way of going
there. At that Place, the servant received "Darshan" [beatific
vision]. In Kutastha – all kinds of droplets like tassels of pearls
and the Light like the light of diamonds – and a place where
there is no moon or sun – the servant receives "Darshan" of
such; and the one who is big with ego – neither does he learn,
nor does he receive "Darshan." -7

**kabir surya samaana chaandme, dvou kiyaa ghar ek
man ko cheetayo gayaa, purva janamkaa lekh -8**

[Bengali:]

Kabir is saying: with the union of the sun and the moon,
one made two houses as one. The restlessness of mind finished
and Awakenedness dawned, by which all that was there from
previous lives was finished off. -8

[Commentary:]

Kabir, with the union of sun and moon, two [houses]
became one house. Then the restlessness of mind finished, and
all that was written from previous lives was finished off . The
sun in the navel merged in the moon at the "taalu mool" [root
in the skull] – meaning: it [sun] became Still in the "taalu
mool." Then sun and moon became One. Then the restlessness
of mind no longer remained, and the fruits of the actions of
past lives were no longer there. -8

kabir pinjar prem prakaashiya, antar rahaa ujaas
mukh kasturi maha mahi, baani phuti subaas -9

[Bengali:]

Kabir is saying: the cage of Love surely became revealed, but That was known only within. It is like when musk is kept inside the mouth, others cannot smell it, but when one speaks, the sweet fragrance of the musk comes out. -9

[Commentary:]

Kabir, a cage of Love became revealed. Its revelation is only happening within. Musk was put on inside the mouth, and it became revealed just as one began to speak. This means - ("pinjar" [cage; chamber]) – the cage is closed on all sides; the bird has no way of escaping. In that same way, upon doing Kriya with love, a cage became revealed, and within that is the self; there is no possible way for him to go anywhere. And the revelation of that cage is happening within only; there is no way of speaking about it. And the musk is covered inside the mouth. As soon as speaking began it became known all around – meaning: whatever one says to anyone – that itself went on to happen. Then, one's mind ran in all directions. -9

kabir jogee huye jak lagi, meti gayi ve chataan ulti
samaanaa aapume, hoy gayaa brahm samaan -10

[Bengali:]

Kabir is saying: I have become a yogi, but like a wealthy miser. Desires have been fulfilled. Being turned back [or: reversed] into myself, I have become the same as Brahman -10

[Commentary:]

Kabir, I have come to know that I have become a yogi, because there is the wealth of a miserly person now. And the looking about – in this direction and that direction – all that was finished. And I have reversed and entered into MySelf, upon which I have become the same as Brahman. Like the way the wealth of a miser is buried in the earth, in that same way, my Wealth is buried in my Muladhar. Seeing this, I came to understand that I have become a yogi. Then the Bliss is within; there is no desire any more to open the eyes and look outside. Before, the sun used to merge with the moon; now the moon is merging with the Sun – in the Self, and I am experiencing: I Am Brahman. -10

kabir kachu karanee kachu karma gati, kachu purbilaa lekh dekho bhaag kabir kaa, kya dost aalekh -11

[Bengali:]

Kabir is saying: I have done some things and some actions are being done also, and whatever was written from previous lives – I have done all that too. Now look at Kabir's fortune: he has become friends with "Alekh" ("Alekh" = God). -11

[Commentary:]

Kabir, whatever I have done, and whatever I am doing – meaning Kriya, and whatever was written from previous lives – now look at Kabir's luck: he has become friends with "Alekh" [God]. "Friend" = one who feels hurt when you are hurt and is happy when you are happy. "Did something" - meaning: Kriya with enthusiasm and the Revelatory Light via the movement of Kriya – and some good acts from previous lives, doing which has brought about this kind of [spiritual] wish – upon doing all these things, one became friends with Kutastha. -11

kabir kaayaa chhip samsaar me, paani boond shareer binaa chhip ki moti, pragate daas kabir -12

[Bengali:]

Kabir is saying: the physicality is the [clam] shell of samsara and the body is the droplet. Servant Kabir is revealing a Pearl without a shell. -12

[Commentary:]

Kabir, the physicality is the [clam] shell of samsara, and the body has come about from drops of water. Servant Kabir is revealing the Pearl without a shell. The two halves of the shell are open. The physicality also has two breaths which are being parted. These have come about from Water-Cause of Brahman. There is no shell, yet there is a Pearl – meaning: the Bindu that can be seen in the Void. Servant Kabir saw and revealed It. -12

kabir yoha moti jani jaanahu, jo poye poni saath
eha to moti shabda ki, jo bedhi rahaa sab gaat -13

[Bengali:]

Kabir is saying: do not have that type of mentality [wrongful type]. Find that type of mentality that is happening from Sound – meaning: happening within the Omkar Sound. That which has permeated the entire body and is happening in the entire body – have your mentality that way. Eat up wrongful mentality like mashed up bread. -13

[Commentary:]

Kabir, may it not be that your mentality becomes like: "let me eat not only only the bread but the one who is also making the bread." Let your mentality be that of the mentality that is from the Sound and that which has permeated the entire body. This means: rajah and tamo gunas exist simply for the sake of pleasure. "Oh now I will be happy, oh now I will be happy" - thinking this on and on, the body is eaten up. Do not have mentality like that. Keep your mental direction in the Omkar

Sound, which is permeating the entire body and happening in the entire body. -13

**kabir man laagaa unmani so, gagan pahucha jaay
chaand bihunaa chaandnaa, tahan alakh niranjan raay -14**

[Bengali:]

Kabir, when mind became caught on the gem* – then one can go to the Void Brahman, where there is no moon yet there is moonlight – meaning: there is Light. It is in that Place that the Supreme Being Brahman resides. -14

[*Translator's note: In dohas 14, 15 and 27 of this section, the spiritual word "unmani" is used. Often this is translated as "no mind." But in this case, it is the "jewel through which Stillness/Void is known," simplified as "gem" and "jewel" in these dohas only. This is because in the commentaries themselves the word "unmani" has been referred to simply as "mani" [gem].]

[Commentary:]

Kabir, mind became caught on the gem, by which one can go to Brahman. Where there is no moon yet there is moonlight, in that place is the "Alakshya" [hidden] Kutastha. -14

**kabir man lagaa unmuni so, unmun manhi
bilag laon bilagaa paaniyaa, paani laon milag -15**

[Bengali:]

Kabir is saying: when mind caught on to the gem – upon going to the gem, mind became separated, like water became separated from salt, and again water merged back with salt. -15

[Commentary:]

Kabir, mind became caught on the gem. And upon going

from the gem, mind became separated. Salt is separate from water, and [again] water became merged with salt. This means: when mind is connected to Kutastha, then mind and ida, pingala, maya and - separate – alas! I do not have to speak useless things – meaning: restlessness does not remain. With salt, foodstuff gets taste. This salt-endowed samsara – from that the water-like mind became separate. But for how long can one keep mind on Kutastha – meaning: not being able to keep mind in Kutastha [one cannot realize] the Particle which is everywhere, like salt, in which the water-like mind merged – meaning: one went on seeing all things as Kutastha. -15

kabir paanihu te puni hem bhayaa, hemo gayaa bilaay
kabiraa jo thaa soi bhayaa, ab kachu kahaa naa jaay -16

[Bengali:]

Kabir is saying: water again became gold. And gold also merges. Kabir says, "Whatever was [originally], that has come about. Now there is no way of saying anything." -16

[Commentary:]

Kabir, water again became gold. After that gold also merges. Whatever Kabir was [originally], he became verily That. Now there is no way of saying anything. ("Hem") precious gold – meaning: that by which many deeds can be done/had. When mind, abiding in the Gold-like Rays of Brahman, is seeing all kinds of supernatural happenings going on, then mind became like precious gold. After that, it came to mind: "Who needs to be crazy? Let me stay now in the Bliss of Intoxication." Kabir Saheb is saying, "That Which I was before, I have become That only." This means: that Supreme Person, Whom I was originally, I have become That only. There is no way of saying anything else – meaning: That Brahman Which I was before, I have become That only, yet in the meantime I saw so many wondrous happenings. -16

kabir surati knaol me baithke, amee saroyar chaakh
kahen kabir vichaar koi, tab shant viveki bhaakh -17

[Bengali:]

Kabir is saying: sit on the lotus of "beautiful desire" and taste the Nectar from the Lake of Ambrosia – meaning: lick it up. Kabir Saheb has discerned and is saying, "That can only be done by peaceful and aware beings. Not others." -17

[Commentary:]

Kabir, sit on the lotus and lick up the Nectar from the Lake of Ambrosia. Kabir Saheb, having discerned, is saying, "When that State is attained, one is peaceful and aware." Whatever one wants to say to oneself, one does so. "Surat" - mind/attention – which goes in other directions. This mind has come about from Kutastha, and the five chakras (lotuses) have also come about from Kutastha. But is the [real] "sitting down" in Kutastha happening [for the aspirant]? One is only witnessing one burst [at times] in Yoni Mudra, that's about all. When one is always in Kutastha, that is when "sitting down" [truly] has happened. Then one went on tasting the Lake of Ambrosia – meaning: being in Kutastha itself is Stillness. As long as there is Stillness, for that long is the drinking of Nectar – meaning: Immortal. Kabir Saheb is saying, "One who is constantly drinking Nectar – he can let himself be known as peaceful and aware." -17

kabir adhar knaol ke upare, parimal shvet subaas amee
knaol par baithike, darshan darash hu laas -18

[Bengali:]

Kabir is saying: on top of the support-free Lotus, within a beautiful and sweetly fragrant white cloth, sitting on top of the

Nectar-Lotus, one went into ecstasy upon seeing Divine Forms. -18

[Commentary:]

Kabir, sitting on the support-free Lotus, wearing a white cloth wrapped all around – meaning: impurities – meaning: "kal" [time or death] – when the Nectar-Lotus blossomed – meaning: when Kutastha was witnessed in Yonimudra, then, abiding in That, witnessing supernatural scenes, mind went on experiencing great ecstasy. -18

kabir avigat kie gati kyaa kaho, jaake gnaao na thnaao
gun bihunaa dekhiye, kyaa kahi dhariye naao -19

[Bengali:]

Kabir is saying: how can I speak about the movement of That Which has no movement?! That Which has no village/town [historical root], no particular place, and Which, when perceived, is seen as having no attributes– how can I give this kind of Land a name?! -19

[Commentary:]

Kabir, how can I speak about the movement of the One Who absolutely has no movement? And where there is no village/town, and the three gunas [primal attributes] are even not there – when there are no gunas, then by what name can I call It (par avastha of Kriya.)? -19

kabir woki gati aas alakh hay, alakh lakhaa nahi jaay
shabd svarupee raam hay, sab ghaat rahaa samaay -20

[Bengali:]

Kabir is saying: His Movement cannot be seen. How can the Unseen be seen? The Omkar Itself is Rama. He has become the Omkar Sound Itself and is residing as such in every body. -20

[Commentary:]

Kabir, the Movement of that Awareness is like this – that Unseen, that Unseen which cannot be seen. Rama is the Divine Sound/Word and has entered in every body and is residing as such – meaning: the Movement that is in the par avastha of Kriya cannot be seen because at that time there is no mind. If there is no mind, then who is there to see? What that State cannot be seen, then how can Its Movement be seen? In this way it is Unseen. For this reason, no one can see that State. And, having become the Sound/Word, He is residing in every body as the Self. -20

kabir jnehi kaaran ham jaat the, soi paaya thaor
so to pheri aapnaa bhayaa, jaako kahte aur -21

[Bengali:]

Kabir is saying: the reason for which I was traveling – I have found out Its location. The One Whom I used to think was separate – He has also become one's own Self. -21

[Commentary:]

Kabir, the One for Whom I was traveling – I got His location. And the One Whom I used to think was separate – look, He became Mine. This means: I understood where that Peaceful Place, for which I was traveling, is – meaning: I became Stilled from that "Alas! Alas!" [feeling]. And the One – meaning Brahman – Whom I thought was separate – He has become My Own. There is no one who is mine. Even life itself is not mine, because when it goes, it cannot be held onto and kept. That separated state in which I was – when that no longer remained separate – it is then that "My Own" happened. -21

kabir may jaano jo milonge, koi aur raam ko dhaay
aapu ramaiya hoi rahaa, sheesh noao kaay -22

[Bengali:]

Kabir is saying: if I had known before that one has to merge with one's own Self, then I would not have gone after another Rama. When I have delighted in MySelf and become Rama Himself, then where will I bow my head? -22

[Commentary:]

Kabir, if I had known that I will merge with MySelf, then I would not have run after another Rama. Later, when I saw that I myself am delighting in MySelf, then to whom shall I bow my head?! -22

kabir makut manohar adhik chabi, bhed na paoe
koy bunknal ko sam karei, gurugam kahiye soy -23

[Bengali:]

Kabir is saying: there are very enchanting scenes guarded in the crown, but no one has inroads to that. One who keeps the tongue always in "samaan" [upright] (this is known via guru) – meaning: everything can be known via the mouth of guru. Otherwise there is no way to know. -23

[Commentary:]

Kabir, there are very enchanting scenes guarded in the crown, the inroads to which no one has. One who keeps tongue "samaan" at all times, and that no one can have any way of getting without guru telling it – meaning: the Crown captures and ends the mind; within it there is much that captures and ends the mind. Such are the scenes within Kutastha, that which no one can penetrate to find. If the tongue is kept in "samaan" [upright] at the "taalu moola" [skull root, or: palate root], one can penetrate (that which is known via the teachings of guru). -23

kabir jnahnaa pawon naahi sanchaare, tnahaa rachi ekagraha acharaj ek jo dekhiyaa, sindh kalejaa deha -24

[Bengali:]

Kabir is saying: the Place where there is no movement of air – I made a house there, but I am seeing an incredible thing: that the state of the body and the heart has changed – meaning: there is no "dhak-dhak" [beating] of the heart. -24

[Commentary:]

Where there is no movement of air – I built a house there, and in that I saw a wonder: that the body and heart were broken into [like a burglary] – meaning: in-breath and out-breath have stopped, and then one is moving in subtle-form from element to element. One can reside in a house. Because of residing in sushumna, sushumna becomes the "house." In that state, I saw a wonder (that which was never seen is called "wonder"): that the "dhap dhap" [beating] of the heart is no longer there. Coming inside, it is going inside too and in the body as well. -24

kabir dhadhas dekho chakor ki, sindh kalej dinha hirdayaa bhitar paithike, laal ratan hari linha -25

[Bengali:]

Kabir is saying: look at the daring of the partridge! She picked the lock of the heart, sat inside the heart and stole the "laal" jewel ("laal" = very precious stone). -25

[Commentary:]

Look at the daring of the partridges!! They pierced into the heart, sat inside the heart and stole the "laal" jewel – meaning:

the way that male and female partridges look at each other, in
that same way – from these two eyes, going on seeing the
("trinetra" [third Eye]) Kutastha Eye, the heart was broken into
[like a burglary] – meaning: it went on inside. After that,
sitting in the heart, the "laal jewel" - which is the substance of
all these valuable exchanges – they stole that – meaning: upon
the happening of "all is Brahman," everything was taken away
– meaning: there were no more separate things left. Then for
whom will there be any exchanges [give and take]? -25

kabir alakh lakhe laalach lago, kahat bane nahi bayan
nij man dhaso svarupa mo, satguru dinhe shayan -26

[Bengali:]

Kabir is saying: the desire that is happening from having
seen the Unseen – one cannot even speak about that, because
at that time mind has stuck onto the Self. It was satguru who
showed this remembrance [or: state]. -26

[Commentary:]

Kabir, upon seeing the Unseen, the desire came to see
[more]. What I saw cannot be said by speech. One's one mind
entered the Self. Satguru showed this place of lying down –
meaning: upon seeing the Supreme Person, a great desire came
about: that I want to see Him all the time. If I say "time" [or:
tomorrow] then it is not that – because He is not a person made
of space, because there aren't arms and legs, yet there are arms
and legs. What He is, there is no way of saying. My mind
entered the Self. Then there was no "mind" as a separate thing.
Satguru gave this place of "lying down." "Shayan" [lying
down] – going to sleep – meaning: being in an unconscious
state. In this State, because of being in That Awareness and
being away from unconsciousness – [thus] being unaware of

all unconscious things – [thus] Being Aware [Chaitanya] – guru bestowed this place. -26

kabir unman laagi shunyamo, nishu din rahe gul tnaan
tan man ki kachu sudhi nahi, paaya pad nirbaan -27

[Bengali:]

Kabir is saying: upon catching on to the gem, I went on witnessing the Void. In that State, day and night there is a pull at the throat. There is no awareness of body or mind. In this State, I received Nirvaana [Absolute-ness]. -27

[Commentary:]

Kabir, upon being locked in the jewel ["unmani" - see note at doha 14 of this section], I went on witnessing the Void. And day and night there is a pull at the throat. There is no awareness of body or mind. In that State, I received Nirvaana – meaning: upon being locked in the jewel above, there was Kutastha Brahman (Voidness). And day and night there is a pull at the throat (jalandhar mudra). Then, upon being in the stupor of intoxication, no cravings remained. Then I received Nirvaana. One who has jalandhar mudra all the time – for him there is Nirvaana. "Baan/Vaan" [arrow] - that by which every jiva [soul] is being pierced – that arrow is no longer there ["Nir-vaana" - no arrow]. -27

LIKHTE ASTHIRATA KO ANG

*On Restlessness**

[*Translator's note: The translators of the work have translated EXACTLY what is in the published Bengali original. It is possible that the readers may think that the titles of some sections do not accurately reflect the material in that section. But it is not up to the translators to decide what was originally meant; therefore the titles have been left as they were found in the published original.]

kabir paylaa premka, antar liyaa lagaay rom
rom me rami raho, amal na aur so hay -1

[Bengali:]

Kabir is saying: the cup of Love has moved inside. Being inside, it is making delight in every nerve. And the more that state happens inside, the more there is Bliss. -1

[Commentary:]

Kabir, the cup of Love has gone inside. Love is dripping from every nerve. And the one who practices more and more Love – he gets more and more Bliss. The cup of Love, which is the par avastha of Kriya, has gone within and It is keeping oneself locked to it. Every hair on his body is being delighted by Still vayu. And one who wishes to stay in that at all times through practice – he gets even more radiance (happiness). -1

245

kabir hari ras eyo piya, baaki rahim chhaak pakaa
kalas ko bhaaraka, bahuri chare nahi chaak -2

[Bengali:]

Kabir is saying: one who has tasted the Nectar of the Lord even once no longer has any fancy for any other drink [or: feeling/sentiment]. It is like when a clay pot is burned, it no longer goes on the potter's wheel. -2

[Commentary:]

Kabir, one who has tasted the Nectar of the Lord no longer has any attraction to any other drink [or: feeling/sentiment]. It is like: the burned clay pot is not put back on the potter's wheel. This means: one who has drunk the Nectar of the par avastha of Kriya – meaning: when the par avastha of Kriya stays at all times, then no pull towards any other sentiment/feeling remains– meaning: no desires remain. In this way, the one for whom that State has become "settled-in" – meaning: it has become a habit – for him there is no more "potter's wheel," which is birth and death. -2

kabir raam rasaayan adhik ras, piyoto adhik rasaal
kabir piyan so durlabh hay, maage sheesh kalaal -3

[Bengali:]

Kabir is saying: having the drink of Rama is a great elixir. If you drink It you will be greatly intoxicated. But drinking It is very costly, because to drink It one has to cut off one's head, meaning: one cannot keep the idea of "me" and such kinds of feelings. -3

[Commentary:]

Kabir, drinking Rama is a great drink. If you drink It there is great intoxication, but drinking It is very costly. If one wants to drink It, the head has to be cut off. "Rasaayan" [drink-making; or chemistry] = that which comes about from liquids. The "Liquid" comes from the eight types of nadis in this body – ida, pingala, shushumna, hastilimba, alambusha, pusha, gandhari, brahmanadi. Of prime importance in these [nadis] are 3 [ida, pingala, sushumna]: like in the outer, when silver, mercury and tin are burned up – like the way via that process gold is brought about – in that same way, when the three on the inner are burned to cinders [there is] the par avastha of Kriya – the gold-like great elixir [or: great intoxication], because other types of [worldly] intoxications can be controlled by the intellect. That [intoxication] is greater than that because after that State there is a feeling: "How happy I was." When one drinks It, there is even more intoxication. By drinking water, the thirst for water is quenched. By drinking the Nectar of Rama all thirsts are quenched. As much as you drink this elixir – meaning: the more you stay in that State – the more there will be the intoxication – meaning: Bliss. Drinking that elixir is very costly. That State says: "If you want to drink Me, then the head must be cut and given." When the head is cut off, it is separate from the body. In that State there is no awareness [or: noticing] of the body. -3

kabir bhnaati prem ki, bahutak baithe aay
shir sope piwe soy, aur so piya na jaay -4

[Bengali:]

Kabir is saying: the Love of the distillery comes after sitting for a long time – meaning: It happens after doing a great deal of sadhana. This too can only be drunk by one who can give his head. It is not possible to drink [That] in some other way. -4

[Commentary:]

Kabir, the Love from the distillery comes after sitting a

long time. The one who can give his head is the one who can drink It. Except for this way, it is not possible to drink It in another way. "Bhnaati" [distillery; alcohol still] = that which has fire burning below, and above, it is becoming steam and going through another pipe. Here, from the distillery of this body, via the [use of] "brahmaagni" [inner fire; digestive fire] in Kriya, the "steam" of vayu goes to the "other pipe" of sushumna. The Love that comes from this distillery - "prem" [love] = without which one cannot live – here it is the Stillness – this [Love/Stillness] does not happen unless one sits for a long time doing Kriya. The one who stays in the head is the one who drinks [It]. There is no other way of drinking this Stillness. -4

kabir hariras mahaghaan jaani kai, maage sheesh kalaar
dil ynochhaa ghant dublaa, baithike gaaoe malaar -5

[Bengali:]

Kabir is saying: know that the Nectar of God is very precious. If one wants the Nectar of God, one first has to give one's head. The body is weak, and the heart is also not good. So one is sitting about singing in [or: using] the "Malhar Ragini" [a particular musical mode used during the rainy season]. -5

[Commentary:]

Kabir, know that the Nectar of God is very costly. To get that Nectar, the head is demanded first. And the heart is bad and the body is weak. Then one is just sitting about singing in the "Malhar" mode [see above paragraph]. "Hari" [Lord] is the one who takes away all. Now, if all is taken away, well then the nectar [or: emotion/sentiment] does not remain. Now this Nectar of non-nectarousness [non-emotion] – the par avastha of Kriya – because this is had after great suffering [or: great effort; great labor], it is very costly. If one desires to attain this State – that State right at the beginning asks for the head – meaning: unless one is bodiless, one cannot attain that State. But the heart is very "ynochhaa" (bad) and the body is also very weak. Now, in order to cool down, I am singing the "Malhar Ragini." -5

kabir hariras maahange piyataa, chori jeeoyanki
baan maathaa saate saai mile, tao laagi sulabh jaan -6

[Bengali:]

Kabir is saying: if the Nectar of God is very difficult to have – if you want to drink That – if that is so, then let go of the hopes of life [or: staying alive]. But if you can cut off your head and offer it, then one day you will have "Saai" [beloved] (the Lord is called "Saai"). Then there will be prosperous gain. -6

[Commentary:]

Kabir, if you want to drink the Nectar of God, then let go of that desire to stay alive. And if the head can be tightly stuck onto, then the Lord is met. And if in that way one can tightly stick onto the head night and day, know that there is beautiful gain. If you want to stay in the par avastha of Kriya, let go of the breath, which is the desire to live. And take it to the head and stick it there. Then you will have the Lord, Who is the Supreme Person. And know that staying in the head day and night is "sulabh" - meaning: know that it is beautiful gain/profit. -6

kabir avadhutaa aavi gatirataa, jaysaa akhil
ajit naam amal maataa rahe, jeevanmukti ateet -7

[Bengali:]

Kabir is saying: the one who is "avadhuta" [saint; ascetic]

– his motion has stopped. He no longer has any desire to conquer any part of this universe – meaning: he has become desireless. And whom and what will he conquer anyway? And what is even there to be conquered anyway? And one becomes intoxicated with the Immaculate Name. One has Immaculate Mentality [or: Immaculate Pearl]. Know that that is even beyond the state of "jivanmukta" [liberated while in the body]. -7

[Commentary:]

Kabir, the one who is "avadhuta" is without motion. And he does not desire to conquer anything of any of the vast universe at all. And from doing that Name, an Immaculate Mentality [or: Immaculate Pearl] comes about. He is beyond even being "jivanmukta." The one who is "avadhuta" is without motion – meaning: he truly has no [inner] movement. And because of being merged with Brahman, because of which there is no thing separate any more to be conquered – who is there to conquer what?! If one does the Name, the answer can be had. By staying in that State, everything manifests even before coming to mind. Then an Immaculate Mentality comes about, and in that State – meaning: one who always resides in the par avastha of Kriya is even beyond the state of "jivanmukta" - meaning: even the "jivanmukta" person wants that State, but the one who always resides in the par avastha of Kriya – he does not want anything at all. This is the reason that he is "beyond" [the state of "jivanmukta"]. -7

kabir aat gnaat kopeenme, manhi na aane shank
naam amal mataa rahe, kahaan raajaa kahaan rank -8

[Bengali:]

Kabir is saying: there are eight knots in [or: holding] the loincloth, and there is no trepidation coming to the mind any more. One is ever absorbed in the ecstasy of the Immaculate Name. In this State, who is a king and who is an ascetic sage? - 8

[Commentary:]

Kabir, there are eight knots in [or: holding] the loincloth; there is no trepidation in the mind. One is just totally absorbed in the ecstasy of the Immaculate Name. From the door of the anus to the navel, one is abiding on the eight-petaled lotus. At that time there is no fear in the mind. There is only the intoxicated ecstasy of the par avastha of Kriya. For him, there is no king, because he does not want anything. And there is no ascetic sage because he does not want any attainments [or: powers]. -8

kabir hariras piyaa tab jaaniye, utre nahi khnoari matvaalaa ghumat phire, tan ki naahi samaari -9

[Bengali:]

Kabir is saying: you will know that one has drunk the Nectar of God when the intensity of intoxication does not leave. One wanders about like a drunkard, yet one has no regard for the body. -9

[Commentary:]

Kabir, you will know that one has drunk the Nectar of God when the intensity of intoxication does not leave. One wanders about like a drunkard. There is no awareness of [or: care for; regard for] the body – meaning: one is [physically] falling down from the intoxication; one does not even care about stopping one's fall. -9

kabir jnoha sar gharaa na dubta, maygal mali mali nahaay deol dubaa kalas so, parkhat saai jaay -10

[Bengali:]

Kabir is saying: in a lake in which the pot does not sink, yet the body is caressingly having a bath. Yet again, the temple-like body sank in the pot-like head. As soon as one looks, it goes away [or: does not remain as before]. It does not stay. -10

[Commentary:]

Kabir, in a lake in which the pot does not sink – meaning: if one holds the nose closed, the life force begins to struggle – this is the "not being able to sink a pot and take even one potful of water." And when there is Stillness, then the mad elephant-mind is caressingly bathing – meaning: it [mind] does not go in any direction. "Deol" (temple) – the temple-like body sank in the pot-like head – meaning: the breath went from the body and became Still in the head. But as soon as one wants to see if it is Still or not, immediately then it is in motion [again]. -10

kabir sabe rasaayan may kiyaa, hariras aaor na koy
ranchak ghatme sanchare, sab tan kaanchan hoy -11

[Bengali:]

Kabir is saying: I have done every kind of alchemy, but if the Nectar of God enters the pot-like body even a little bit – if that happens, the entire body becomes gold. But except for the Nectar of God the body does not become gold with anything else at all. -11

[Commentary:]

Kabir, I have done all alchemy. "It" has happened by the Nectar of God and absolutely nothing else at all. If even a little bit of the Nectar of God spreads in the body, then the entire body becomes gold. Ida, pingala, sushumna – the alchemy of these three – that which happens by uniting two or three substances – the union ["yoga"] that happens by making "one" - meaning: that which is the par avastha of Kriya – that I have done by the Nectar of God and absolutely nothing else at all. The body that has partaken in the par avastha of Kriya even a little bit – that body becomes gold. -11

kabir ekastha chhaak chhakaaiya, ekastha piyaa dhoy kal kalanti bhaathi jinha piyaa, rahaa kaal lne shoy -12

[Bengali:]

Kabir is saying: straining [as in a sieve] once and washing once, and after drinking It, the one who again drinks that which is bubbling in the distillery [alcohol still] – that person is lying down with [or: in the way of] "kal" [time; death]. -12

[Commentary:]

Kabir, straining the pure substance once, washing it and after drinking it, there is a bubbling in the distillery – one who drinks that, he has taken over [as in "usurped"] the road of "kal" and is lying there – meaning: the par avastha of Kriya, which, upon happening once, again one washes it via Brahman and drinks it – meaning: after the par avastha of Kriya happening once, and again after Kriya – one who enjoys that state – its [par avastha's] bubbling sound of the Still vayu – which is loaded in the head – one who drinks that – he is [in the way] of the road of kal – meaning: the time [kal] which is going by – one is holding that in one's lap – meaning: one is Still. -12

kabir kahat shunat jag jaat hay, bikhayan shujhe kaal kahe kabir re praaniyaa! baani brahma sahhaal -13

[Bengali:]

Kabir is saying: talking and talking, hearing and hearing,

the world is going by. Because of being in the poison of worldly matters, "kal" [time; death] is not able to be seen. Kabir is saying to them [jivas], "O living beings! The Speech of Brahman – meaning the Omkar Sound that is going on – manage [or: take care of] That" – meaning: hold on to That. - 13

[Commentary:]

Kabir, talking and hearing, the world is going by. Being in worldly matters, "kal" is not able to be seen. Kabir is saying, "O living beings! Manage [or: take care of] the Sound of Brahman" - meaning: one is listening to this and that, but the one who is the world itself – meaning: the one who is inhalation and exhalation – he is continuously going by. Being involved in worldly matters – meaning: "my son," "my rule over my land" – all of these thoughts are making one unable to see "kal." Kabir Saheb is saying, "O living beings (those who have the life-force)! Manage the Omkar Sound, which is the Speech of Brahman, which is automatically going by in the current." To keep [or: hold] it with conscious effort is called "saamlaan" [manage; take care of]. Here [it means]: listen to the Omkar Sound. -13

kabir rato maataa naam kaa, piyaa prem aghaay
matvale didaar ke, maage mukti balaay -14

[Bengali:]

Kabir is saying: being engaged in the Name, one became absorbed in intoxication. Because of drinking and drinking the Nectar of Love in the throat, one attained the state of a drunkard. Then he said, with complete disregard to liberation, "Liberation! Let my enemies take that. I don't need it." -14

[Commentary:]

Kabir, being absorbed in Amorous Acts, one became the Name's own. And one went on drinking the Nectar of Love in the throat again and again. Drinking like that, he looks out with the eyes of a drunkard. That which you call "liberation" - let my enemies take that. This means: upon the continuous doing of the guru-given Kriya, gradually one became absorbed in Kriya, and upon being absorbed, one became owned by the Name, which is the par avastha of Kriya. And then, one became loaded only down to the throat – meaning: stayed in the throat. Then he became a drunkard with the eyes – meaning: no attraction for worldly matters remained for the eyes. A person in this kind of state wants/says, "Let my enemies take liberation. The fun in which I am; that is actually best" [or: "Let me just stay in the fun I am having"]. -14

kabir rato maataa naam kaa, mad kaa maataa naahi
mad kaa maataa jo phire, se matvaaraa naahi -15

[Bengali:]

Kabir is saying: it is by being engaged amorously in the Name that one has become intoxicated. One is not a drunkard from alcohol. One is not talking about a person who gets drunk by drinking alcohol. This drunkard is actually a very worthy drunkard; he does not say a bunch of nonsensical things; he actually just sits there quietly – meaning: by oneself being in one's Self, one has become a drunkard. -15

[Commentary:]

Kabir, upon being engaged amorously in Kriya and becoming intoxicated – the one who becomes owned by the par avastha of Kriya is not a drunkard from alcohol. The one who goes about with his ego claiming, "I am a drunkard" - he is actually not a drunkard [in God], because the real drunkard [in God] stays quiet. -15

kabir matvaala ghumat phire, rom rom bharipur
chote aash shareer ki, tab dekhe daas hazur -16

[Bengali:]

Kabir is saying: the one who is a drunkard [in God] is roaming about here and there, but every one of the fibers in his body is full of Divine Energy. When the desires of the body end, then the one who is servant will see "hazur" - meaning Lord. -16

[Commentary:]

Kabir, the one who is a drunkard [in God] – he is wandering about with every one of the fibers of his body filled [with Divine Energy]. When the desires of the body leave, then one sees "hazur" [lord] – meaning: one's own Form (the Supreme Person). Servant Kabir is saying – meaning: one has become intoxicated in the par avastha of Kriya and is wandering about in the follicles of every hair. When both the body being there and not being there are felt as the same, then the Supreme Person becomes visible. Servant Kabir is saying [this]. -16

kabir prem piyaalaa bhari piyo, jar naa karo jatan
aayo chhaak jab jaansi, sohaage dharaa ratan -17

[Bengali:]

Kabir is saying: fill up the cup of Love and drink It. And why are you not taking care to drink That? When you have strained [as in a sieve] and come to know, then hold on to the Jewel-like Kutastha. -17

[Commentary:]

Kabir, fill up the bowl of Love and drink It. Why do you not take care about that? When you came to know the Substantial Thing after straining [as in a sieve], then you lovingly embraced the Jewel. This means: the par avastha of Kriya – fill up the cup of Love and drink It – meaning: always reside in the par avastha of Kriya. Take a little bit of care about that State, because just by taking care one can have that State. When you began to see the Substantial Thing – meaning: you went on seeing the Subtle Brahman in everything, then you became transfixed to [or: put on] the Priceless Jewel, which is Kutastha. -17

kabir bhnouraa baari parihari, mari bilanme aay paaon chandan ghar kiyo bhuli gayaa ban raay -18

[Bengali:]

Kabir is saying: the bee has left the wet [or: humid; moist] garden. It has come to the hole and is staying there. He has made a home inside the Immaculate Sandalwood, and has forgotten the one who is the king of the jungle. -18

[Commentary:]

Kabir, the bee has abandoned the garden and is staying covered in the various holes. And, after making a home in the Immaculate Sandalwood, he has forgotten the jungle – the bee which is the king of the jungle. The bee-like mind has abandoned the honey of the pleasures of the flowers of worldly things/matters in the garden of samsara. First in the hole of Kutastha, [then] in Its atomic form – the hole in the Star; after that in the hole of the sushumna; after that, cutting through the tongue-knot, the heart-knot [and] the Muladhar-knot, he covered himself in those three holes in Immaculate Sandalwood ("chandan" [sandalwood] = immaculately white;

he set up house in the White Form of Brahman) – meaning: residing there, the mind who is the king of the jungle of samsara – he completely forgot about all the pleasures of the world. -18

kabir amrit keri, raakhi satguru chhori aapu
sarikha jo mile, taahi piyaaoe ghori -19

[Bengali:]

Kabir is saying: the one who is satguru has kept the Nectar of Immortality separate [or: only for special purpose]. If he finds someone the same as him, he [then] stirs It up and feeds [that person]. -19

[Commentary:]

Kabir, satguru has kept the Nectar of Immortality separate. If he finds someone the same as him, then he stirs It up and feeds [that person]. This means: the satguru has kept separate [or: kept it to himself] that which enables one to be in the par avastha of Kriya at all hours of the day. If he finds the disciple to be fit for it and the same as himself, then he speaks of the method by which that State can remain for all hours of the day. -19

kabir amrit piye so janaa, jaake satguru laage
kaan ve to agochar mil gay, man nahi aave aan -20

[Bengali:]

Kabir is saying: the one who drinks the Nectar of Immortality is the one at whose ear satguru is connected. It is for him only that the Hidden Substance has been found. Then mind no longer goes in other directions. -20

[Commentary:]

Kabir, the one who drinks the Nectar of Immortality is the

one to whose ear satguru is connected. It is for him only that the Hidden [Reality] has been found. Then mind no longer goes to other things. This means: one always drinks the par avastha of Kriya – it is he only who is fulfilled – the one who constantly listens to the Omkar Sound. And it is that person only that has found the Hidden [Reality]. The "Hidden" cannot be known by mind, ear, nose, eyes – by none of such ways – meaning: becoming desireless, one attained the All-Form-ness, All-Pervading-ness, All-Powerful-ness – meaning: God-ness happened – then mind does not go to any thing, because to go to a thing means visibility [or: look; perception] has happened, and as soon as visibility [or: look; perception] happens then one does not stay in the "Hidden." -20

kabir saadhu cchip hay, satguru svaati bund trikhaa gayi ek bund te, kya le kare samund -21

[Bengali:]

Kabir is saying: it is the sadhu [sage] who is the shell, and the satguru is the bindu [dot; drop] of the "svaati" star [the fifteenth of the twenty-seven stars in Hindu astrology]. All thirst that was there has all been quenched by one drop. Now what is the need to have an ocean?! -21

[Commentary:]

Kabir, the sadhu is the shell, and the satguru is the bindu of the "svaati" star. If the thirst is quenched by one drop, then what need is there to have an ocean?! This means: like the way a clam-shell opens its mouth and then closes its mouth, in the same way, the sadhu is taking the mind back again and again from wherever it goes and settling it back in the Self. The One Who is Kutastha is the "svaati" bindu.

One who remains in the One Particle [Bindu [drop]] of Kutastha, he becomes desireless. Then what need has he for the innumerable-wave-filled ocean of samsara?! -21

LIKHTE LOKO ANG – SAKSHI [WITNESS/DIRECT EXPERIENCE]

Elucidation on "Loka[s]" (special state[s] [or: "planes of consciousness"])

[On] the state[s] attained upon Stillness coming about, and the signs of the Great Beings who have attained that State

[Translator's note: There is another chapter later in the original published work also titled "Likhte Loko Ang." It has been marked by the translators with a "[2]" next to the title in order to distinguish it from this section of the same name.]

kabir kaaya kaondal bhari liyaa, ujal nirmal neer
piyat trikha na bhaajai, tirikhaavant kabir -1

[Bengali:]

Kabir is saying: in the water-pot of the body, I have filled up with Bright and Pure Water. [Even] after drinking that, the thirsty Kabir's thirst was not quenched. -1

[Commentary:]

Kabir, I have filled up the water-pot of the body with Bright and Pure Water. Even then the thirsty Kabir's thirst was

261

not relieved. This means: I have completely filled up this water-pot-like body with the Bright and Pure Water of Stillness (Brahman) – meaning: all of the vayus in the body have become Still. Even then the thirst has not gone, because at that time Kabir Saheb is feeling, "So now I have come to this particular State [or: Plane]. Now if there is some other "lok" (state) that exists, let that happen also." -1

kabir man ultaa dariyaa milaa, lagaa mali mali snaan
thaahat thaaha na paaiyaa, tirikhaa rahi amaan -2

[Bengali:]

Kabir is saying: mind found the reverse current of the river. Catching onto that itself, it went on bathing thoroughly. But it could not find the end of that. And the thirst is remaining just as it was. -2

[Commentary:]

Kabir found the reverse current and went on bathing thoroughly in that. But he could not find the end in that. The thirst still remains just as unresolved as it was. This means: guru gave the reverse current of Kriya to the mind. Mind went on bathing thoroughly in that – meaning: going on doing Kriya again and again, one kept taking full dips in order to be fulfilled – meaning: one attained the par avastha of Kriya. But one could not find the boundaries of the par avastha of Kriya, and the thirst that says: "What is that State, and where does It exist at that time?" - that remained where it was. -2

kabir pandit se ti kahi rahaa, kahaa na maane
koy aao gahaayeh ko kahe, bhaari aacharj hoy -3

[Bengali:]

Kabir is saying: I told the pundits this, but no one at all minds my words. And if someone actually says [to aspirants],

"Come!" At that itself they become very astonished. -3

[Commentary:]

Kabir, I told the pundits, but no one minds my words. If someone says, "Come! It has pierced [me]! I mean 'It' has 'happened' to me!" - then they become very astonished. -3

kabir jore baseyeh tan maha, taa gati lakhe na koy
kahe kabiraa sant jan, badaa achantaa hoy -4

[Bengali:]

Kabir is saying: the one who forcefully sits down in this body itself – no one can see the movements. Kabir Saheb says, "Only the saints see that and watch in awe." -4

[Commentary:]

Kabir, no one sees his [or: its] movement – meaning: if there is no Stillness, then the movement cannot be seen. Kabir Saheb is saying that saints become Still, witness the movement, and become filled with great awe and wonder. -4

kabir ghatme rahe shujhe nahi, karan so shuna na
jaay milaa rahe aao na mile, ta so kahe basaay -5

[Bengali:]

Kabir is saying: "It" is actually in this very body, but no one understands. It cannot be heard via the ear. It is already merged with oneself, but no one merges with it. In this kind of state, how can one be made to stop moving and sit [in meditation]?! -5

[Commentary:]

Kabir, this Self [Atman – True Self] is in the body, yet no one is able to see It. It is residing as merged with oneself in the body, but no one is merging with It. The self [ego] that is like this – how can one sit it down – meaning: make Still? -5

**kabir karan kahe karne shune, bhanak pare nahi kaan
ayse sant na ha sutise, paao hi brahma ginaan -6**

[Bengali:]

Kabir is saying: [people] speak via/for the ear and listen via the ear: "there is no use of listening to the "bhan bhan" [humming] sound." The saints all listen to the Sound of the Omkar Resonance, and in Bliss, they attain the Knowledge of Brahman. -6

[Commentary:]

Kabir, one speaks by the ear and listens by the ear – no use for the "bhan bhan" sound [humming sound] seems to be apparent. All saints listen to this type of "bhan bhan" sound and attain the Knowledge of Brahman. No one speaks if he does not hear in the ear. It is for this reason that talking is done by the ear. If one is deaf, he does not have the [normal] ability to speak. ("Bhanak" = that by which cotton is spun.) There appears to be no use/ function for the sound which is like a "bhanak" going on day and night. All saints listen to this type of "bhan bhan" sound and attain the Knowledge of Brahman – meaning: the Omkar Sound. -6

LIKHTE HERAT KI ANG

Witnessing [or: Looking to Find] Truth

kabir herat herat he sakhi, herat gai heraay
bund samaana sindhume, so kita heraa jaay -1

[Bengali:]

Kabir is saying: "O Friend! While searching and searching for You, I even lost the 'searching'! The Bindu that I was seeing – even that I cannot see any more. When That [Bindu] has merged with the ocean-like Brahman, where am going to I find It [as a separate thing]?" -1

[Commentary:]

O Friend! Searching and searching – the searching itself was lost. The ocean merged into the Ocean. How can That be seen now? This means: while searching for Kutastha, the Bindu was seen. From looking and looking at the Bindu, there was intoxication and the Bindu was no more seen. Then, because of that Bindu entering the ocean-like Infinite Brahman, where can It be found now? -1

kabir herat herat he sakhi, rahaa kabiraa heraay
sindhu samaanaa bundme, so kita heraa jaay -2

[Bengali:]

Kabir is saying: "O Friend! While searching and searching

265

for You, Kabir Saheb himself was lost [no longer found]. Because of the Bindu entering the Ocean – even That could no longer be seen." -2

[Commentary:]

O Friend! Searching and searching – Kabir Saheb himself was lost [no longer found]. The Ocean entered the Bindu [drop]. How can That be seen? This means: searching and searching in Kutastha, the doer of the searching itself – Kabir Saheb – no longer remained as a separate thing. The ocean-like Brahman is in Atomic-Form within the Bindu [drop]. How can That be seen? Because of the happening of "all is Brahman," Kabir Saheb himself became Brahman as well. If there is no one who is separate, who will search for whom? -2

kabir bund samaanaa sindhume, so jaane sab loy
sindhu samaana bundme, bujhe birla koy -3

[Bengali:]

Kabir is saying: that the bindu [drop] is like [or: with] the ocean – everyone knows this. But that the ocean enters the bindu – very few people know this – meaning: those who know [this], those types of people are very rare. -3

[Commentary:]

Kabir, that the bindu [drop] enters the ocean – everyone knows this, but that the ocean enters the bindu – very few people know this – meaning: upon looking and looking at the Bindu in Kriya, the par avastha of Kriya is attained. This is known only by Kriyavans. And very, very few people know that Brahman is in that Bindu. -3

kabir samudra samaanaa bandume, gou khur ke asthaan
icchaa rup samayiaa, bahuri na paaoe jaan -4

[Bengali:]

Kabir is saying: upon the ocean entering the bindu, that place began to look like the hoof of a cow. In the place that is like the hoof of a cow, the desire-mind entered that and then was not able to know anything again. -4

[Commentary:]

Kabir, the ocean entered the bindu. The place where it entered – that place is like the hoof of a cow. Then the desire-mind entered the cow-hoof. Then this side cannot be known again – meaning: Brahman – the par avastha of Kriya – He entered the Atom. That place is like the hoof of a cow. Then no desire remained any more. And mind goes to nothing of the world at all any more. -4

kabir ek samaanaa sakal me, sakal samaanaa taahi
kabir samaanaa bujhi me, jahaa dosro naahi -5

[Bengali:]

Kabir is saying: the One is "one" with all this, and all is also "one" with that One. Going to understand that "samaan" ["same-ness"], Kabir Saheb found that there is no more "two" there. All is One. -5

[Commentary:]

Kabir, One has entered into all. And everything has entered that One as well. Kabir Saheb entered into that Knowing where no one exists as a separate [anything]. This means: the "One" that is self-Self became Still in: (1) Kutastha; (2) the par avastha of Kriya; (3) the Atom/Particle of Brahman; [and] (4) everything, because in the One Brahman-Atom are the three worlds. And the Universe itself is made up of the Brahman-Atom [or: the Universe itself is manifesting within the Brahman-Atom]. Entering the One Brahman-Atom is verily the entering into the entire Universe. Then Kabir went on knowing truly everything, went on seeing and hearing [everything], because there is no "second" anyone there. How long does it take for the Self to know the Self? -5

kabir guru nahi chela nahi, nahi murid nahi peer
ek nahi duja nahi, tahaan bilame daas kabir -6

[Bengali:]

Kabir is saying: in that place, there is no guru and no disciple either. There is no "murid" (the disciple of a "pir" [Muslim saint]). There is even no "pir" there either. Where there is no "one," from where will "two" come? In this State, Kabir Saheb rests. -6

[Commentary:]

Kabir, in that place, there is no guru or disciple. There is no pir or murid [see above paragraph]. Because there is no "one" there, how can there be "two"? This is the place in which Kabir Saheb resides. This means: in the place (in Brahman) where there is no guru – because there is no one to know [anything], that there can be someone to teach him; and there is no disciple there either because there is nothing to know at all. And in the State where "I" am not, then it is not possible for a "two" to exist. Kabir Saheb is locked in that State. -6

kabir birccha jo dhnure beej ko, beej birccha ke paahi
niojo dhnure brahma ko, brahma jio ke maahi -7

[Bengali:]

Kabir is saying: the tree is searching for the seed, but the seed is in the tree itself. Yet the searching is going on. In this way, all are searching for Brahman, but the One Who is Brahman is within the jiva [individual] itself. -7

[Commentary:]

Kabir, the tree is trying to find the seed, and the seed is in the tree itself. And the one who does not know the "Seed," is trying to find Brahman. But Brahman is within every jiva [individual]. In the tree of this body, mind is trying to find out: "From where have I come?" And the Seed of Kutastha is in the body itself – meaning: immediately when the self [ego] becomes Still, Kutastha is seen. And the one who does not know that this Seed-Kutastha is in the Self – he is searching: "Where is Brahman?" And Brahman is within every jiva. -7

kabir aadi hotaa so ab hay, pher phaar kachu naahi je
vo tarivar ke beej me, daar paat phal cchnaahi -8

[Bengali:]

Kabir is saying: that which was in the beginning is here now. This has no coming and going. Like: in the seed of the tree are the branches, leaves, fruits, shade – all is there – nothing has gone – it is like that. -8

[Commentary:]

Kabir, that which was in the beginning – that same thing is also here now. There is no coming and going [change] with that – that seed of the tree in which branches, leaves, shade – all are verily there. This means: at the time of birth, the Self was Kutastha. Now that it is still exactly the same – meaning: that Atman [Self] and Kutastha are there. No coming and going [nothing different] has happened with that. Like what is this? It is like: fruit is born from a tree; within that fruit is again the branches, leaves, fruits, seeds and even the shade of the tree. -8

LIKHTE JARNA KO ANG

[On Knowing and Speaking about Mystical Matters]

bhaari kaho to bahu dare, haalukaa kaho to jhut mai nahi jaano raam ko, disht dekhaa nahi mudh -1

[Bengali:]

Kabir is saying: if you say that It is "heavy," then there is great fear, and if you say that It is "light" [not heavy], then it is a lie. I do not know Rama; if Rama was in my fist, then I could see. -1

[Commentary:]

If I say "heavy," then there is great fear, and if I say "flimsy," then it is a false statement. I do not know Rama; if He was in the fist, I could see. If I say that Brahman is "heavy," then there is great fear; I may get crushed. And saying that It is "flimsy" is a false statement, because when there is nothing without Brahman, then compared to what substance is It "flimsy"? Because of this, I naturally had to say that I do not know. If It was in the fist, then I could open the fist and see. -1

kabir dithaa hay to kya kaho, kahon ta ko pati aay hari jayse tayse rahaa, tum harkhi harkhi gun gaay -2

271

[Bengali:]

Kabir is saying: if I say, "I have seen," then who will believe it anyway? There is no way I can reveal It via words. The Lord is remaining as He is. You go on singing the Lord's praises. -2

[Commentary:]

Kabir, if you say, "I have seen," then – It is Unspeakable – I cannot reveal It. And if I do speak, then who will believe (that Kutastha is in you, within It is the Atom Star, within that are the three worlds etc.)? The Lord is remaining as He is – meaning: the One Who kills [or: takes away] the three afflictions – that par avastha of Kriya – He is always there. You (meaning: servant Kabir is telling himself) sing His praises while being in Bliss. Before, I did not know that the Seed was in this tree. Now, seeing It, there is Bliss. -2

kabir aysi kathani mati katho, kathone dharo chhapaay
bed kitebon naa likho, kahot ko pati jaay -3

[Bengali:]

Kabir saying: do not ever speak about these things. Keep those statements secret. Do not write vedas [scriptures], books and such, because who will believe your words anyway? -3

[Commentary:]

Kabir, do not intend to speak about these things. Keep that kind of speaking secret. And do not just write vedas [scriptures] and books. And just because you say such things, who will believe you – meaning: I myself will not do any practicing of Truth, yet I will speak about spirituality – do not have your intention be for these kinds of talk. Do not let those types of words come out of your mouth any more – meaning: do Kriya and thus do good to yourself. And do not write vedas [scriptures] and books, because if you actually speak about the Truth, then no one at all will believe your words. -3

kabir kartaa ki gati aur hay, to chal apne anumaan
dheere dheere paao dharu, pahuncche gaa nije thaam -4

[Bengali:]

Kabir is saying: the Lord's movement is of another kind [or: the Way of the Lord is of another kind]. You keep going [continue] with the understanding of the Self. Gradually get a hold of the Feet of the Self. It that happens, then for sure you will reach Your Own Place. -4

[Commentary:]

Kabir, the Lord's movement is of another kind [or: the Way of the Lord is of another kind]. You keep going [continue] with the understanding of the Self. Gradually grab a hold of the Feet. You will reach Your Own Place – meaning: the movement in [or: the Way of] the Supreme Self is different, verily. The benefit that has come about from doing Kriya – take that as a sign and understand, and continue going with Kriya. Upon gradually becoming Still, you will reach that Place which is Your Own – the par avastha of Kriya. -4

kabir pahunchhoge tab kahahuge, ab kachu kahaan
jaay ajahu bhelaa samadrame, boli bigaare kaay -5

[Bengali:]

Kabir is saying: when you get There, then speak. Right now there is nothing to speak about and nothing can even be said. The boat is still on the ocean. First reach the Shore and speak after that. Otherwise there can be conflicts coming about from talking – meaning: what is spoken may not be correct. -5

[Commentary:]

Kabir, when you get There, then naturally you can speak. Right now it is not possible to say anything, because the Kriyavan who is greater than you will cut up [dismiss] your words. And you have not gained any Power that you can exercise any command over that subject. And when there is the par avastha of Kriya at all times, then no one at all will have the possibility of cutting up [dismissing] your words. The boat is still on the ocean; words will create problems. Like when there is a storm on the river, the boatman tells everyone to remain quiet because the chaotic behavior can possibly cause the boat to sink. And if the shore is reached, then everyone can freely jump about. In that same way, if you talk now and be a hero for a couple of people, then you will become enslaved by your pride and drown. First reach the Shore – meaning: abide in the par avastha of Kriya at all times. Speak afterwards -5

kabir jaani bujhi jar hoe rahe, bal teji nirbal hoe kahen
kabir tehaa daas ko, pallaa na pakare koe -6

[Bengali:]

Kabir is saying: the one who has understood after directly knowing is abiding as if inert – meaning: he is abiding in a Still condition. Power and energy are there as if without any ability to move. Kabir is saying, "No one at all can get a hold of that person" – meaning: no one can get to that person. -6

[Commentary:]

Kabir, the one who has done Kriya and then understood after directly knowing is abiding as if inert – meaning: there is no more any desire to speak, because one has become Immaculate after doing Kriya. Kabir is saying that a person who is this type of servant – no one at all can grab a hold of his "pallaa" (the edges of his clothing). -6

kabir baad vibaad beekhaya ghanaa, bole bahut upaadhi
maun roop gahi hari bhaje, jo koi jaane saadhi -7

[Bengali:]

Kabir is saying: by talking a lot, the knowledge of subjects may increase, and a lot of talk is made about many different scholarly things. And the one who does sadhana [spiritual meditation] meditates upon the Lord silently. It is only he who has known. -7

[Commentary:]

Kabir, in talking a lot, outward subjects come forth with intensity. Through a lot of talking, another kind of understanding [wrong understanding] comes about. Only a few persons know the type of sadhana which is silent meditation on the Lord. As soon as there is talking, there is bondage in the answering and responding about subjects. And one ends up looking at the bad side of someone who is spoken about as a good person. -7

kabir saakshi ek kabir ki, shuni shikhi nahi jaay
ranchak ghatme sanchare, tou ajar amar hoy jaay -8

[Bengali:]

Kabir is saying: Kabir does not learn only by hearing about one witnessing [or: one direct experience]. When That will spread throughout this body, only then will there be the Imperishable and Immortal. Otherwise nothing at all happens. -8

[Commentary:]

Kabir, do not just listen and learn from one witnessing [or: one direct experience]. The reason is because whatever has been said in the teachings of witnesses – if That ever spreads throughout the body once, then one becomes Imperishable and Immortal. -8

LIKHTE LOKO ANG [2]

The Subject of Spiritual States [or: Spiritual Planes]

kabir surati tekuri lau lejuri, man niti daar
nihaar kaul ku aami prem ras, peeoe baarbaar -1

[Bengali:]

Kabir is saying: bring out the thread from the spindle of the Still attention, and keep mind thrown down always on that. If that happens – the Well that is in the Lotus, the Nectar of Love is there also – if that happens, you can drink again and again. -1

[Commentary:]

Kabir, if one pays attention to the spindle then the "lejuri" (thread) comes out evenly. Throw down mind in that place and see. If that happens, then you will get the Nectar of Love. Drink That again and again. Kutastha is the heavy round object in the spindle [like that of a spinning wheel] and from the Muladhar to the Sahasrar is the metal of the spindle. The thread of spiritual experience comes from this spindle; throw mind upon that, and remain seated and see (the three worlds). And drink again and again the Nectar of Love that is in the Well of the Lotus in the Muladhar (the abode of Kulakundalini). -1

**kabir ganga yamun ke antare, sahaj shunya hay ghaat
tnahnaa kabira mat rachon, muni jan joe baat -2**

[Bengali:]

Kabir is saying: there is a naturally void field between the
Ganges and Yamuna [rivers]. Kabir Saheb has created a
Temple at that place. "Muni" - those who have become
"mouni" [mute; silent] because of the self abiding in the Self –
they are called "muni" - they desire to go to that place. -2

[Commentary:]

Kabir, there is a riverbank between the Ganges and the
Yamuna [rivers] which is Void and natural [or: simple]. At
that place, Kabir Saheb has created a Temple, a place for
which "munis" [sages] search. Between the ida and pingala is
the bank of sushumna, which happens from the performance of
"sahaj" [that which happens with ease; natural; simple] Kriya.
That is Void-filled (the par avastha of Kriya). Just as taking a
bath by the riverbank is fulfilling, although only for a short
time, taking a bath at the bank of sushumna verily brings
Eternal Fulfillment. At that very place, Kabir Saheb has
created a Temple – meaning: at the back of the head, there is a
triangular place where the anterior [and posterior] stem[s] of
the sushumna begin. "Munis" [sages] (those who have become
"mouna" [mute; silent] after doing Kriya – meaning: no desire
to speak comes about) search for the road to that place. -2

**kabir jehi bansi ghan sancharai, raay pancchi naa udi
aay motaa bhaag kabir ka, tnahaa rahaa lau laay -3**

[Bengali:]

Kabir is saying: when the flute began to permeate and
spread intensely – meaning: [when] the flute is playing on,
then the bird does not fly away like mustard. Kabir is abiding

as merged in the fat part – meaning: instead of going to the subtle part, one is merged in the physical part. -3

[Commentary:]

Kabir, when the subtle – meaning: fine – sound of the flute plays, then the bird does not fly away like mustard. Instead of being in the subtle part, Kabir Saheb is abiding as merged in the fat part. When the sound of pranayam becomes exceedingly fine [like silk thread], then the minuscule Bindu becomes steady. Instead of putting mind on that Bindu, Kabir Saheb [has put mind] on the fat part – meaning: that vayu, which has come from that Bindu and has gradually become prominent – he is abiding with mind on that. If one stays in the subtle, feelings take mind in other directions. -3

kabir lao laagi tab jaaniye, kabhi churi na jaay
jeeyat to laagi rahe, muye maahi samaay -4

[Bengali:]

Kabir is saying: know that "laya" [merging; melding; mixing as one] has taken hold when one cannot at all free oneself of It. One remains with It constantly while alive. Even if one leaves the body, he leaves as merged. "Laya" does not go away regardless of anything happening at all. -4

[Commentary:]

Kabir, when "laya" [see above] takes hold, one comes to know that "laya" never leaves as long as one lives. And when [the body] dies, one becomes One with Brahman. The one from whom the par avastha of Kriya stays for all hours of the day and night – it is only he who knows that that Condition never leaves whatsoever. As long as he is alive, up to that time he is locked in that State. And if he casts off [the body] then he merges in Brahman. -4

kabir jaysi laagi yo raso, taysi nim hay
cchor koti koti jori ke, kya laakh karor -5

[Bengali:]

Kabir is saying: as much as one is receiving Nectar, so much is the bitter "neem" [margosa leaf] of maya going away. In this way, if one gathers It together – hundreds of thousands of times, millions and millions of times– then It stays for a long time. -5

[Commentary:]

Kabir, as much as the par avastha of Kriya went on happening, so much the bitter maya went on leaving. In this way, upon the par avastha of Kriya happening millions and millions of times, It stays for a long time. -5

kabir jayse upje per so, taysi nim hay jor aapne
tan ki kyaa kahei, taare parivaar karor -6

[Bengali:]

Kabir is saying: as this tree grows, so does the "neem" [margosa] gain strength. What more will one say about one's own body? One is rescuing so many families – meaning: saving them. -6

[Commentary:]

Kabir, as much as the tree grows, so grows the strength of the "neem." And what will one speak of regarding one's own body? He is taking care of hundreds of thousands of families. As much as a one is doing Kriya, so much is the strength of the "neem" [referring to bitterness] – meaning: there is disenchantment with worldly things, and nothing else at all [other than Brahman] feels good any more. Yet because of the teaching/initiation given by that type of person, millions and millions of people are being saved. -6

**kabir jaysi prathame lao lagai, taysi dhurle jaay
jaake hirdaye lao basai, so mohi maahi samaay -7**

[Bengali:]

Kabir is saying: as much as the attraction/interest there is to have "laya" [merging] – however far that attraction/interest takes one, one must go that far. One in whose heart the attraction/interest of "laya" has set in – that person is I MySelf, and has merged with MySelf. -7

[Commentary:]

Kabir, like the way that the attraction/interest first happens – however far that attraction/interest takes one, one must go that far. One in whose heart the attraction/interest resides – that person is I, and enters Me Itself. The kind of attraction/interest that happens immediately after having had initiation (taking it up as an addiction), as far as that attraction/interest can go – meaning: the par avastha of Kriya – so far (meaning: so that that State remains at all times) must one go. One in whose heart the par avastha of Kriya is staying at all times – meaning Stillness – that which says "I, I..." in him – that "I" has merged in That/Him/Stillness. -7

**kabir jab lagi kathani ham katho, churi rahaa jagdeesh
lao laagi pal naa pare, ab bol naa nahi deesh -8**

[Bengali:]

Kabir is saying: as long as I am speaking, for so long is the Lord of the World far away. And when "laya" [melding] took hold, then I am not without [Him] even for an instant now. And there is no desire to speak even arises. It is difficult to try to speak even. -8

[Commentary:]

Kabir, as long as I am speaking, for so long is the Lord of

the World far away. And when "lao" ["laya" - merging; melding] took hold, then there in no being without [Him] for even an instant. Now I do not see anything to talk about. For as long as I am speaking and talking, up to that point is the Lord of the World far away. And when "laya" took hold in the par avastha of Kriya – meaning: It is there at all times – then, there is great suffering in being without that State for even an instant. In that State, there is no desire to speak anything any more. -8

kabir satguru tatu lakhaaiya, granth hi maahi mool lao laagi nirmal bhayaa, meti gayaa samshaya shool -9

[Bengali:]

Kabir is saying: the one who is satguru – it is true that he showed It to one. But the Essential Thing is in the "granthi" [gathering place; knot] itself. Now because of "laya" [merging] has It/One become Immaculate. And the spike of conflict has also gone. -9

[Commentary:]

Kabir, it is true that satguru showed It to one, but the Essential Thing is in the "granthi" [see above] itself. When "laya" took hold then It became Immaculate and the spike of conflict no longer remained. Satguru showed it by giving initiation/teaching, but in the Essential Thing is already in the three "granthis" - meaning: the par avastha of Kriya, and if one abides in the par avastha of Kriya at all times, then the spike of conflict (what is this? what is that?) no longer remains, because everything verily is done. -9

PATI BARTAA KO ANG

On Devotion to the Beloved

kabir prita laagi meri tujhte, bahu guniyaa lay kant
jao hnaasi boli aur te, to nitahi rangaayo dant -1

[Bengali:]

Kabir is saying: "preeti" [dearness/love] is born in me for You, because You are a Lover with so many great qualities. When I laughed and talked with others, I wanted to show the goodness and always showed my teeth [smiled greatly]. -1

[Commentary:]

Kabir [says]: I have fallen in Love with You, because You are a Lover with so many great qualities. And because of having to talk to others I have always shown my teeth [smiled greatly]. This means: I am locked in Love with You [Brahman]. ("Prita" [beloved; dear one] = one without seeing whom I cannot live; I am here, I am here but if I do not see [You] once, my being begins to feel not right.) As soon as one sees [his/her Beloved], one runs, and filling one's heart up with seeing [the Beloved], there is Contentment. Forget about any need to speak at that time. The reason for falling in Love with You is because You are the Beloved, and from Loving You, all of Your qualities – Brahmaa [creator], Vishnu [sustainer], Mahesh [transformer/destroyer], the Experiential Substance, Omkar Sound and such [are known]. But constantly ("svabhaav" - characteristic) showing my teeth [smiling

283

greatly] and speaking is a beautiful thing. In that way, sadhus [sages] naturally have the characteristic of speaking pleasantly. -1

kabir chaitati raho na bisaro, to pad darshi thaay
eha ang bnadro bhalaa, jab tujh so miliyaa jaay -2

[Bengali:]

Kabir is saying: always think of It; do not forget — meaning: always keep It in mind; may it be that mind stays on Your Lotus Feet. If this body becomes like that of a monkey, even that is good if I can remain One with You. Otherwise everything is totally useless. -2

[Commentary:]

Kabir, think on it; do not forget. May it be that mind stays in the Vision of Your Feet. If in the process of being One with You my body becomes like that of a monkey, even that is fine. Witnessing Kutastha, the mind begins to wander to other directions; then it comes to mind [that one is wandering]; and mind tells mind to always do remembrance; do not forget ([one] is saying this while watching Kutastha). May it be that mind stays in the Vision of Your Feet. And if upon being in "laya" [merged state] with You the body becomes like a monkey, that is even beneficent. -2

kabir naynaa bhitar aautu, tneha nayan jhapehu
naahi dekha aur ko, naa tu dekh na dehu -3

[Bengali:]

Kabir is saying: You enter my eyes. When You enter, then the eyes close. Then no one else can be seen at all. You also do not allow anyone else to be seen. -3

[Commentary:]

Kabir [says:] You enter the eyes. When You come in, then the eyes close. Then nothing else at all can be seen, and You also do not allow anyone else to be seen. The Supreme Person is actually invisibly within everyone's Eye. Kabir Saheb is saying, "I am seeing You from time to time. I am not satisfied with that. Now You please enter into my eyes – meaning: let me see [You] at all times. When You come in, then the eyes become covered [with You]. Then I do not see anything else at all. And You also do not allow anyone else to be seen – meaning: it is experienced that You are all. -3

**kabira rekhaa ek sindur ki, kajraa diyaa na jaay nayan
na raam rachaar hay, dujaa kahan samaay -4**

[Bengali:]

Kabir is saying: there is a streak of vermilion left, but collyrium [natural eyeliner] cannot be put on. And well, Rama is appearing in the Eye [or: in my sight]. Then how there be a "second" anything? -4

[Commentary:]

Kabir, there is a streak of vermilion left. Collyrium cannot be put on, and Rama is appearing in the Eye [or: in my sight]; how can a "second thing" enter? Subtle body – meaning: the self/Self – he is abiding in Kutastha like the flame of a lamp. At that time, the collyrium-like "mind in other directions" is not happening any longer. One is not seeing anyone apart from the One Who is delighting one's sight, because the Self has appeared. "Rachana" [manifestation; creation] – meaning: that which is seen as beautiful by the eyes and that which grabs the mind away. When one is in the Self – meaning: when the One Who is presiding over all is in front of oneself, then how can a "second" anything enter the mind? This is because there is nothing except the Self – meaning: all is Brahman. -4

kabir aat prahar chaushat ghadi, mere auran
koi nayananha me tum hi baso, nid na aave soi -5

[Bengali:]

Kabir is saying: I am alone during the eight periods and sixty-four time-divisions of the day and night. [Or: I am alone all day and night.] I have no one else. You have come and sat in my sight. This is why sleep is not coming. -5

[Commentary:]

Kabir, there is no one at all for me during the eight periods and sixty-four time-divisions of the day and night. [Or: There is no one at all for me at any time.] And You are sitting in my sight. Because of this sleep has not come. After first staying in Kutastha a little bit at a time, gradually one stays in that State for all eight periods of the day and night [all day and night], when mind goes in other directions from time to time only. After that, gradually, [the State happens] always – because other than You, I have no one at all. And You are "sitting" in my sight. There is no Stillness in standing; this is the reason why [Kabir Saheb] has said "sitting." Because of this, sleep does not come any more, because when there is attention on some thing, sleep does not come. -5

kabir nid dekh jab pursh ko, ulti aapu uthi jaat
taate nikat aave nehi, mudhan te na bharaat -6

[Bengali:]

Kabir is saying: when the "person" goes to sleep, then the it automatically gets upturned [or: the self [ego] gets upturned] and is gone. It does not come to one. And there is no fear of unconsciousness either. -6

[Commentary:]

Kabir, when the "person" goes to sleep (meaning: the par avastha of Kriya), then there is an upturning – meaning: "all is Brahman" happened. Then the self was removed – meaning: there is no more a separated "I". Remaining in that State at all times, no sleep comes any more, and there is no fear of unconsciousness from being upturned. -6

kabir saai mere ek tu, dujaa aur na koy
dujaa saai tab kaho, jab kali dujaa hoy -7

[Bengali:]

Kabir is saying: the One Who is the Beloved – He is my only Lord; there is no second one at all. If you say that there is [or: when there can be] a second Lord, then there will be a second bud. -7

[Commentary:]

Kabir [says:] my Lord is only You. There is no second one at all. And I could say that there there is a second Lord only if one [the very same] flower could bloom in two totally different buds. -7

kabir baar baar kyaa ankhiyaa, mere man ki
shoy kali to uthli hoyegi, saai aur na koy -8

[Bengali:]

Kabir is saying: what things will see with my eyes again and again? The One Who is my mind – well, He is lying down [resting]. But when the bud emerges, then it is necessary to see the Lord, because I have no one else other than the Lord. -8

[Commentary:]

Kabir [says:] "ankhiya" [eyes] – what will I see in other directions [away from the Lord] with my eyes – again and again? He is resting in my heart. When the bud has come about, then it will bloom one day, but I have no Lord other than my One Kutastha, and no one else. -8

kabir balihari wo dukh ki, jo pal pal raam kahaay wo
sukh ko maathe shilaa, jo hari hirdayaa so jaay -9

[Bengali:]

Kabir is saying: I give praise to that kind of suffering, [the kind] because of which one says "Rama, Rama" at every moment. And the one for whom the Name of the Lord has left the heart – even if he lives in happiness, that is not good at all – meaning: crush that kind of happiness by putting a heavy stone on its head. -9

[Commentary:]

Kabir, the suffering that makes one say, "Rama, Rama" from moment to moment – praise be to that suffering. And beat the head of that happiness with stones, that [happiness] which does not have the Lord in one's heart. The happiness that is there from staying in the par avastha of Kriya at every moment – praise be to that happiness. "Love" - because of which one loses one's own power to the one he/she loves – meaning: one becomes a slave to the one that he/she loves. And one in whose heart the Lord (the par avastha of Kriya) is not, yet desire is there – the happiness that comes about from that desire – hit that [happiness] on its head with stones. -9

kabir rahe samudrake beechmo, rate piyaas piyaas
sakal samudra tinu ka gane, ek svaati bund ki aash -10

[Bengali:]

Kabir is saying: one is living in the sea yet is going about saying "I am dying of thirst." Only because of the longing for the star-droplet, one feels the sea to be like grass [and not water]. -10

[Commentary:]

Kabir, one lives in the sea, yet is going about saying, "I'm dying of thirst; I'm dying of thirst." One feels the entire sea to be made of grass, just because of the longing for one Bindu [droplet] from the Star. Because of not being able to relieve one's thirst while being in the sea of samsara, one is saying, "I'm dying; I'm dying," even though there are many things in samsara which there to quench one's thirst. That person feels that the sea of samsara is made of grass [which cannot quench thirst], because he longs for the One Star-Bindu Brahman. -10

kabir sukh kaaran ko jaat the, aage miliyaa dukh
jaahu sukh ghar aapne, hamre dukh sammukh -11

[Bengali:]

Kabir is saying: the reason for which I was actually going was happiness, but I met with pain first. The home of happiness is in the MySelf itself, but in front of me is pain. -11

[Commentary:]

Kabir, the reason for which I was going was happiness. Before that there was pain. The home of happiness is in MySelf, but in front of me is pain. I was going with the hope of drinking the Star-Bindu of Brahman. But before that there was pain (Kriya). The happiness which is the par avastha of Kriya is within MySelf verily, but facing me is pain in the form of Kriya [practice]. -11

kabir dojak to ham angayaa, so daraa nahi mujh
vihinti na mero chaahiye, bnaajhu piyaare tujh -12

[Bengali:]

Kabir is saying: I have covered up the place of hell. I have no fear of that. I do not want any happiness or pain – nothing [like that] at all. I want You and only You. O Beloved! Even if I remain barren – even that is fine with me. I do not want children and such things – nothing [like that] at all. I want You and only You. There is nothing else at all that is necessary. -12

[Commentary:]

Kabir [says:] I have covered up hell. I have no fear because of that, and I do not want heaven either. (When I do not want happiness, pain, boy, girl – when I do not want anything whatsoever – then it is called "bnaajhaa" [barren].) Even I live as a barren person – even that is fine. But You are my Beloved. If You are here, that is all that matters. -12

kabir jo vohi ek na jaaniyaa, to sab hi jaan ajaan
jo vohi ek hi jaaniyaa, to sabe ajaan sujaan -13

[Bengali:]

Kabir is saying: the person who does not know the One – everything that person knows is in the realm of ignorance, because when the One is lacking, there is nothing there at all. And the person who has known that One – he actually has known everything, verily. There is nothing left unknown at all, because just as without the One there is nothing, then by knowing that very One, all is known. And if that One has not been known, then nothing at all has been known. -13

[Commentary:]

Kabir, the person who does not know the One – for him everything is verily unknown. If he knows that he knows that One, then that [previously] unknown substance becomes "sujaan" [known well; or: known thoroughly]. "One" - the Self which is the Life of the World – the person who does not know Him – whatever that person knows is all ignorance. This is because the One Who is the Life of the World is verily in everything and everywhere. Without Him there is nothing at all. Thus, if a person does not know Him, knowing about something and ignorance are both the same. The person who knows that One ("jaanaa" [knowing] = as long as attention is on something, for that long is that thing known) – meaning: the person who has his attention on Him at all times – that person has come to know all unknown things fully and well – meaning: revelation in front of oneself even before thinking about it. -13

kabir jo vo ek na jaaniyaa, tao sab jaane kyaa
hoy ekhite so hot hay, sab te ek na hoy -14

[Bengali:]

Kabir is saying: when there has been no knowing that One, then what is the use of your knowing everything? It is like: one plus one makes two, and another one makes three. In this way, if there is one, then there is two, and even then you are saying "two" by joining "one" with "one." If the first "one" does not join with the latter "one," you cannot say "two." And that "two" that you are saying – that is also your delusion [mistaken perception], because at first there is "one" and afterwards there is also "one." There is nothing that exists other than "One." So you are only forcing yourself to say "two." In reality, there is only "one" and no "two." That "One" is verily everywhere. Everything that you are seeing is also that same "One." The person who has not known about that "One" through direct knowing/experience – that person has actually not known anything at all. That person only says with the mouth, "I have known everything." But he has known nothing at all. Yet with the mouth he is saying, "This is a house. That is a tree. This is a human being. That is a cow. This is a man. That is a woman [etc.]." He is speaking about many forms. What "gunas" [primal qualities] are in those things or what substance there is even – he knows nothing of that, yet he has said, "I have known everything." In reality, he has not known anything at all. Because if that were so [that he had known everything], then he would not busy himself with "cow," "horse," "home," "house," "man," "woman" and all these "upadhi[s]" [identifications/identities] Identifications/identities are absolutely nothing. They are temporary. In the aforementioned identities there is an Eternal Substance in subtle form, which is the Presider everywhere. Bones and flesh – [just the same as] bricks and stones – they are all nothing at all. Bones and flesh do not eat and do not move about. If that were so then a carriage could be pulled by a dead horse; a child could come forth from a dead woman and man, because everything is still there in the dead state – hands, feet and such, nose, ear, tongue, skin, reproductive organs – all are there, but without the One, none of them are doing anything. Wherever each were, they are lying in that same place. The form/expression of "One" is what "two" is. When there is Knowledge of the One, then forms and expressions no longer remain. Then everything is One. Bones and flesh are only the form/ expression of that "One" only. Form is the shadow of that "One" only. Just as a shadow is actually nothing, in the same way, form is also nothing. Whatever is happening is happening from "One." That "One" must be known. Otherwise all knowing is useless. Then again, [knowing the One] does not come about without sadhana [spiritual meditation practice]. It can be known via sadhana. It cannot be known by studying the shastras [scriptures] and such. This is verily true: without the direct imparting of the practice from a satguru [true preceptor; or: preceptor of Truth] the Knowledge of the One does not happen. -14

[Commentary:]

Kabir, when that "One" is not known – meaning: "all is Brahman" did not happen, and no knowledge of the gunas [primal qualities] of things was had, then what actually was gained by [the so-called] knowing everything? It is like knowing "that is wood," but you do not know its guna because of not knowing the One from Whom that wood has come into existence. From "One" - meaning: from that Brahman – all has come into existence. And everything not becoming one means that the Knowledge of Brahman has not happened. -14

kabir ek saadhe sab saadhiya, sab saadhe sab jaay
ulteeke sinche mool ko, tao phule phale adhaay -15

[Bengali:]

Kabir is saying: by doing the "sadhana" [practice/inner cultivation] of "One," the "sadhana" of everything is done. It is like: by upturning one root and sowing it brings about the full harvesting of flowers and fruit. And doing the "sadhana" of everything actually means no cultivation of anything, because in how many places can one mind become still? Having a bunch of lovers is not good; people call such a person "whore." It is not possible to please everyone equally, and mind also does not behave the same way towards everyone/everything. One becomes a big god; another becomes a small god. Thus, no "sadhana" [devoted engagement] is given to anyone actually. For this reason, "sadhana" [spiritual practice] must be for "One" only. It is on "One" that mind must be kept fixed. People will also call that person "satee" [faithful]. Sadhana will also be right [fruitful]. Mind will also stay right. -15

[Commentary:]

Kabir, doing sadhana [see "Bengali" section above for

various definitions] of One is verily doing the sadhana of all. And doing sadhana of all means that everything becomes upturned. The root that is sowed brings about the full harvest of flowers and fruits. In this case, the "sadhana of one" was done, because in everything/everyone is that "One" verily. If sadhana [dedication] is given to everything, then everything goes away – meaning: by doing "this person/being/thing is a god; that person/being/thing is a god," the restlessness of mind remains just as it was. It does not remain still in any place. An example of this is the prostitute: it is like the way that she destroyed her youthful vitality by having ten lovers, yet when the time of trouble came for her, no one came to her. And the faithful and devoted wife served her one husband and spent her whole life in happiness. A person who upturns the root and sows it – meaning: does Kriya – he has the full harvest of flowers and fruits – meaning: from the Flower of Kutastha, the Fruit comes forth – meaning: the person will become desireless. -15

kabir sab aayaa us ek so, daar paat phal phul
kabir paache kyaa rahaa, jab pakraa nij mool -16

[Bengali:]

Kabir is saying: everything has verily come about from "One" - branches, leaves, fruits, flowers – everything you see. Kabir is saying, "Now that I have got hold of my Root, what is left after that?" -16

[Commentary:]

Kabir, everything has really come about from that "One" - branches, leaves, fruits, flowers. Kabir Saheb is saying, "What is left after getting hold of my Root?" From the Kutastha, the vayu of sperm goes to the yoni [womb] – head, arms, legs etc. - meaning: this body comes into being. Now that I have got hold of that Kutastha Itself, then whether this body is here or not – both are same. -16

kabir mool kabiraa gahi chare, phal khaayaa bhari pet chor sahuki gami nahi, jeo bhaoe teo let -17

[Bengali:]

Kabir is saying: grabbing a hold of the root, climbing the tree, one filled his belly by eating the fruits. Thieves and wealthy people are the only ones who cannot go to that place. "Sahu" ("sau") is what a wealthy person is called. Even a wealthy person cannot go there. Whatever comes to mind, one does that. If the desire to lie down comes, well, right then one lies down. -17

[Commentary:]

Kabir cut/pierced through the root, climbed up and ate a bellyful of fruit. A thief, and "sahu" - meaning: "wealthy person" - both of these have no way of going to that Place. However one thinks/feels, lie down like that. Cutting/piercing through the root – meaning: piercing through the area from Muladhar to Sahasrar, continuously doing Kriya, one filled one's belly by eating the Fruit of the par avastha of Kriya – meaning: one stayed in that State at all times. "Thief" - one who takes someone else's thing by picking a lock and without telling anyone. "Sahu" - wealthy person – meaning: one who is always engrossed in feeling "it is my wealth"; [referring to both types:] one whose mind unknowingly goes away from the Self to other places. The wealthy person's mind is also away from the Self and always on riches. Both of these [types of people] have no way of going to that Place. And in that state, whatever feeling comes to one – one stays in that feeling – meaning: if there is the desire to stay lying down, well, one stays lying down etc. -17

kabir jab man laagay ek so, tab niruari jaay
saadar doy mukh baajti, ghan tamaa bakhaay -18

[Bengali:]

Kabir is saying: when mind caught on to the "One" - it is actually then that it found the road. And cordiality and polite speech are words of the mouth. If anything more than the usual happens, they get hurt. -18

[Commentary:]

Kabir, one whose mind is on the One par avastha of Kriya – he has found the road – meaning: "Oh I've found the road. Now I must travel on this." And those who just stay with sweet words, polite speech and only words of the mouth – they only keep getting hurt. It is like this: upon first meeting, "May I please come in?" and such polite and courteous statements are made. Later in conversation, one person says, "You are a liar." And then after this statement there is fighting. -18

kabir aashaa to ek naam ki, chuji aash niraash
paani maahi ghar kiyaa, soko mare piyaas -19

[Bengali:]

Kabir is saying: that which can be hoped for [or: desired] – well, that is only for the One Name. And the second desire is to be desireless. I have actually made my home in water, yet I am dying of thirst in the form of desire. -19

[Commentary:]

Kabir, well, the first and foremost desire is for the One Name – meaning: for the par avastha of Kriya. After that the second [desire] is [for] non-desire– meaning: the state of being without desire. (As long as the desire for non-desire exists, for so long non-desire does not happen – meaning: when desire no longer remains in the par avastha of Kriya, then that

[desireless] state is enjoyed.) I have made my home in water –
meaning: "all is Brahman" has happened. Now there is no
thirst for things – meaning: I have become desireless. -19

**kabir kali yug aahike, kiyaa bahut so mit jinha
dil bandhaa ek so, tinho sukh paraa nit -20**

[Bengali:]

Kabir is saying: "Kali* Yuga" [the age of ignorance and
duality] has come and has made itself a great friend. But the
person whose heart is tied to the One – what can it do to him? -
20

[*Translator's note: "Kali" connected here with "yuga"
[epoch; or: dual], as in this case, DOES NOT, in any way,
refer to the well-known Goddess "Kali," Whose Name is
pronounced with a long "a", i.e. "Kaali." The Goddess Kaali is
beneficent and the destroyer of ignorance, whereas the epoch
"kali" [as mentioned in this doha] is an epoch of ignorance, or:
period of duality.] -20

[Commentary:]

Kabir, "Kali Yuga" [the age of ignorance and duality] has
come and spread itself throughout as a friend. The person
whose "antahkaran" [inner being] is connected to the One has
Eternal Happiness. "Kali"* [see translator's note above] =
"sin" - meaning: mind in other directions. "Yuga" [epoch; or:
dual] = "two" - meaning: ida and pingala. These two breaths
have come and made themselves very friendly – meaning: has
kept a person in matter, lust etc. The person whose inner being
is in the one – meaning: tied to the sushumna – meaning: the
person who is "locked" [in God] is eternally happy, verily. -20

**kabir patibarta ko sukh ghanaa, jaake barat hay ek
nam mayli bibhchaarinee, taake khasam anek -21**

[Bengali:]

Kabir is saying: there is great happiness in being a faithful and devoted spouse to the Beloved. Because the devoted spouse's vow is to One. And the unfaithful/loose lover whose mind is dirty has many paramours [to fulfill]. -21

[Commentary:]

Kabir, being a faithful and devoted spouse to the Beloved brings deep happiness. That spouse's vow is to One, and the person whose mind is dirty is an unfaithful/loose lover who has many paramours. ("Patibrata" [devotion to the spouse/beloved]; "pati" [spouse/beloved] = Kutastha + "brata" [faithful devotion] = living always in propriety. The person who regularly and properly abides in Kutastha has Supreme Happiness. The fruit of his/her devotion is "One" - meaning: being merged in Kutastha.) And the person whose mind is dirty – meaning: the person who does not stay in Kutastha and goes in other directions – that person is a loose lover (one who participates in sensual embrace with several lovers). The person whose mind is dirty worships this god and that god and a bunch of them, yet has no firm faith in any one of them. That person has many paramours (desire[s]). -21

kabir patibarta ko ek hay, bibhchaarinee ko doy
patibarat bibhchaarinee, kahu ko bhalaa hoy -22

[Bengali:]

Kabir is saying: the faithful and devoted spouse/lover is One, and the unfaithful/loose lover is "two." Now, among the faithful and devoted spouse and the loose lover, who is better? -22

[Commentary:]

Kabir, the faithful and devoted spouse/lover is One. The

unfaithful/loose lovers are "two." Tell me, between the faithful and devoted spouse/lover and the unfaithful lover, who is better? The faithful and devoted spouse/lover is the person who has become One, and the unfaithful/loose lover is the person who has not become One. So who is better among these two? -22

kabir patibartaa mayli bhali, kaali kuchili kuroop
vo ke mayle roop par, woaro kot svaroop -23

[Bengali:]

Kabir is saying: the devoted spouse/lover is still great even if he/she is looks unseemly. Millions of beautiful ones are cut down in front of his/her ugly outer appearance. -23

[Commentary:]

Kabir, the devoted spouse/lover is great [even if] unseemly. Even if she/ he is not fair looking and is ugly – hundreds and hundreds of beautiful ones get cut down next to his/her unseemly appearance. -23

kabir patibartaa tab jaaniye, rati na khande
nayan antar so saanch rahe, bole mithi bayan -24

[Bengali:]

Kabir is saying: you will know that "patibrataa" [devotion to spouse/ lover] has happened when not for even a single pleasure does mind go in directions other than the Beloved. It is then that "patibrataa" has properly happened, when there is trueness and purity within and one speaks sweet words with the mouth. -24

[Commentary:]

Kabir, know that "patibrataa" has happened when not a single pleasure exists other than the Eyes of the Beloved, and when there is "sattva guna" [purity] within and one speaks sweetly. When with every blink of the eye one sees nothing else but the Eye of Kutastha, know that that is when "patibrataa" has happened, not by showing off to other people. And when one sees the Infinite Beneficence of the Brahman-Beloved, then naturally one becomes soft in manner and speaks sweet words. -24

kabir baale bhole khasam ki, bahut kiyaa bibhchaar
satguru rahe bataaiyaa, param purukh bhartaar -25

[Bengali:]

Kabir is saying: in childhood, because of delusion, I did all kinds of loose behaving. But when satguru told me the way, then I came to know the Supreme Being as the Caretaker and Beloved. The One Who nourishes is the One Who is "bhaataar" [sustainer; supporter] or "swami" [husband; beloved]. The Nourisher of the world is that Supreme Being. He is actually residing in me verily. I now know this by satguru's grace. Now I must keep it like this. -25

[Commentary:]

Kabir, in childhood, because of mistakes – meaning: not knowing – I did a great deal of loose behaving – meaning: because of not knowing my Beloved (God), I accepted many gods as my lovers. After that, when satguru told me the way, my Beloved – meaning: the nurturing and supporting Supreme Being – meaning: I came to know the Supreme Person. That Supreme Person is actually Me Myself. "Bhartaar" [nourisher; one who fills] – breath is rising from the navel, filling up with that in the Muladhar via Kriya, there is fullness from the Muladhar to the Sahasrar. When one is completely filled, no gap can be seen. It is like seeing the oil at the tip of a pot filled to the brim with oil. In that same way, upon vayu going from

Muladhar to Sahasrar and thus becoming filled up to the top with the Brahman-Oil, one sees everyone and everything as Brahman, and it is Brahman who is seeing everyone and everything, and it is He Who is nourishing and taking care of everyone and everything. -25

kabir bhed jo leoe baithi ko, sab so kare pukaari
dharaadhare so dharkutee, adhar dhare so naari -26

[Bengali:]

Kabir is saying: one who has penetrated the aforementioned Thing – he is shouting to tell everyone. One who has been able to grab hold from the earth element to the Void – he has found a Hut for his Abode. And the one who has grabbed on to "adhar" [non-holding] ("na dhar" [non-hold; insubstantial]) – he is "woman" [worldly attractions]. -26

[Commentary:]

Kabir, "bhed" [penetration] = "entering" - one who has sat and pierced the Muladhar is joyfully shouting to tell everyone. "Dharaa" [holding] – meaning: one who has been able to grab hold from the Muladhar to the Brahmarandhra – he has found a Hut – meaning: a Place to reside, and is one who has grabbed hold of the Void. "He is woman [attached to world]" – meaning: those who have [worldly] intoxications and such did not get the Supreme Person. One cannot have the Supreme Person unless the Muladharknot is cut. -26

kabir may sewok saamrath ko, koi purabka bhaag
shoyat jaagi sundaree, saai diyaa sohaag -27

[Bengali:]

Kabir is saying: I am the servant of Oneness. Even that has happened because of the fortune that has come through from past lives. The Beautiful One was going to sleep. She awakened. "Sai" [beloved] – the Beloved Lord caressed Her in Love. -27

[Commentary:]

Kabir [says:] I am the servant of Oneness. Because of some fortune gained from past lives, the Beautiful One, who was asleep, awakened. Then the Beloved caressed Her in Love. "Sundaree" [beautiful one] = that by which mind is pleased – that is what is "the beautiful one" to a person, like a female donkey is to a male donkey – among humans [the beautiful one] is laughter for some, woman for some, sweets for some – when all of these things are appearing, then there is sleep. "Sai" [beloved] = the Lord, Supreme Person put vermilion on the Beautiful One with loving caress – meaning: because of some good fortune from past lives, I am abiding in the par avastha of Kriya. Before I was lying asleep. Upon the break of that "sleep" - meaning: upon the coming about of the experience "all is Brahman," the Supreme Person Beloved Lord put on the forehead the Vermilion of the Still Flame – meaning: the Tilak of the Flame of the Lamp went on being lit at all times. -27

kabir may sewok saamarth kaa, kab hi naho akaaj patibartaa nangee rahe, tao wohi piyaako laaj -28

[Bengali:]

Kabir is saying: I am the servant of Oneness. I never do any useless work. The devoted spouse/lover stays naked in front of the beloved. In fact, it is the beloved who feels bashful. The devoted spouse/lover has no feelings of any kind of shame, because the devoted spouse/lover has surrendered mind, life, vanity – all – to the beloved. Other than the beloved, he/she does not know anything else at all. So why should there be any bashfulness/shame? -28

[Commentary:]

Kabir [says:] I am the servant of the par avastha of Kriya – meaning: I take great care of that which keeps the par avastha of Kriya present, and no useless work happens from me. "Kaaj" [work] = dutiful acts; abiding in the par avastha of Kriya; "akaaj" [useless work] = not staying in the par avastha of Kriya and putting mind in other directions – meaning: let me reside in the par avastha of Kriya always. When the wife becomes naked in front of the husband, the husband feels bashful, although everyone knows that the husband belongs to the wife [or: they belong to each other]. In that same way, if the devotee does not stay in His/Her Self's Beloved Brahman and stays elsewhere, then it is Brahman's shame. -28

kabir tu tu kahe to duri ho, dui kahe to aaon
jnyo hi rakhe tyo rahon, jyo deoa so khaon -29

[Bengali:]

Kabir is saying: if you say, "you, you," then He is far away. And if you say "far away," then He is near. In whatever state/condition He keeps you, be in that state/condition. Whatever He gives to eat, eat that. -29

[Commentary:]

Kabir, if you say "you, you," well then It is far away. And "far away" cannot be said, because He is within me. Stay as He keeps you. And eat what He gives you to eat. This means: if upon seeing the Supreme Person in front of me, I say, "You are the Beloved Lord. You are the Supreme Person. You are the Lord," in order to get close to Him, then He keeps moving away and stays eternally far. And there is no way of saying "far away" because whatever condition He keeps within myself, I stay in that condition, meaning: sometimes He is in front of me: sometimes He is not there. Eating is for the sake of satisfaction/fulfillment – meaning: in whatever state/condition He keeps me, I am satisfied/fulfilled with that. -29

kabir jo gaawe so gaawaniyaa, jo jore so jor patibartaa
aao sadhu jan, yeh mali mah hay thor -30

[Bengali:]

Kabir is saying: someone who sings is called a "singer." But there are better and inferior ones among them. Just because one sings does not mean that one is a singer. There are stages of learning and the stage of being a teacher. Those things have to be judged. In the stage of learning, one cannot be called a singer. It is possible to call one a singer when he/she is at the stage of being a teacher. In the same way, as much as you can gather together [or: realize], gather together [or: realize] that much – meaning: however much you can make effort, make that much effort, because not everyone is a devoted spouse/lover or sadhu [sage]. In Kali Yuga [age of ignorance [see doha 20 of this section], there are very few devoted spouses/lovers and sadhus. -30

[Commentary:]

Kabir, one who sings is a singer. There is no judgment of good and bad. In that same way, one who does Kriya is a yogi; he has no judgment of good and bad any longer. Whatever you can get, do that – meaning: as much as you can do, do that much, because in Kali Yuga, persons who are devoted spouse/ lover [types] or sadhus are hardly found. "Patibrataa" [in this case: devoted spouse/lover] = one who stays in Kutastha. "Sadhu" [sage] = one who always practices Kriya. -30

kabir paramesar aaye paahunaa, shunya sane hi daas
khatras bhojan bhakti karu, jo kabhi na chore paash -31

[Bengali:]

Kabir is saying: the Supreme Lord has come. Feed Him six nectars. And give Him great devotion. And do not leave His company. Servant Kabir is truly in the company of the Void. -31

[Commentary:]

Kabir, the Supreme Lord (Stillness) was not here at one time. He is now a guest here. Servant Kabir is saying: He is Only Void, which I love. Now that the Guest has come, feed Him the meal of the six, and give Him devotion, so that in no way will He ever leave you. -31

kabir uchi jaati papiha, naoe na neechaa neer
ki surpati ko jaachai, ki duhkha pahe shareer -32

[Bengali:]

Kabir is saying: the swallow keeps its head upward and drinks only the water from the sky. Although there is much water below, it does not drink that. And it also does not beg for water from anyone. It prays to Indra, the king of the gods for water from the clouds. For as long as it does not receive water from the clouds, for so long does it tolerate great suffering and continues to wait in the hope of receiving water from the clouds. Still it does not drink the water from below. It does not care even if it loses its life. -32

[Commentary:]

Kabir, just as the swallow keeps head upward to receive water and never drinks the water from below, and as it keeps praying to Indra [king of the gods] for water from the clouds – and it does not care whether the body stays or perishes because of thirst – it does not feel bad about that (the swallow tolerates so much suffering for the sake of receiving water from the clouds), in that same way, there is the one-pointed desire of the devotee: "I will drink the Nectar dripping from the Sahasrar and be fulfilled; I will not use the cold things from below – meaning: from the world." And he is constantly praying to Kutastha, "O Lord! Please bestow Nectar and save my life." For this reason, he does not think of the suffering of the body as suffering. -32

kabir may ablaa piu piu karon, nirgun mera piu shunya sanehi raam binu, aur na dekho piu -33

[Bengali:]

Kabir is saying: I am just a helpless woman, just crying again and again, "O Beloved! O Beloved!" My Beloved is "Nirguna" [beyond qualities]. Other than Atma-Rama [Self] along with the Void – well, I do not see any other Shiva [God] – meaning: the Self is One and Only Shiva, the Beneficent One. Other than That [Self], there is no other Shiva. -33

[Commentary:]

Kabir [says:] I am helpless – meaning: Prakriti – crying, "O Beloved! O Beloved!" My Beloved is "Nirguna" [beyond qualities]. Affection to/from anyone or anything other than Atma-Rama is of no use. I do not see anything but the Self. In other words, I do not see any other Shiva [God] other than Atma-Rama [Self]. -33

kabir patibartaa brata kumbhajal, pati bhaji dhare bishvas aandishaa chitaoe nahi, sadaa jo piu ki aash -34

[Bengali:]

Kabir is saying: what is devotion to the Beloved like? It is like the full pot of water – meaning: just as the water in a full pot remains unmoving, in the same way the the vow of the devoted spouse/lover also remains unswervingly proper and correct; it does not sway in any direction. One stays with the desire/hope for the Beloved only. One does not notice anything in any other direction. -34

[Commentary:]

Kabir, "patibrataa" [in this case: devotion to the beloved] – meaning: the vow of the devotee – is like the water in a [full] pot – meaning: just as the water in the full pot remains unmoving, in the same way, the devotee remains Still in the par avastha of Kriya. And whatever one has come to understand from meditating on the Beloved – one has faith in that only. That person does not take his consciousness/heart in any other direction. He is always there for the Substance of the Supreme Person – meaning: "There! My Beloved Supreme Lord is coming!" -34

**kabir pati bartaa kayse rahe, jayse choli paan tab
sukh dekhai pio ka, jab chit nahi aaoe aan -35**

[Bengali:]

Kabir is saying: the devoted spouse/lover stays like this: like "choli" ("kanchuli") [bodice], or "paan" [betel leaf]. Just as: if a bodice is tied tightly there is a pull on the chest, and like the way a slight pleasant satisfaction comes from chewing the betel leaf – it is like this for the devoted spouse/lover. The consciousness/heart does not go in other directions and stays pulled to the Beloved, and then he/she comes to know what the Beloved actually is. -35

[Commentary:]

Kabir, the devoted spouse/lover is like a bodice and the betel leaf – meaning: the "pulling feeling" that is there by putting on a bodice tightly or by chewing the betel leaf – that kind of pulling feeling is felt by the devoted spouse/lover also.

When this state happens, then the consciousness/heart does not go in other directions, and one comes to see what the pleasure of being with the Beloved is. -35

CHETAWANI KO ANG

On Awakening [Realization]

**kabir naobat aapni, din dah lehu bajaay eha pur
paat na yeh gali, bahuri na dekhahu jaay -1**

[Bengali:]

Kabir is saying: the "nahabat" [concerted drum-music] that you are hearing – keep on playing it for ten days [or: a few more days]. It is not complete [or: not the end]. If one goes on this Road, after that, nothing is seen nor is anything heard. -1

[Commentary:]

Kabir, keep on playing (hearing) the "nahabat" [concerted drum-music] of the Omkar Sound for ten days [or: another few days]. This listening to the Omkar Sound is the not the complete lesson. And this is not a "road" either, because once one goes on it, [nothing] can be seen again – meaning: [nothing] can be heard. -1

**kabir jehi ghar naobat baajti, may gal baandhe doaar
ekai hari ke naam binu, gaye bajaaoni haar -2**

[Bengali:]

Kabir is saying: "nahabat" [see above doha] is playing in the house. In order to listen to it, I have tied up the throat and the door – meaning: I am listening to the Sound properly. But what is the use of even that? Without the One Name there is no other way. ("Naam" [name] = a particular State which cannot

309

be sounded by the mouth [or: cannot be explained by speech; cannot be spoken]) Without That [Divine Name] the jiva [soul] has no possibility [of emancipation]. The Sound also has an end. But the Name has no end. The Name is Unspeakable and "Nirguna" [beyond qualities]. The one who has experienced the aforementioned State directly himself – it is only he that knows. But it is impossible to speak about it. It is like mute people, who cannot say good, bad etc. about anything – it is like that. -2

[Commentary:]

Kabir, when "nahabat" is playing in the house, I have pressure on the throat – meaning: when the Omkar Sound is heard, there is intensity on the throat-area. The soul who is playing [the "nahabat"] without doing Kriya goes away – meaning: those who listen to Omkar Sound [in that way] – they die. -2

kabir jinha ghar naobat baajti, hot chatisho raag te mandil khaali pare, baithan laage kaag -3

[Bengali:]

Kabir is saying: the house in which the thirty-six Raginis [particular musical modes] and "nahabat" are being played – that house becomes empty. And crows come and sit on that person – meaning: those who listen to the Sound do not even go in the direction of the aforementioned State. They die. And when death happens, crows come upon that person's body and peck and eat the flesh. -3

[Commentary:]

Kabir, the temple in which "nahabat" is playing, and the "nahabat" from which the thirty-six Ragas [particular musical modes] are springing forth – that house is empty, and crows are coming there – meaning: those who only listen to the Omkar Sound without remaining in the par avastha of Kriya – they die, and after death, crows peck and eat the body. -3

kabir dhol damaama dundubhi, sahnaai aaru bheree
ao sar chale bajaaike, hay koi laaoe pheri -4

[Bengali:]

Kabir is saying: "dhol," "damamaa," "dundubhi" [different types of drums], "shahnai" [oboe-like horn] and "bheree" [kettle-drum], and many other types of sounds that can be heard – they are going on playing, but is there anyone who after "it happening" once, can again bring "it" back? -4

[Commentary:]

Kabir, "dhol," "damamaa," "dundubhi," "shahnai," "bheree" [see above] (this is the Omkar Sound) were all played and are gone; one has a break – meaning: while listening to the ten types [or: various types] of Omkar Sound, one died. Is there someone who can bring that person back into the dead body – meaning: because of death, as there is no life-force spreading in the body, there is no Omkar Sound, but that person who is in the par avastha of Kriya – he can, because in the par avastha of Kriya, one is dead according to outer appearances. In that State, that person can effortlessly hear the Omkar Sound. -4

kabir thoraa jeeo naa, mare bahut mandaan
sab hi ubhaa melsi, kya rank kya sultaan -5

[Bengali:]

Kabir is saying: life is truly very short, and one is roaming about so much. This is in both the poor man and the emperor. -5

[Commentary:]

Kabir, life is very short. In this short life, one has traipsed over a lot of places – meaning: one is roaming about once here, once there. This is in both the poor man and the emperor. -5

kabir ekdin aysaa hoyegaa, sabhte pare bicho
raaja raana chatrapati, saabdhaan ko nahi so -6

[Bengali:]

Kabir is saying: one day, it will be such that one will have to separate from all. Whether king, royal ruler, monarch, they all have it [coming], but they are not wary. -6

[Commentary:]

Kabir, one day such a time will come that there will be separation from all. That separation is to happen for kings, rulers, monarchs – all, but the one who is wary does not have separation – meaning: because of outwardly being dead while in the par avastha of Kriya, his separation has already happened. -6

kabir ujar kheraa theekri, gadi gadi gaye kunbhaar
raaon sarikhaa chali gayaa, lankaake sardaar -7

[Bengali:]

Kabir is saying: the one who is Prince [or: young being] has made many different kinds of bright-colored outfits. Ravana, the leader of Lanka and other such powerful and brilliant outfits have come and gone, but the Prince Self has remained as It was. -7

[Commentary:]

Kabir, the Prince has made quite a lot of bright-colored outfits. So many like the leader of Lanka – Ravana – have come and gone – meaning: like the attractive, powerful and beautiful leader of Lanka, many beautiful body-outfits have come and gone, and the Prince Self is ever continuing to create them [or: rolling through them]. -7

kabir uchaa mahal banayiaa, chune kali dheraaye
eke hari ke naam binu, jab tab pare bhulaaye -8

[Bengali:]

Kabir is saying: I built a high palace and whitewashed it with powdered and wet limestone, but without the Name of God, that state is uncontrollably forgotten from time to time. -8

[Commentary:]

Kabir, going to the head is known as "building a high palace" - meaning: when one rides up on top of the head (like a bowl coated with limestone becomes firm, and the kind of clean whiteness that happens when wet limestone is applied), then one feels firm and experiences oneself as Pure White. After that, if one is without the Name of God, one uncontrollably forgets – meaning: not doing Kriya in the par avastha of Kriya, that State is uncontrollably forgotten from time to time. -8

kabir kahaan garbiyo, chaam lapeta haad hay
aor upar chhatrapati, te bhi dhekhaa khaad -9

[Bengali:]

Kabir is saying: where is your pride now? There are nothing but bones in the body which are covered by skin. The Monarch Who resides above is standing straight up and watching. -9

[Commentary:]

Kabir, where is pride now? The bones are covered by skin and that is all. There is a Monarch residing above. I have seen

Him be straight up – meaning: Still. -9

kabir kahaan garbiyo, uchaa dekhi awaas
kalhi parei bhnui lotnaa, upar jaame ghaas -10

[Bengali:]

Kabir is saying: where is your pride now? I see that your house is high up. But tomorrow, verily, it will have to crash down to the ground in pieces. It will be on the ground in pieces in such a way that grass will grow on top of it. -10

[Commentary:]

Kabir, where is your pride now? Your house is very high up. Verily tomorrow it will fall down to the ground and grass will grow on top of it. This means: well, Brahman is in Brahmarandhra, after merging there, you will come down to the Muladhar and then you will see all the funny things going on on the Earth. Now where is your pride? -10

kabir kahaan garbiyo, kaal gnahe shir kesh naa
jaani kahan maari hay, ki ghar ki pardesh -11

[Bengali:]

Kabir is saying: where is your pride now? "Kal" [time; death] is holding you by the hair on your head. He will kill you at home or in a foreign land. There is no knowing where he will kill you. -11

[Commentary:]

Kabir, where is pride now? "Kal" [time; death] is holding you by the hair. There is no knowing whether he will kill you at home or in a foreign land. For this reason, remain always in Brahman, because Immortality is in Brahman. Do not let That go. -11

kabir uttim khseti dekhike, garbe kahaan kishaan
ajahu jholaa bahut hay, ghar aawe tab jaan -12

[Bengali:]

Kabir is saying: what is the gain in the farmer being proud as he looks at his excellent farm? Today you are seeing that there is great harvest, but there are still many problems involved. When the fruit of the harvest is brought in the house, then you will know that it is an excellent farm. -12

[Commentary:]

Kabir, what is gained by the farmer looking upon his excellent farm and being proud of it? There are still a lot more chores to be done. When all the harvest is brought into the house, then you will know that the farm is good meaning: do not be proud by just getting a little bit of Bliss from Kriya, because there are still a lot of chores to be done – meaning: there is still much "jholaa" [hard work] (Kriya) left to do. If It is brought into the house - meaning: if there is Stillness and attainment, then you will know that all has happened [well]. -12

kabir jehi ghar preeti na prem ras, aao rasanaa nahin
naam te nar aaye sangsaar me, upaje khsape bekaam -13

[Bengali:]

Kabir is saying: the house in which there is no contentment or the feeling of Love, and where there is no mention of Loving – that type of person is uselessly moving about in samsara. -13

[Commentary:]

Kabir, the house in which there is no affection or the feeling of Love, and Loving is not even mentioned once – that house [person] is uselessly coming to this samsara, being born once, dying once [and again and again] – meaning: one who sees the Supreme Person (God) facing him within his own body (meaning: plane), and does not have affection rise in him by knowing that this is verily the Supreme Person, and one who is not abiding in the par avastha of Kriya at all times and not drinking the Nectar of Love – meaning - Immortal Ambrosia – that person is uselessly taking birth and dying, like grass, in the "coming and going" form of this samsara. -13

**kabir aysaa yeh samsaar hay, jaysaa maaltee phul
din dashke beohaar me, jhnute rangan bhul -14**

[Bengali:]

Kabir is saying: this samsara [worldly life] is like the "maaltee" [a kind of jasmine] flower – meaning: just as the "maaltee" flower enchants people for a while with its beauty and fragrance, and after a short time, there is nothing – in the same way, this samsara is also only for a few days, enticing people with false color and glitter. -14

[Commentary:]

Kabir, just as the "maaltee" flower pleases the mind for few days with its beauty, in the same way, samsara [worldly life] is also for a few days only. That for which you are becoming attached – that itself does not stay. -14

**kabir dhuri sakelike, pot bandhi yeh deha dewas
chaarikaa peknaa, ant kheha ki kheha -15**

[Bengali:]

Kabir is saying: this body is like a bundle made of dust. You have been sent to be here for a few days and you are showing off your grandness. In the end dust is just the same dust it was. -15

[Commentary:]

Kabir, this body is like a bundle made of dust – meaning: like there are all kinds of lines on dust/mud and like how it is covered up with a piece of cloth – in that same way, skin is on top of nerves and tendons, and inside there is the dust/mud-like flesh, within which are all kinds of lines made up of bones. For a few days it is showing "pekna" [flash and show] – meaning: like the way a magician shows his flashy tricks – meaning: that which is actually not real is thought to be absolutely real, and in the end dust is the just same dust it was. -15

kabir chaari pahar dhandhe gayaa, tini pahar rahu
shoy ek pahar bandregi karo, jo janm saoarth hoy -16

[Bengali:]

Kabir is saying: four parts of the day and night [out of a total of eight] were spent on work, and three more parts were spent on sleeping and lying about. The one part that is left – do not waste that one part; call God – meaning: do sadhana [spiritual meditation]. If this happens, then this birth [life] will be a success. -16

[Commentary:]

Kabir, four parts of the day and night are spent on work, and you sleep and lie around for three more parts, but if you spend the time in the remaining one part of the day doing Kriya, this birth [life] will be a success – meaning: you will see Your Own Form. -16

kabir raati gawai shoi kari, dewas gawai khaai
heera janm amol hay, kauri badle jaay -17

[Bengali:]

Kabir is saying: I have spent the night sleeping, and I have spent the daytime eating. Alas! This priceless diamond-like birth [life] is being exchanged for a bunch of coins [or: small change; or: cowrie shells]. -17

[Commentary:]

Kabir, you spent the night sleeping and the day eating. And you exchanged this priceless diamond-like birth [life] for some small change (meaning: "O money!")! -17

kabir mandil khaak ka, jadiyaa heera laal
dewas chaarik pekhna, binashi jaaygaa kaal -18

[Bengali:]

Kabir is saying: the temple-body will burn to ashes. You are being uselessly vain by putting on diamonds, emeralds and all such ornaments. You have been sent for just a few days, yet you are showing off meaninglessly. One day you will attain your destruction via "kal" [time; death]. -18

[Commentary:]

Kabir, this temple of ashes – meaning: the body, because if it is burned it turns to ashes. You are wrapping this body up with diamonds, precious stones, filigree wrappings and all such ornaments and being so vain. All of this is the magician's flash and show – meaning: the old person puts dye on his/her hair and shows that he/she is young – and all such things! Because of associating with "kal" [time; death], you will attain your destruction. -18

kabir svapnaa raiyanka, ughari gayaa jab nayan
jeeu paraa bahu lutme, naa kachu len na den -19

[Bengali:]

Kabir is saying: after the dream, the eyes turned [opened]. The jiva [person] became very worried then. But neither was there anything one had nor was anything given –

nothing was fruitful at all. -19

[Commentary:]

Kabir, the eyes opened after dreaming at night. The jiva [person] became greatly crestfallen – meaning: many kinds of thoughts came and grabbed hold. No giving and taking, nothing fruitful happened at all – meaning: neither was Kriya received nor was Kriya given – nothing fruitful happened at all. -19

kabir i hay chitawanee, jou niruaree jaay jo
pahile sukh bhogiye, so paache dukh khaay -20

[Bengali:]

Kabir is saying: one who does not leave that kind of pride and vanity [aforementioned] – and because of no awakening happening to oneself, one who goes to enjoy pleasure, later that person has to suffer misery. -20

[Commentary:]

Kabir, one who does not have the aforementioned awareness, and attends to having pleasure first – he later suffers. -20

kabir aajuki kaalnahme, jangal hoyegaa baas
upar uparaa ki rahenge, thor charantaa ghaas -21

[Bengali:]

Kabir is saying: whether it is today or tomorrow, your living space will become a jungle. You will roam about above. Not being able to find the right location, you will eat grass in the end. -21

[Commentary:]

Kabir, today or tomorrow your living space will become a

jungle – meaning: you will not be here after a few days. And you will roam about above – meaning: not being able to enter in any matter; one will go to this sage and then to another sage and so on. And then you will go around eating grass – meaning: you take birth in the body of an animal. -21

kabir muye ho mari jaahuge, koi na legaa naao
ujar jaai basaai ho, chhori santaa gnaao -22

[Bengali:]

Kabir is saying: if you live as dead, then you will die. No one will mention your name even. After being extirpated, again another will be set up – away from the village [residing place] of sadhus. -22

[Commentary:]

Kabir, you are dead now and you will die. No one will mention your name. After this one is extirpated, another will be set up. All of this is happening away from the village [residing place] of sadhus. Someone who is dead – now how can he die again – meaning: those who do not know who dies and what death is – these people are living as dead, because by not knowing these things, they are believing "I will die," "the boy just died" etc. But the Self is the Indestructible Divine. And those who are truly alive – meaning: those who know the Self – they do not die. It is so because they have come to know the Self as Indestructible and think of this body as insignificant. "Let me do something great. My name will last. And everyone will talk about me" - but nobody actually does that. [The ignorant person] will leave this body and take residence in another body – meaning: because of not being in the place of saints [aforementioned sadhus], which is the par avastha of Kriya, he will get another body. -22

**kabir haad jvare jeo lakri, kesh jvare jeo ghaas sab
jag jvarataa dekhi ke, bhayaa kabir udaas -23**

[Bengali:]

Kabir is saying: like wood burns, so are the bones burning. Like grass burns, so is the hair burning. Upon seeing the whole world burning, Kabir Saheb has become dispassionate about it all. -23

[Commentary:]

Kabir, the bones are burning like wood. Hair is burning like grass, and, upon seeing the entire world burning – meaning: seeing that all the moving things of the world have their end – Kabir Saheb became dispassionate about it all – meaning: he rode up above, in the par avastha of Kriya. -23

**kabir raakh nihaaraa baharaa, chireeyanha khaayaa
khet aadhaa pardhaa ubre, cheti shake to chet -24**

[Bengali:]

Kabir is saying: because of looking outside, birds are eating up the farm. If you can get up above the half and become Awakened, then do it. -24

[Commentary:]

Kabir, because of keeping attention outside, birds are have eaten up the farm – meaning: because of giving mind to five different things [or: a bunch of different things], the desire-birds are eating up the body-farm. "Kshet" [farm; land] – that from which there is emergence. Run for more than half; then you will rise above. If you can have Realization now, then do it. -24

**kabir jo janme so bhi mare, hambhi chal nehaar mere
piche jo paraa, tinha bhi bnaadhaa bhaar -25**

[Bengali:]

Kabir is saying: one who has taken birth – of course, he will die. But I will go away. The one who will come after me – he will also be tied to the weightiness. -25

[Commentary:]

Kabir, those who have taken birth – of course, they will die. But I will go away, and those who come after me will also be tied to the weightiness– meaning: those who take birth are the ones who will die. Kabir Saheb is saying, "I have Brahman-Knowledge. I will not die. I will go on to That Brahman. This is because: those who die take birth again. And those who have Knowledge, they merge with Brahman upon casting off the body. They do not take birth again. And one who will do Kriya like me will tie to the weightiness that is there in the par avastha of Kriya." -25

kabir may budhaani baap budhaanaa, ham bhi maajh budhaay kewatiake naao jneo, sangjoge mile aay -26

[Bengali:]

Kabir is saying: mother has drowned; father has also drowned. I too was drowning in the midst of it. Through a divine connection I found a ferryman's [or: fisherman's] boat and I was saved. -26

[Commentary:]

Kabir, mother has drowned; father has also drowned. I too was drowning in the midst of it. While drowning, a ferryman's [or: fisherman's] boat connected [to me] and I was saved – meaning: in the par avastha of Kriya, Prakriti-Mother drowned. Kutastha-Father also cannot be seen. I also drowned in the midst of it and was saved. - meaning: gasping for air and trying to stay afloat in this ocean of the world, I found the Boat of the par avastha of Kriya and was saved. -26

kabir dewal haad kaa, maaste bnaadhaa aan khar
khar taa paayaa nahi, dewal kaa sahi daan -27

[Bengali:]

Kabir is saying: the temple of bones is held together by flesh. Within this, there is God. But I looked for Him in that temple and could not find him. The reason for not getting him is the lack of teaching/initiation by satguru. Without the teaching/initiation, it is not possible to know. -27

[Commentary:]

Kabir, Kutastha is within the temple of bones. [The temple] is held together with flesh. Standing and standing [or: being straight], I found Him within MySelf. This is the sign of a "temple" [or: this is why it is called a "temple"]. -27

kabir dewal dhahi paraa, it bhari saykor chiteraa
chuni chuni gayaa, milaa naa duji dor -28

[Bengali:]

Kabir is saying: because of the temple collapsing, the bricks are lying about here and there. Spirit/Consciousness has eaten it thoroughly to the last crumb. But I cannot find the door to the place I have to go. -28

[Commentary:]

Kabir, because of the releasing of [divine] intoxication due to Kriya, the temple fell down – meaning: when there is [divine] intoxication, the vayu that is normally there is not there any more, and the brick-like nerves and tendons have let go and are spread about. And Kutastha has eaten all of this thoroughly to the last crumb. Now I cannot find the door to go to that place any more. -28

kabir raam naam jaaneo nahi, bemukh aanhi aan
ki bhushaa ki kaatraa, khaate gayaa paraan -29

[Bengali:]

Kabir is saying: you did not get to know the Name of Rama. Turning away from That, you became engaged in other things. You spent away life eating nothing but chaff and refuse – meaning: you uselessly ruined your life. You could not do anything at all. -29

[Commentary:]

Kabir, you did not get to know the Name of Rama. And turning away from the Name of Rama, you put your mind on other things. And you spent away life by eating chaff and gravel – meaning: not knowing what the par avastha of Kriya is, you gave your mind to the things of the world after all. And "bhushaa" [chaff] – meaning: unclean food – meaning: talking, and "kaatraa" [gravel] (crushed rocks) [meaning:] difficult discussions – you went on doing this until your death. -29

kabir raam piyaare chorike, kare aur ko jaap
bishyaakeraa putra jo, kahe kon ko baap -30

[Bengali:]

Kabir is saying: you left Beloved Rama and went on worshiping another [or: others]. What can come of that anyway? It is like being the son of a prostitute. There is no knowing who is the father. Who will you call "father"? -30

[Commentary:]

Kabir, one who leaves Atma-Rama – meaning: Kriya – and worships another (one who [worships] another god) is like the son of a prostitute. Who is he going to call "father"? This is because Kutastha Himself is "Father." -30

kabir jinha hari ki choree kari, gaye naam gun bhuli
tehi bidhane baadur rancho, rahe urdhamukh jhuli -31

[Bengali:]

Kabir is saying: one who has stolen the Lord and has forgotten about the beneficence of the Name of the Lord – the Ruler has made that person a bat, always hanging with the face turned upwards. -31

[Commentary:]

Kabir, one who has stolen the Lord and who has forgotten the Name and the beneficence of the Lord has been made into a bat by the Ruler, and those beings are hanging with their faces turned upwards. This means: "Hari" [Lord; God; One Who ends all] = the One Who has taken away everything within and without in the par avastha of Kriya – those people who have stolen away this "Hari" - meaning: those who do not do Kriya and those for whom that State remains unrevealed – the Ruler has made them into bats and they are hanging with their faces turned upwards – meaning: they are looking in the direction of the sky and crying, "Alas! Alas!" in order to fulfill their desires. -31

kabir raam naam jaaniyo nahi, baani binaathi mool hari
tyaji ihaai rahi gayaa, ant parimukh dhool -32

[Bengali:]

Kabir is saying: you did not get to know the Name of Rama. The root cause of speech is the "binaathi." ("Binaathi" = taking a [medium-sized or short pole], lighting fire on both of its ends and showing acrobatic stick-handling, like sophisticated stick-twirling – that is called "binaathi"; this type of stick [and stick-show] is mostly prevalent in the western provinces.) You left the Lord. In the end when you die, there will be dirt on your face. -32

[Commentary:]

Kabir, well, you did not get to know the Name of Rama. Speech, which is taking place because of fire above and below – the root of this speech is the par avastha of Kriya. If one leaves the Lord, one remains here. And when one dies, there is dirt on the face. ("Binaathi" = a [medium-sized or short] pole which has its two ends lit by fire, and it is held in the middle and twirled to show stick-play.) In this case, below is the fire of lust and such; above is the fire of Brahmarandhra. Speech is taking place because of this "binaathi." -32

kabir raam naam jaaneo nahi, laagi moti khori kaayaa haandi kaath ki, naa woh chare bahori -33

[Bengali:]

Kabir is saying: well, you did not get to know the Name of Rama, and you could not ride on top of the wooden pot-like body either. -33

[Commentary:]

Kabir [says:] you did not get to know the par avastha of Kriya. You stayed with the fat wood-like body. And you could not even ride on top of this wooden pot-like body. Now how are you going to get to the other shore? -33

kabir raam naam jaaneo nahi, chukeo ab ki ghaat maati milan kunhaar ki, ghani sahegaa laat -34

[Bengali:]

Kabir is saying: well, you do not even know the Name of Rama, and this was such a great opportunity, but you lost that too. You did not understand properly. The potter checks if the clay is right or not by using his feet (the potter prepares clay by using his feet). As long as it is not right, he keeps kicking and kneading it. -34

[Commentary:]

Kabir, because of not knowing the par avastha of Kriya, you lost the opportunity of this human birth. But as long as the clay is not forming the way the potter likes, he is kicking it over and over. -34

kabiryeh sangsaarme, ghanaa manikh mat heen
raam naam jaaneyo nahi, aaye budhaapa din -35

[Bengali:]

Kabir is saying: in this samsara [world; society] many people have lost "mat" [spiritual direction] ("mat" - scripturally proper acts). You did not get to know the Name of Rama either. Thus old age came. -35

[Commentary:]

Kabir, in this samsara, because of the lack of the "mat" [firm spiritual way] of the Name of Rama, many people have become weak. And because of not practicing the Name of Rama, they have "jaraa" - meaning: old age has come for them.

"Mat" = that which has been prescribed to do by all of the shastras [scriptures] – that is "mat."
"Raam naam" [the Name of Rama] = the par avastha of Kriya. -35

kabir kahe kyaa tum aaike, kahe karoge jaay
it ke bhaye na wo ke, chale janm jahraay -36

[Bengali:]

Kabir is saying: what have you done after coming here, and what will you do even if you go there? Neither did you do anything of this side, nor did you do anything of that side. You uselessly wasted your life. -36

[Commentary:]

Kabir, what did you do after coming here and what will you do even if you go there? You did not get to know anything of this place – meaning: the par avastha of Kriya – and you did not get to know anything [of That] here at all, not to even speak of "there." Thus, life passed away uselessly. -36

kabir ek hari ki bhakti binu, dhrik jeewan sangsaar
dhuaakaa dhaurhar jyo, jaat na laage baar -37

[Bengali:]

Kabir is saying: it is meaningless to continue to live on in this samsara without the One Name of God. Just go – it is like the plough, which does not take long to cut a groove in the ground. -37

[Commentary:]

Kabir, living is meaningless without devotion to the Name of Rama. Just as it does not take long for the plough to cut a groove into the ground, in that same way, it will not take long for you to go. -37

kabir jagat maaha man raanchiaa, jhnute kul ki laaj
tan binshe kul binshe, rate na raam jahaaj -38

[Bengali:]

Kabir is saying: one has enjoined one's mind to the world and the vanity of the pride of lineage. The body is being destroyed. The lineage will also be destroyed. Then the ship of the Name of Rama, by which one can cross ocean of this illusory world – That is no longer spread about – meaning: That did not happen. -38

[Commentary:]

Kabir [says:] you have kept the mind "raanchiaa"

(enjoined) to the vanity and pride of lineage – meaning: "I've taken birth in a respectable lineage. So I want to live in a respectable social circle and do high level work" - you are saying these things and have become enamored with samsara. Both your body and your lineage will be destroyed. Possessing and living with these temporal things – you did not spread – meaning: did not practice – the One Name of Rama – meaning: Kriya, the ship to take one across the ocean of this illusory world. -38

kabiryeh tan knaachaa kumbh hay, chot laage phuti jaay ekai hari ke naam binu, jab tab jeeu jahraay -39

[Bengali:]

Kabir is saying: this body is like a pot made of unfired clay. As soon as there is a jolt, it will break. Without the One Name of God, the jiva [individual] will die just at any random moment in time – meaning: it will suddenly die one day. -39

[Commentary:]

Kabir, this body is like a pot made of unfired clay. A hole is made on it by the slightest strike. Without the One Name of God – meaning: without the par avastha of Kriya, all jivas [individuals] are dying just at any random moments in time. -39

kabir yeh tan knaachaa kumbh hay, liye ki ratn hay saath thakka lagaa phuti gayaa, kachu nahi hayaa haath -40

[Bengali:]

Kabir is saying: this body is like a pot made of unfired clay, and you are carrying this around with you. But it can break with the slightest jolt. Then you will have nothing in the hand [or: you will have nothing]. -40

[Commentary:]

Kabir, you are going about carrying the body which is like a pot made of unfired clay. A slight jolt will cause a hole in it – meaning: it will die. Then nothing at all will come to the hand – meaning: nothing will go with you. -40

kabir yeh tan knaachaa kumbh hay, moodh kare bishwas kahe kabir bichaarike, nahi palak ki aash -41

[Bengali:]

Kabir is saying: this body is like a pot made of unfired clay. Only absolute idiots believe that this kind of a body will remain forever and will never go away. But Kabir Saheb has discerned that there is not even a moment's security [or: any hope] with this body – meaning: this body can end in the blink of an eye. -41

[Commentary:]

Kabir, absolute idiots believe in this body, which is like a pot made of unfired clay – meaning: they always attend greatly to what feels good for the body. Kabir Saheb has discerned the matter and is saying that the body [can be gone] in the minuscule amount of time that it takes to blink an eye. Do not put your hopes on it. -41

kabir paani maahkaa budbudaa, dekhat gayaa bilaay aysaa hi jeeyaaraa jaayegaa, din dash thogari lagaay -42

[Bengali:]

Kabir is saying: just like the bubbles in water disappear within the blink of an eye, in the same way, this life will go. You are just roaming about for a few days only. -42

[Commentary:]

Kabir, just like bubbles in water are lost in the blink of an eye, in that same way, this life will go. You are just roaming about like bubbles for a few days only. -42

kabir kabir yeh tan jaat hay, shake to thor lagaayo
raajaa raanaa sabh gayaa, kaahu na rahiyaa thaayo -43

[Bengali:]

Kabir is saying: this body is going away. If you can, keep it held/leaned to a boundary/wall. Kings and rulers have all gone away. Not one of them could stay Still. -43

[Commentary:]

Kabir, this body is going away. If you can, hold it off – meaning: keep it leaned against something – meaning: be Still. Kings and rulers and such have all gone away. Not one of them became Still. -43

kabir yeh tan jaat hay, shake to lehu bahori
nangee haathete gaye, jaake laakh karor -44

[Bengali:]

Kabir is saying: well, this body is going away. If you can do so, bring it back, because hundreds of thousands, millions and millions have left empty-handed and naked. -44

[Commentary:]

Kabir, this body is going. If you can do so, bring it back and keep it. Those who had hundreds of thousands, or even millions and billions [of rupees [currency]] – they also left empty-handed. -44

kabir baasar sukh nahi bayen sukh, naa sukh svapne
maahajo nar bichhure raam so, tinha ko dhoop na
chhnaha -45

[Bengali:]

Kabir is saying: those people who have live having forgotten the Name of Rama have neither happiness during the day nor any happiness at night. There is no happiness in dream either. They have neither sun nor shadow. -45

[Commentary:]

Kabir, those people do not have happiness at night, day and not even in dream. And they do not have sunlight or shadow (meaning: nothing but sorrow and pain, because those who have both sunlight and shadow – if there is discomfort from the sun, they can find relief in shadow) – those who have forgotten Atma-Rama [Self] and live with mind in other directions. -45

kabir din gnaowaayaa mupat me, duniyan na laagi saath
paao kulhaadi maariyaa, gaafeel apne haath -46

[Bengali:]

Kabir is saying: you have spent the day in useless activities. This world will not go with you. By needlessly being unmindful, you struck your own feet with your own axe. -46

[Commentary:]

Kabir, you uselessly spent the day. The world will not go with you. Striking you own feet with your own axe yourself, you are living in a state unmindful of YourSelf. -46

kabir yeh tan ban bhayaa, karm jo bhayaa kulhaar
apne aapu ko kaatiyaa, kahen kabir bichaar -47

[Bengali:]

Kabir is saying: this body has become a complete jungle, and work has become like an axe. After discerning, Kabir

Saheb is saying, "Cut out all the jungle of acts [with the desire for results] from inside yourself." -47

[Commentary:]

Kabir, this body has become a jungle (because of doing acts with the desire for results). Acts without the desire for results is the axe. Automatically, by doing work without the desire for results, one should cut out all of the work with the desire for results. After discerning, Kabir Saheb is saying this. -47

kabir kul khoye kul ubre, kul raakhe kul jaay
raam akul kul metiyaa, sabhkul gayaa bilaay -48

[Bengali:]

Kabir is saying: if lineage is destroyed, then again the lineage can be had. If lineage is preserved, then the lineage ends. When Ramachandra [Lord] resolves lineage and non-lineage, then all lineages will be extinguished. -48

[Commentary:]

Kabir, if the Self is lost, all lineages are had. If the Self is kept, all lineages end. Because of getting Rama Nakul [the Lord of no boundaries/no lineages], all lineages have ended, and in That Un-lineage Itself all lineages have ended. -48

kabir duniyaa ke dhnokhe mua, chalaa jo kul ki kaap
tab ka ko kul laajsi, jay lay dhare mashaan -49

[Bengali:]

Kabir is saying: everyone is just about dead because of being hoodwinked by the world. People are just going on by ear and lineage – meaning: people are doing all false and useless activities because of hearing by ear only, but when you are taken to the cremation ground, then where will the vanity of your lineage be? -49

[Commentary:]

Everyone is dying from the hoodwinking of the world (meaning: the false "mine, mine"). Going on because of hearing [about what to do] from the lineage – meaning: going on doing work because of hearing things, one eventually died. Then which lineage will you be proud of, when they take you to the cremation ground? -49

kabir kul karanee ke kaarane, hangsaa chale bigoy
tab ka ko kul laajsi, jab chaari charan ka hoy -50

[Bengali:]

Kabir is saying: is your life for the sake of doing the work of your lineage? When you ride the Swan – when you are riding on four shoulders [pall bearers], then for whom is a lineage and for whom is pride?!! -50

[Commentary:]

Kabir, the reason for life is the Self. And you are leaving the Swan and going. Then which lineage will you be proud of, when four sets of feet carry you away on their shoulders? -50

kabir kul karanee ke kaarane, hoye, raha nal sum
tab kaako kul laajsi, jab yam dhumaa dhum -51

[Bengali:]

Kabir is saying: you have become miserly in order to keep the activities right for your lineage. But when the Lord of Death comes and takes you away with great fanfare, then for whom will there be any lineage and for whom will there be vanity? All will remain here [or: all will be just lying there uselessly]. -51

[Commentary:]

Kabir, because of selfish reasons, people have become miserly and are acting from vanity – meaning: whatever worshiping and ceremony/ritual people are doing are for the sake of avoiding a negative view from society, because everyone definitely thinks: well, all of these things that I am doing [pious acts] – from not one of them am I getting the benefits according to what the shastras [scriputres] say. When the Lord of Death takes one away with great fanfare, then for which lineage will you have your pride? -51

kabir kul karalee ki paagree, kup kathor taa maahi
bnaachi chalaa so upraa, nahi to budaa taahi -52

[Bengali:]

Kabir is saying: the pot of the work prescribed by lineage is inside the well. If it rises up from there then it is saved. Otherwise, it drowns. -52

[Commentary:]

Kabir, within a very hard well is the pot of oneself with work prescribed by the lineage. One who is saved rises above. Otherwise, he dies in that [typical stuff of the lineage].

In the very hard well of samsara, the pot of work done with the desire for results in the form of the ego – meaning: the ego is only acting with the desire for results. In this hard samsara – the dark well of samsara in which nothing is able to seen - yet there are many types of jolts like the deaths of sons and daughters etc. - one who can survive all these jolts and rise up to do Kriya – it is he who is free from the well of samsara. And one who remained immersed in doing acts with the desire for results really drowned in that – meaning: he became enslaved to going through birth and death again and again. -52

kabir jetaa dar hay jaat ki, tetaa hari ki hoy dhol
damaamaa dei chale, chalaa na pakare koy -53

[Bengali:]

Kabir is saying: the amount of fear that you have for your race/caste, have that amount of fear for God. If have that amount of fear for God, people will try to go with you, beating drums loudly, but no one at all will be able to catch hold of you. -53

[Commentary:]

Kabir, the amount of fear that you have for your race/caste, if you have that amount of fear for God, then people will beat drums loudly, and no one at all will catch hold of you – meaning: because of having fear of lineage/ caste, one cannot associate with either someone of a low caste or a good sage – etc. One cannot do many good works. If this kind of fear were there for the Self (meaning: if I do bad things, the Self will be angry; if the Self is angry, I will have misfortune etc.), then all people would praise you, and no one at all would be your enemy. -53

kabir kewal raam ko, tu mati chore ot naato
aharal ghan bikhe, ghani sahegaa chot -54

[Bengali:]

Kabir is saying: the only work is Ramachandra [Lord]. Do not leave his shelter. If one leaves this work and gives mind to other things, one will have to suffer the pain of going through life and death again and again. -54

[Commentary:]

Kabir, the only work is Rama [Lord; Self]. The cover that is between Rama and you – do not let go of that, because if you let that go, you will fall down – meaning: if you leave

Kriya and put mind in other directions, you will forget Kriya. If you do not do this work, then with what do you have any connection/relationship? And if you leave this work and remain in worldly things, and thus bow down to the Lord of Death, you will have to withstand a plethora of attacks – meaning: again and again you will have to take birth and die. - 54

kabir kewal raam kar, sujgari baa jhaari kul
badaai budsee, bhaaree parsee maari -55

[Bengali:]

Kabir is saying: Now that you have come to this beautiful world, do the work of the Only-ness of Ramachandra [Lord]. If this happens, your [bondage to] lineage and your vanity will all drown. And it will also kill a very weighty neighbor. -55

[Commentary:]

Kabir, now that you have come into this beautiful world, do Kriya. If you do this, [bondage from] lineage and vanity will drown. Killing a big neighbor – meaning: the individual self, which is the neighbor of the Supreme Self – merging that individual self with the Supreme Self is the "killing." If there is no individual self, no lineage or pride can remain. -55

kabir kaayaa manjan kyaa kare, kapdaa dhoyan
khoy ujal bhaye na chutsi, jo man mail na khoy -56

[Bengali:]

Kabir is saying: what are you doing cleaning your body and washing your clothes? Cleaning your body will not get rid of the dirt from your mind. If the dirt from your mind does not go, you will not get the Natural/Real State. -56

[Commentary:]

Kabir, after cleaning the body, washing clothes and making everything bright, you are not still able to get rid of [dirt] – meaning: you are not able to be free until the dirt from the mind goes. "Dirt of the mind" - if mind does not remain in Mind – if it just goes in other directions, it is dirty [or: that is the "dirt of the mind"]. -56

kabir ujal pekhe kapraa, paan supaari khaay ek
hari ke naam binu, bnaadha jampur jaay -57

[Bengali:]

Kabir is saying: with clean clothes, and chewing betel, you are going about dressed like an aristocratic gentleman. But without the One Name of God, you will have to go to the city of Death. Friends and family will not be able to keep you. -57

[Commentary:]

Kabir, there is dirt within, but you are showing off outside with bright clothes and chewing betel. Without the One par avastha of Kriya, you will be tied up and taken to the city of Death. "Tied" = the Lord of Death by whose slightest indication everyone has to die – why is it necessary for him to "tie up" anything? "I will go to heaven. I will take birth in the house of royalty. I will enjoy being rich." Because of all such desires of the mind, instead of being free from them, one is being "tied" to the repetition of births and deaths. -57

kabir dar pnotedi paag so, mati mayli hoy jaay paag
bechaari kyaa kare, jo shir nahi maati khaay -58

[Bengali:]

Kabir is saying: there is the fear of tying the turban crookedly because accidental rubbing will make the pearl untidy. Now what fault is it of the turban? If the head does not get into the earth, then there will be no crooked and straight. It will be all right then. -58

[Commentary:]

Kabir, there is the fear that the turban will be tied crookedly, because the pearl can rub against the forehead and hair and become dirty. What has the poor turban done? So that the head is not eaten up by the earth – meaning: one will die. The gentleman's turban is on the head. If that becomes crooked, vayu will become distorted. This is the great fear – that turban. -58

kabir mandil maahi paudte, parimal ang lagaay
chhatrapatike raakhme, gadhaa lote jaay -59

[Bengali:]

Kabir is saying: because of remaining lying in the temple, the body has become pure. And even an ass can lie down by the Monarch. -59

[Commentary:]

Kabir, I am lying down in the temple and I have put perfume on the body. And the donkey is lying down on the dust of the Monarch. Living with the Supreme Person in the temple of this body and becoming One with That, the body has become Pure. And in the Atom of the Monarch Kutastha, an ass like me (because I do not understand anything at all) is lying down. -59

kabir gaudhan maahi paudte, parimal ang lagaay
svapnaa sam dekhat rahe, gayaa so bahuri bilaay -60

[Bengali:]

Kabir is saying: "gaudhan go" [cattle as wealth] = in the continuous process of doing a certain act via a guru-bestowed technique with the tongue, the body became pure. I was seeing many things like a dream, but what I was seeing did not come back again. -60

[Commentary:]

Kabir, going on meditating continuously with the tongue up, I was seeing so many pure things, like a dream. That which went did not come back again – meaning: the form that went away did not come back again. -60

kabir khasaamal pahintai, khaate naagar paan
tebhi hote maanavee, karte bahut gumaan -61

[Bengali:]

Kabir is saying: wearing well-washed linen clothes, chewing betel, dressed up like an aristocratic gentleman and being completely intoxicated with pride, you continuously look for holes in others. One does not see one's own faults, and in mind there is always the thought, "We are [civilized and proper] human beings" [or: "We are elite people."] -61

[Commentary:]

Kabir, those who go around wearing good silk and eating good betel – they think, "We are [civilized and proper] human beings." [or: "We are elite people."] They think this and are very proud. -61

kabir jangal dheri raak ki, upar ghaas patang
tebhi hote maanavee, karte rang berang -62

[Bengali:]

Kabir is saying: a jungle-like condition [overgrowth] has come about on top of the mound of ashes, and a great deal of grass has grown on it and insects are living there. They are also joking and making so much fun, saying, "We have again become [civilized and proper] humans" [or: "We have again become elite people."] -62

[Commentary:]

Kabir, there is a mound of a jungle of ashes. On top of that there are grass and insects. They have also become humans [elite people], and how much fun and jocularity they are making – meaning: this samsara [life in the world] is nothing but the ashes of ashes, because everyone will have to be burned to ashes. On this samsara of ashes [or: ashen samsara] there is grass – meaning: joking and making fun – on that itself people are all going around once to this thing, once to that thing. All of these people have become "civilized" and are making "rang" [color] – meaning Brahman – into "berang" [off -color; off-color attitude] because of being absorbed in worldly things. -62

kabir mera sangee ki nahi, sabhe saarathee loy
man parateet na upje, jeeu bishraam na hoy -63

[Bengali:]

Kabir is saying: I do not have any companion at all. Those who are there at all – they all want to be drivers [and not passengers]. Because of not having faith in the mind, the jiva [person] is not able to get any rest. -63

[Commentary:]

Kabir, I have no companion. Everyone wants to be a driver (of the chariot). Because of not having faith in the mind, there is no rest in life either. This means: I myself am non-existent in the par avastha of Kriya, then how in the world can I have a companion? No one at all wants to be just the passenger on the chariot – meaning: people do not want to abide in body in the Still State. Verily everyone wants to be the driver [charioteer] and drive the body – meaning: people always want to remain restless [or: in motion]. Without being Still, there can be no faith in the mind. If there is no faith, there is no Peace. -63

kabir thal charantaa mirgalaa, eru jo bedhaa soh ham to paathi basi rahaa, pheri karegaa kaunha -64

[Bengali:]

Kabir is saying: the deer is grazing about. The one who has pierced it [as if with an arrow] is also me. And I am a traveler sitting about. Who cares to hawk? -64

[Commentary:]

Kabir is moving about on the Earth. He is also the one who pierced the deer [as if with an arrow]. Me, well I am a traveler who is sitting about. Who needs to move? This means: the mind that is going about in the body became pierced by the Self and became Still. And the Self who did the piercing, He also became Still. I am a traveler – meaning: I was moving, but mind was pierced by the Self – meaning: upon doing pranayam, I am abiding as Still in the par avastha of Kriya. Now who is going to move? -64

kabir it ghar ut gharwonaa, banijan aaye haat karma phiraanaa bechike, chaliye apni baat -65

[Bengali:]

Kabir is saying: leaving my house, I have come to the house of another. It is like the way merchants go to the market, do their own work of trading, and again come back to their own street. It is like that. -65

[Commentary:]

Kabir, one has left one's house and has come to this other

person's house as a merchant to do business in the marketplace. After having come, one sells rice, beans/legumes and such and goes back to one's own street. This means: because of acts done in the house of the body in the previous life, one has come to the house of another – meaning: you have taken this [present] body. Because of having become a merchant and doing business in the marketplace of this samsara [life in the world] (meaning: exchanging one substance for another substance or for money) – meaning: because of having to experience the fruits of acts from the previous life, do the work of this time and sell the rice and legumes/beans and such, and go back to your own street – meaning: act without desire and merge with Brahman. -65

kabir maarag upar daurnaa, sukh nidri naa shoy
paraa paraaye deshraa, waisi thor na khoy -66

[Bengali:]

Kabir is saying: if you want to run on the road, do not go for pleasure and sleep because this Country is after all the other lands. Thus, do not waste it by going needlessly to sleep – meaning: do not waste time. -66

[Commentary:]

Kabir, run on the road. Do not go for pleasure and sleep. That Country is after all other lands. Do not waste time in bad places. This means: come and go on the road of sushumna. Do not go for pleasure and sleep because that Country is beyond all other lands, and do not waste time in bad places – do not leave Kriya and then put mind in other directions. -66

kabir naao jo jhari, kurso kheowaan haar haluke
haluke tari gaye, bude jinha shir bhaar -67

[Bengali:]

Kabir is saying: the boat that is there is full of holes, like a sieve. The oar of the boat is also not rowing well. Those which were of the light type were saved. And one who had heaviness in the head – it is he who drowned. -67

[Commentary:]

Kabir, the boat is like a sieve and the oar is not rowing well. "Haluke, haluke" [lightly, lightly] = slowly, slowly, one went across to the other shore. And one whose head is heavy drowns. This means: The boat of the body is full of holes like a sieve – meaning: the nine doors. It is this that is making people go about wrongly. One whose mind is only slightly in bad directions, but mostly in good directions can slowly, slowly, go to the other shore. And one whose head is full of bad acts – meaning: one whose intentions are only in bad directions – he drowns – meaning: he takes birth again and again. -67

kabir raam kahante khijhi mare, kushree hoy gali jaay ghukar hoyeke aao tare, naak budante khaay -68

[Bengali:]

Kabir is saying: [there are those who] burn up [become irritated] when it comes to practicing the Name of Rama. They become ugly and melt. One has incarnated as a pig and is eating with his nose sunk in [food; mud]. -68

[Commentary:]

Kabir, [a type of person] burns up when saying "Rama." He becomes ugly. And he incarnates as a pig and eats with his nose sunk in [food; mud]. Those who become irritated at saying the Name of Rama become ugly – meaning: because of being immersed in worldly things, their minds and bodies become ugly and melt – meaning: just as when metal melts and goes to one side and then to another side, in that same way, the minds of people addicted to worldly matters are not still for even one moment. They incarnate as pigs – meaning: like the way pigs gather together with each other's bodies and live in dirt and mud, in that same way, all those people roll around in the mud of worldly experiences. And like the way that a pig eats with its nose sunk in [food; mud], they also partake in liquor, meat, prostitutes and such, and causing ruin to others, sink their noses in and eat. -68

kabir jaa mat saa mat taa mataa, taa mat laao n saao
raam bina sab bharm hay, raajaa, raanaa, raao -69

[Bengali:]

Kabir is saying: the prevalent ideology has been established by kings, rulers and lords. Without the Name of Rama, verily all of them have fallen into delusion/ignorance. -69

[Commentary:]

Kabir, the ideology is the same as the mentality of the maker of the ideology. Destroy that ideology. Without Rama [Self] verily everyone is deluded - "raajaa," "raanaa," "raao" - meaning: kings, rulers or lords – whatever ideology they have used – that very ideology has been established [as the "proper" way]. Destroy that ideology, because without the Name of Rama – meaning: without knowing Atma-Rama [Self] (there is no other way of knowing Atma-Rama besides Kriya) – all are lying about in delusion/ ignorance. -69

kabir yeh pur paatan deshoa, paanch chor dash doar
man raajaa garme lahe, sumiri lehu kartaar -70

[Bengali:]

Kabir is saying: this country – meaning: the country of the

body – is covered. Within it there are five thieves and ten doors. Within the castle of this body, mind resides as king. In this state, take up the remembrance of the Lord. -70

[Commentary:]

Kabir, this country is completely covered. Within it there are five thieves and ten doors. Mind is residing as king in the castle. Take up the remembrance of the Lord. This body is completely covered. Within this there are five thieves and ten doors, within which mind is sitting as king. You are the Lord – meaning: take up the remembrance of the Supreme Self. -70

kabir pipri lunaay phul binu, kul binu lunaay na
jaay ekaa ekee maanasaa, dhnaapaa dinho aay -71

[Bengali:]

Kabir is saying: a banyan tree without flowers is seen, but that cannot be seen in any place other than Kulakundalini. Going on watching that in aloneness, mind becomes Still and then mind attains samadhi. -71

[Commentary:]

Kabir, there is a banyan tree without flowers. Without the root it cannot be had. The alone mind becomes covered – meaning: within the Bindu, something like a banyan tree can be seen, which has no flowers. That tree cannot be had without Kulakundalini. By continuously looking at that tree, mind becomes alone and samadhi happens. -71

kabir may to hi bhaunraa barjiyaa, ban ban baasan
lehu aatkegaa koi bel so, talfitalfijeeu lehu -72

[Bengali:]

Kabir is saying: the bee of my mind is bound to desire and is going from one forest to another forest – meaning: upon seeing it going about with many different kinds of desires, one is telling one's mind, "O mind. Do not become engrossed with temporal desires like this. Who knows when in some vine of desire your wings will get caught? If that happens you will struggle in desperation and lose your very life." -72

[Commentary:]

Kabir Saheb is telling his own mind, "Mind-bee, do not roam about this forest and that forest – meaning: do not become enamored with many different kinds of desires, because your wings will get caught in some vine, and in desperate struggle your very life will go out – meaning: some desire will trap you, and because of your desired not being fulfilled, you will die, crying, 'Alas! Alas!'" -73

kabir bejhaa bhnau rathaa, let kalihu ko baas
so to bhaunraa uri gayaa, chori baari ki aash -73

[Bengali:]

Kabir is saying: the bee of the mind – well he used to be bound and smell the fragrance of the flower-bud, but that bee has given up the desire of the water-like honey and has flown away. -73

[Commentary:]

Kabir, the bee was bound and used to smell the bud of the flower. That bee has flown away, renouncing the desire for water-like honey – meaning: having been bound to lust, children and such flower-buds of worldly things, mind used to smell [their fragrance] – meaning: it was engrossed in worldly things. That Mind-Self flew away – meaning: renouncing the desire for the minimally satisfying water of samsara, He cast off the body. -73

kabir maanik mati knaakraa, naam na hosi
koy aysaa saheb sei le, duno dinkaa hoy -74

[Bengali:]

Kabir is saying: rubies and pearl are pebbles; none of these are the Name. Serve such a "saheb" [noble being] that both this life and the afterlife stay right. -74

[Commentary:]

Kabir, rubies and pearls are pebbles; none of these are the Name. Serve such a "saheb" [noble being] that both sides are done. This means: rubies and pearls have come about from pebbles [earth element]. None of these are the par avastha of Kriya (the Name). Serve such a Lord that both this life and the afterlife stay right. -74

kabir baarbaar to so kaha, shunre manua neech
banijaar ke bayel jo, pere hi maahi mich -75

[Bengali:]

Kabir saying: "Hey, you lowlife mind! You will not listen even after telling you again and again. You are like the oxen of the ox-cart traders. Traveling on and on, you will die on the road itself." -75

[Commentary:]

Kabir [says:] "O you lowlife mind! I am telling you again and again that [you are like] the tradesman's oxen who die from just the travel, right on the road itself." This means, "O lowlife mind! I am telling you again and again: like the way the tradesmen take the oxen from land to land with the greed for wealth and the oxen die from the incessant travel without getting any profit themselves, in that same way, you are getting life and death again and again without any profit for yourself." -75

**kabir banijaare ke bayel jneo, tnaadaa utraa jaay ye
kahuke dunaa bhaye, ek chale mool gnaowaay**

[Bengali:]

Kabir is saying: it is like this: if the load on both sides of
the ox of the oxcart trader is put all to one side, it becomes
twice as much [on that side]; and because of not being
squarely on the back, the pack falls down. Then nothing
remains on any side. All gets destroyed. -76

[Commentary:]

Kabir, it is like this: when the two sides of the load of the
ox of the ox-cart trader go to one side, then it becomes twice as
much as the original one on one side, and when one goes
away, the root is lost. We have two loads: one is of the world;
the other is of the Spirit. Putting these two loads together as
one it becomes twice as much. And when one goes away, the
other goes to its root – meaning: if one goes to the worldly
things, the afterlife is ruined; and if the afterlife goes, then this
life goes. -76

**kabir dariyaa kshaara deha hay, chaari bed tehi maahi
koi sant bebekee bnaachi hay, naa to budaa taahi -77**

[Bengali:]

The water in this body-river is salty, and within this are
the four Vedas as well. There are some sages and wise persons
who have remained alive. All others have drowned. -77

[Commentary:]

Kabir, the water of this body-river is salty, and within this
body are the four Vedas. Some saints and wise ones have
remained alive. Otherwise everyone else has drowned. Like
the way salty water in a saline/brackish river is unsatisfactory,
in that same way, all of the desires of the body not being

fulfilled are all unsatisfactory. Within this saline body there are the four Vedas – to/on the front, to/on the right, to/on the back [or: to/on the west] and to/ on the left – Omkar Kriya. Some saints have remained alive. Otherwise, all other people have drowned and died. -77

kabir purkhanee nyayaaraa sabhante, sabhe kahe sujh maahi upajat binu sat yei sandaa, aaye theer koi naahi -78

[Bengali:]

Kabir is saying: the Being is apart from all phenomena, and everyone has said, "Only look within yourself." And because of doubt arising from seeing life and death happening, no one at all is able to be Still. -78

[Commentary:]

Kabir, the Being is apart from all. Everyone says, "Look within yourself." Because of the doubt coming about [from seeing that] everyone is being born and being destroyed in the end, no one is able to be Still. The Supreme Person is apart from all. Verily everyone says, "Search within yourself." Everyone on Earth is being born and dying, yet the Being is in all; this is the doubt. Because of its [the doubt's] coming about, no one at all is able to be Still. -78

kabir pnaach tattva kaa putraa, taa baha panchhee paun rahane kaa aachraaj gino, jaat aachambhaa kaun -79

[Bengali:]

Kabir is saying: within the body of this doll made of five elements is a bird. The incredible thing in this situation is that the bird stays. What is so unusual about it flying away? It can just go. -79

[Commentary:]

Kabir, within the doll made of five elements is a bird. The fact that the bird is actually staying within this [body] is the wondrous thing. [But] people become stupefied when it leaves he body. Within the body of five elements is the Self. The incredible thing is that the Self is staying within the body. But people do not become awed by that. And dying, which is certain – everyone thinks that that is the unusual thing. -79

kabir pnaacho ke madhime, phiri dhare shareer
jo pnaachko bashee kare, soi laagad teer -80

[Bengali:]

Kabir is saying: in these five elements, the jiva [soul] is taking on a body again and again. But the one who can bring the aforementioned five elements under his control – it is he who lands on the shore – meaning: ends the coming and going. -80

[Commentary:]

Kabir, a body is taken on again and again in these five. One who brings the five under his control – it is he who lands on the shore – meaning: bound by the fruit of previous actions, one is taking on a body again and again. One who brings these five elements – meaning: the five senses – under control – it is he who lands on the shore. -80

kabir chet nihaaraa chetiyaa, aur jo cheto jaay kahe
kabir cheto nahi, bahuri bahuri pacchtaay -81

[Bengali:]

Kabir is saying: it is still possible to become aware of the One Who is making the person conscious. But Kabir Saheb is saying, "If you do not do that, then you will fall into the hands of birth and death again and again. -81

[Commentary:]

Kabir, become aware of the One Who is making the person conscious – meaning: surrender your "chitta" [individual consciousness] to/in That, because it is still possible to become awakened. Kabir Saheb is saying, "If you do not offer up your chitta now, then you will have to suffer again and again." The Self Who is making one conscious – surrender the chitta to That. If you surrender chitta to the Self during this life, then there is beneficence. And if you do not surrender chitta to the Self during this life – meaning: if you do not do Kriya – then you will fall into the hands of birth and death again and again. -81

kabir bhay binu bhaawai na upje, bhay binu hoy na preeti jabhi darsho bhay gai, tab meti sakal ras reeti -82

[Bengali:]

Kabir is saying: without fear there is no enamored feeling; without fear there is no dearness either. When one sees that fear is gone, then all pleasure and enjoyment finish as well. -82

[Commentary:]

Kabir, without fear there is no enamored feeling; without fear there is no dearness either. When you see fear, fear goes away. Then all pleasure and enjoyment end. If there is no fear of death, one does not think/feel lovingly about the Self – meaning: one who has the fear of death takes care of the thing that prevents death – meaning: there is no death if one resides in the Self. For this reason that person resides in the Self. If there is no fear of death, dearness for the Self does not come about. Seeing death – meaning: the Being that goes away – seeing That – meaning: upon becoming Still and attaining Immortality, fear went away. Then all the pleasures and enjoyments of the world were finished – meaning: nothing at all feels good except the Self. -82

kabir bhay so sabh hi bhakti kare, bhaye poojaa joy bhay maare yeh jeeu ko, binu bhay kaaj na koy -83

[Bengali:]

Kabir is saying: everyone practices devotion because of fear, and everyone worships because of fear as well. If there were no fear, no one at all would do anything. And it is this very fear that kills the jiva [individual]. Without fear no work takes place. -83

[Commentary:]

Kabir, everyone practices devotion in fear. Worshiping is done in fear. Fear kills all jivas [individuals]. Without fear no work takes place. Guru is saying, "If one does not do Kriya, one will die." One does Kriya because of this fear. "Pooja" [worship] = the "pull" from the door of the anus to the nose. Feeling that one may die because of not being "in/with" this "pull" – because of this fear one conducts worship. Many people die just from the fear generated by hearing "a tiger is approaching." Without fear no work takes place. -83

kabir dar paarash dar param guru, dar karanee dar saar dartaa raha so ubare, gaafeel khaayaa maar -84

[Bengali:]

Kabir is saying: fear is actually the touchstone. It is fear that is the supreme guru. Fear is actually action. It is fear that is the fundamental element [or: fear is all]. Without fear nothing at all takes place – meaning: because of the fear "I will have to die," people call God. "That" [the Supreme Substance] is attained by calling God – meaning: God Himself happens. Thus fear is really the touchstone. Fear is the supreme guru, because if one does not do what guru has given [to practice], it will be a great sin. There will be birth and death again and again. There will be transgression of guru's teachings. There are many fears like this. For this reason fear is actually the supreme guru. If there was no fear, no one would do good works. And one who does not have this fear will take a beating. He will die. -84

[Commentary:]

Kabir, fear is the touchstone. Fear is the supreme guru. Fear is action, and it is fear that is the essential thing [or: fear is all]. One who fears, crosses over to the other shore. And one who does not fear takes a beating.

"Paarash" [touchstone] = that which turns iron into gold. "Iron" is mind going in other directions. With the fear of the teaching of the guru, one goes to the "gold" of the par avastha of Kriya. Thus fear is truly the touchstone. Because of the fear of transgressing the teachings of guru, one does the Kriya of the Self and goes to That which is after the Self, the Supreme Self – meaning: Kutastha. One who has fear of transgressing guru's teaching is the one can do this – meaning: he goes to/in the sushumna. And one who does not abide by guru's teachings suffers many kinds of suffering while alive and dies an untimely death. -84

kabir khaali mili khaali bhayaa, bahut kiyaa bakwaad bnaajhaha laawe paalnaa, taame kaun sawaad -85

[Bengali:]

Kabir is saying: by getting emptiness, you have yourself become empty. Emptiness is characterized by useless actions – meaning: by getting uselessness, you have yourself become useless. You are not good for anything at all. And you have also done a lot of meaningless talking and arguing. Even in that you did not find any happiness. You are like a barren woman who cannot have a child yet you have a swing in which to swing the child. What kind of enjoyment will you get from the swing without having a child? This means: you have done a lot of false arguing and are still doing it. Intoxicated by pride, you are only seeing the faults of others. You do not even know what you are. Why don't you take a look at your own faults for a change? You will find that you are blind even though you have eyes. You are having to walk with the help of holding someone else's hand, yet you do not admit that you are blind. Instead, if someone calls you "blind," you curse at him and get ready to hit him. Is this good? Whatever anyone does, whatever anyone says, what harm is there in it regarding you? Look at your own actions. Try to do that by which the fruit of a "child" can be had. Search for a satguru. If you get a satguru, the fruit of the "child" will be born. Then you will bow automatically [or: you will automatically be humble]. Then you will have the pleasure of buying a swing. And if you have received the practice of meditation from a satguru, then leave all that nonsensical arguing, and go on practicing that [meditation]. -85

[Commentary:]

Kabir, by getting emptiness, you have yourself become empty. And you are just making a lot of argumentation. You yourself are barren, yet you brought a swing to play with your child. What kind of pleasure is in that? One who stays in the fun of the world and does not have devotion and reverence becomes empty. And he dies arguing, like a barren woman bringing a swing to play with her child – meaning: there is no witnessing of the Supreme Person, yet one gives teachings on religion and spirituality – meaning: one is murdered by this useless talking [or: one spews blood from all this talking]. What is there to be desired in this type of thing? -85

More to be published.*

Note: During Yogiraj's life, this much was published. Although "More to be published" is written, nothing [of Kabir commentaries] further was published.**

[* and ** Translator's note: The clause and the statement above are in the version worked on by the translators.]

AVINASHI KABIR GITA

Spiritual Commentary

Yogiraj Sri Sri Shyama Charan Lahiri Mahasaya

English translation by Yoga Niketan

Avinashi Kabir Gita

Contents

AVINASHI KABIR GITA

(Translated from the original 1894
Bengali version which was)

Published by
Panchanon Bhattacharya,
a disciple following the guru-disciple
lineage of Sri Sri Gurudeva
[Sri Shyamacharan Lahiri Mahasaya]
and with His blessings

Arya Mission Institution*
Calcutta 80/1 Muktaram Babu Street

Bengal year 1300 (1894 C.E.)

[*Editor's note: Refers to the original Arya Mission
Institution which was founded and run by Sri Panchanon
Bhattacharya. That original Arya Mission closed its doors
many years ago.]

FOREWORD*

[*Translator's note: literally
"ANNOUNCEMENT" in Bengali]

By the Grace of Guru, the spiritual commentaries on the Kabir Gita is hereby published. Sriyukta Babu Kumudnath Maitra Mahasaya has greatly filled us with enthusiasm by having taken on the entire financial burden of this publication. And we express our gratitude here for that. We pray to God that he enjoys a long life of beneficent service to the world.

The Publisher

Sri Panchanon Bhattacharya

AVINASHI KABIR GITA

[Translator's note: In this first section of this publication, the dialogue between Dattatreya and Kabir [called here as "Avinashi" [meaning the Eternal Indestructible]] takes place, and is written, mostly in Hindi [transliterated in Bengali script] and sometimes Bengali. The commentary chapter that follows this section – titled simply "Kabir Gita" - is in Bengali. The commentary chapter is the explanation of the meaning of the dialogue and how it applies to the sadhak.]

[Translator's note: Certain definitions: the words "pavan" and "vayu" refer to both air and vital air in all cases. "Pavan," as will be seen, refers particularly to the Still vayu. The word "jiva" has several meanings, each used very specifically by the author. Clarifications to the specific meanings have been made in brackets following the word "jiva."]

[Translator's note: All material within parentheses "( )" are in the original, including the parentheses. All material within brackets "[ ]" are the translator's, including the brackets, provided for the purposes of clarification].

Dattatreya said: What is mind? What is "pavan" [air or vital air]? What is "Shabda" [divine sound]? What is "prana" [life; life-force]? What is "Brahman" [Absolute]? What is "Hansa" [the Pure Soul; or: the mystical sohang/hangsa; I Am That]? What is "kal" [time or death]? What is "jiva" [the individual; or: the offspring; or: the life of]? What is Shiva [the Universal Being]? What is "Niranjan" [the Effulgent]?

Avinashi said: Mind is restless. Pavan [air] is the transition. Shabda is the Void. Prana is Niranjan [the Effulgent]. Brahman is Mercy. Hansa is "Avinashi" [the Eternal Indestructible].

Dattatreya said: Where does mind reside? Where does pavan reside? Where does prana reside? Where does Shabda reside? Where does Brahman reside? Where does kal reside? Where does the Void reside? Where does the jiva reside? Where does Shiva reside? Where does Niranjan reside?

Avinashi said: Mind resides in the heart. Pavan resides in the navel. Shabda resides in the Anahata. Prana resides in Niranjan. Brahman resides in Brahman Itself. Hansa resides in the "gagan" [heavenly sky]. The Void resides in "anupa" [mystic lake; or: incomparable]. Kal resides in "kamal" [mystic lotus]. Niranjan resides in the sushumna [the center nadi of the three primary nadis in the spine].

Dattatreya said: If there were no heart, then where would the mind reside? If there were no navel, then where would air reside? If there were no "anahata" [anahata chakra; heart center], then where would Shabda reside? If there were no Niranjan, then where would prana reside? If there were no "Brahmanda" [universe], then where would Brahman reside? If there were no prana, then where would Hansa [Soul] reside? If there were no anupa, then where would the Void reside? If there were no kamal, then where would kal reside? If there were no air, then where would be the jiva? If there were no moon, then where would Shiva reside? If there were no sushumna, then where would Niranjan be?

Avinashi said: If there were no heart, then mind would be in "anupama" [incomparable; highest]. If there were no navel, then air would be in Niranjan. If there were no anahata, then Shabda would be in anupama. If there were no Niranjan, then

Brahman would be in Avinashi. If there were no Brahmanda, then Brahman would be in the Light Form. If there were no "gagan" [heavenly sky], then Hansa would be in Avinashi. If there would be no anupa, then the Void would be in Omkar. If there were no kamal, then kal would be in the Void. If there were no kal, then the jiva [personal consciousness] would be in Shiva. If there were no sushumna, then Niranjan would be in Brahman.

Dattatreya said: What is the "jiva" [in this case: vital life] of mind? What is the jiva of Shabda? What is the jiva of prana? What is the jiva of Brahman? What is the jiva of Hansa? What is the jiva of kal? What is the jiva of jiva? What is the jiva of Shiva? What is the jiva of Niranjan?

Avinashi said: The jiva of mind is air. The jiva of air is "samnyas" [abidance with]. The jiva of samnyas is Shabda. The jiva of Shabda is prana. The jiva of prana is Brahman. The jiva of Brahman is Hansa. The jiva of Hansa is Avinashi. The jiva of Avinashi is the Void. The jiva of the Void is anupa. The jiva of anupa is kal. The jiva of kal is jiva. The jiva of jiva is Shiva. The jiva of Shiva is Niranjan. The jiva of Niranjan is the One Brahman.

Dattatreya said: Whence [from where; or: in what] does Niranjan arise? [Alternate translation, the manner of which can be applied to all questions in this paragraph: "What is the source of _____?"] Whence does Shiva arise? Whence does jiva [individual] arise? Whence does kal arise? Whence does the Void arise? Whence does Brahman arise? Whence does Hansa arise? Whence does prana arise? Whence does Shabda arise? Whence does breath arise? Whence does air arise? Whence does mind arise?

Avinashi said: Niranjan arises from "anila" [wind]. Shiva arises from Niranjan. Kal arises from Shiva. Omkar arises from Kal. The Void arises from Omkar. Hansa arises from the Void. Brahman arises from Hansa. Prana rises from Brahman. Shabda rises from prana. Air rises from Shabda. Breath rises from air. Mind rises from breath.

Dattatreya said: Where [or: to what] is mind "samana" [merged as one]? Where is air samana? Where is Shabda samana? Where is prana samana? Where is Brahman samana? Where is the Void samana? Where is kal samana? Where is jiva samana? Where is Shiva samana? Where is Niranjan samana?

Avinashi said: The body runs; mind is samana with air. Air is samana with Shabda. Shabda is samana with prana. Prana is samana with Brahman. Brahman is samana with Hansa. Hansa is samana with "surati" [attentive faculty of spirit]. The Void is samana with Omkar. Omkar is samana with kal. Kal is samana with jiva. Jiva is samana with Shiva. Shiva is samana with Niranjan. Niranjan is samana with the Self. The Self is samana with the Self.

KABIR GITA

The meaning of the word "Kabir" is "kaya" [body; alternate meaning: spirit], and the meaning of the word "Gita" is: abiding in the par avastha of Kriya [poise after the performance of Kriya], and singing about – meaning describing – the experiences in the par avastha of the par avastha – that is called "Gita." That Gita is this: the sage Dattatreya (who is a special incarnation of Mahadeva) is asking Kabir Saheb [Sir Kabir] and Kabir Saheb is responding to him accordingly. Upon gathering that wisdom together, a thorough explanation is being given. As much as was possible [to expound upon in words] has been explained here. Of course, explanation happens via the mind. Everything is from mind, and everything is also in mind. So, what is that mind? When mind does not stay in mind, meaning: when mind goes to other things – restlessness comes about only when mind goes to other things – meaning: when mind is not at a state of Stillness, mind is restless. One can see the [quick] movement of lightning. But the movement of mind is far faster than that of lightning. It is so fast that it is like this: first mind goes and then some substance is seen. Always, mind believes the poison-like worldly things to be ambrosia, runs and runs after those things, and goes on tolerating the suffering brought about [by such running] and returns to this predicament again and again. This type of mind (who cannot find find Peace in anything) must take up the unabated practice of pranayam, which is received via initiation from a guru, and he must constantly contemplate upon the Self.

371

The residing place of that mind is the heart, the heart that is within all jivas [sentient beings]. The proof is: hridayambujamadhyastham jnanajneyasvarupakam [in the middle of the lotus of the heart resides the known and the knower Itself]; indriyanam manashchasmi [among the senses, I am the mind]. This, the Still Mind which is Brahman, is in the heart of all. When there is no heart, He resides in the anupa [the incomparable; or: mystic lake] of Brahman – meaning: that Brahman which has no comparison to anything (the par avastha of Kriya). That which is experienced by every Kriyavan after that "avastha" [poise state] in an intoxicated way. The jiva [vital-life] of this mind is "pavan" [vital air]. Pavan – meaning: the Still vayu [vital air] which is absolutely pure – because it is only when mind is Still that it has happiness or Peace. The jiva of Peace is "samnyas" [abidance with] – meaning: Peace is not attained without the par avastha of Kriya. The jiva of that samnyas is the Sound of the Omkar Resonance. The place where vayu goes and merges – in the very place still the mind in Stillness totally and do not think about anything. This Still mind comes about from breath – meaning: via pranayam – the pranayam which is only found through the teachings of a guru. That Still mind merges in the Still pavan – meaning: the Still pavan is Brahman.

This Still pavan is wondrous. People naturally have a desire to know it. What is it? It is the transition point between life and death. Its abode is in the navel. Almost all people die if breath happens from the navel. Therefore, the transition point is verily in pavan. When pavan is not in the navel, it stays in Niranjan Kutastha [the Effulgent Kutastha], which is called "Aditya Hriday" [Primal Heart]. The Omkar [divine resonance], which is also in the body – that too is attained through the teachings of guru. Pavan rises from Shabda [divine sound; divine resonance] – meaning: the Still vayu comes about from the Omkar Resonance – meaning: [Still] pavan. Breath emerges from that pavan, and breath merges back into that Still pavan – meaning: [Still] pavan's or Still vayu's mother is Brahman, from Which it emerges, and pavan becomes Brahman and merges back in Brahman – meaning: the par avastha of Kriya.

Shabda [divine Sound], which is the Void – when the restless mind becomes Still from all sides and abides in the Void – at that time the Sound of the Omkar Resonance is heard, and all of the sounds from the external world merge into the Void, sound against the organ of the ear and all sounds can be heard. Therefore, all sounds that you hear are all the Void. Therefore, the "Mahayana" [Great Void] is Brahman, and Shabda is Itself Brahman in this way. That Shabda is in the "anahata" [anahata chakra; heart center], the place from where ten types of Sound appear, without any effort on one's part. Such as: drum, flute, lute are the first sounds that are perceived, after that, bells and thunder, the blowing in conch shells, cymbals, gong, "daf" [big frame drum] and the lion's roar – these are the ten types of Sound. These reside in the anahata. Everyone and everything is bound by ordinary sounds. Thus these ten kinds of sounds are "proper" [right ones for spiritual attainment]. The Unstuck Sound comes about from the performance of Kriya, hearing which, a person becomes filled with wonderment, and the possibility of becoming disengaged from maya [the illusory phenomena] becomes a reality. The sad thing is this: if the practice of the Kriya of Self is not done, one falls below – meaning: one's intelligence and direction goes towards the lower. When Shabda is not in anahata, then It remains ever locked above. Because of being locked above, one hears from far distances in the universe. That hearing comes about automatically, without any effort. The "jiva" [vital-life] of this Shabda is prana [vital force], because without prana, nothing at all can be heard. Shabda emerges from prana, and merges back into prana itself – meaning: it merges into Brahman in the par avastha of Kriya. This prana is the Still-vayu Brahman Itself as the Brahman-Atom. Its outer manifestation is in the Form of Light. By Light, all things in a dark room are seen, and when there is Revelatory Light within that Atom, Omnipresence, Omniscience and Omnipotence happens, and the eight siddhis [perfections; or: supernatural powers as described in the Yoga Sutras of Patanjali] come about automatically. This prana is the energy in the Still vayu. When the time of death comes, whatever the state of mind is at that time is the state that is attained. This Prana-Fire incinerates all karmas via Kriya in the par avastha of Kriya.

Now, what is prana? Prana in prana [life into life] is Nirvana [Final Release]. Via Omkar Kriya, prana is settled in the Fearless Niranjan. If one resides in Kutastha Brahman, no fear at all remains any longer. Everyone has a great fear of death. But Brahman has no death. Thus, by merging in Brahman, one is liberated even while alive in the body – meaning: "jivanmukta" [liberated while living in the body]. Automatically, there is fearlessness. Niranjan is the holder, and prana resides in Niranjan. If there is no Niranjan, prana resides in Avinashi Brahman [Eternal Indestructible Brahman]. The jiva of Avinashi resides in Brahman. Brahman emerges from Brahman and merges in Brahman, in the way that water merges in water – meaning: the par avastha of Kriya, Brahman Itself.

What is Brahman? Brahman is verily the Mercy towards jiva [person]. Here "mercy" means the endowing of Kriya, from which there is beneficence for prana [life] – meaning: the Still vayu (sarvabhuta hite ratah [[one becomes] favorably disposed to beneficence towards all]). The residence of

Brahman is in the universe – meaning: it feels as if the head is heavy. If there is no universe, It stays in Itself – meaning: It stays in Its Own Self, the Supreme Person. The jiva [vital-life] of Brahman is "Hansa" [Soul; Spirit; the mystic mirror of "Soham" [meaning: I Am That], because if there is no Hansa, where can Brahman be? Hansa emerges from Hansa – meaning: the son emerges from the father. And merging is in Hansa – meaning: when that son bears a son, the [first] son then becomes the father. Thus the jiva in Brahman is Hansa. The emergence of Hansa is from Hansa, and Hansa merges back in Hansa. Hansa merges in dhyan [meditation], and dhyan merges in Omkar – meaning: at that time in the body, this whole body becomes Brahman in the par avastha of Kriya.

Hansa is Itself Brahman and Brahman is verily Avinashi. "Hansa" – meaning: the Void that is within the Void – of course, it is He Who is verily Brahman. And of course, there is no "nash" [ending/destruction] of Brahman. "Nash" is associated with things. When there is nothing in existence other than Brahman, then how can there be different and separated things? If there is [only] One, then there is the Eternal Avinashi Hansa – meaning: Brahman, Who is that Hansa, is in the Bindu [mystic spot] in the "gagan" [inner sky]. And if there is no gagan, Avinashi resides in Hansa. What is the jiva [vital-life] of Hansa? The jiva of Avinashi is the Void, because within the Void is Brahman. If there is no Void, then how can Avinashi Brahman reside in the Void? Thus the jiva of Avinashi is the Void. And the jiva of the Void is Anupa Brahman – meaning: it is the par avastha of Kriya. The jiva of Anupa Brahman is kal [time; death], because everything happens in kal [time]. The emergence of Hansa is from the Void, and the merging back happens in the body, which is Omkar's form – meaning: in the par avastha of Kriya, even the Void does not exist.

What is kal? Kal is that one who presides in the lotus. When there is no lotus, he lives in the Void. The jiva [vital-life] of kal is jiva [alive individual being]. Kal emerges from this body which is Omkar's form, and the merging of kal is in kal itself. The kal of all kals is "mahakal" [great time] Brahman Supreme Space Supreme Sky Consciousness Sky Itself in the par avastha of Kriya.

That Void Great Sky – where is His place of residence? It is in Anupa Brahman. When there is no Anupa, It resides in the body which is Omkar's form. The jiva [vital-life] of the Void is Anupa Brahman, which is the par avastha of Kriya. This Void emerges from kal and merges in the jiva [alive being] – meaning: in the par avastha of Kriya, the Void actually merges in the jiva [person] him/herself.

Jiva [individual consciousness] is in pavan – meaning: the Still vayu. If there is no pavan, it is in Kutastha Brahman Shiva. And the jiva [vital-life] of jiva [individual consciousness] is Shiva [Universal Consciousness]. And the emergence of jiva [individual consciousness] is from Shiva – meaning: it has come about from Kutastha, and Shiva merges in Brahman – meaning: in the par avastha of Kriya, the jiva [individual consciousness/person] merges in Brahman. If is of course "done" – when Shiva merges in Brahman – meaning: the par avastha of Kriya. That Shiva is in the head in the form of the moon. When there is no moon, He is in Kutastha Niranjan [Effulgent]. The jiva [vital-life] of Niranjan is Niranjan. The emergence of Shiva is from Niranjan and His merging back is in Niranjan.

Where does Niranjan reside? He resides within sushumna [the center nadi among the three principal nadis in the spine]. If there is no sushumna, Niranjan resides in Kutastha. The jiva [vital-life] of Niranjan is the One Brahman. The emergence of

Niranjan is from "anila" [wind] (the Still vayu), the merging back is in the Form of the Self, and the Self [merges] in the Self – meaning: in the par avastha of Kriya.

Amongst all of the 11 [divine aspects] written above, it is Hansa Who is the "madhyavarti" [central; that which connects the others] Narayan [Personal Lord] Supreme Space Itself. In the gagan [mystic sky], Avinashi is in Avinashi. It is He who is the essence in the jiva [alive beings] and is holding the world [alternate translation: manifesting as the world]. In the form of the Great Void/Space, He pervades the world/universe. There is no possible way of comparing Him with anything, because it is He Who is manifesting as everything. For this reason one of His names is "Sarveshvar" [God of all]. From the Void, He does everything in kal [time]. And the Resonance of gagan merges in Omkar, the Resonance which is going on all the time. It can be heard simply by being attentive [or: simply concentrating].

Because of this Hansa being central, these: mind, pavan, Shabda, prana, Brahman – these five, and kal, the Void, jiva [individual consciousness], Shiva, Niranjan – these five – altogether these ten - are there.

When "Hansa" (Still vayu) takes on restlessness, His name becomes "mind." When mind enters into the Still vayu, in the transitional space, [Hansa] takes on the name of "pavan." When pavan takes recourse in the Void, or [in other words] it enters the Void, [Hansa] takes on the name of "Shabda." Here, Shabda is the Omkar Resonance – that Resounding Omkar Sound, whose Stillness is verily Nirvana Itself – upon entering that, [Hansa] takes on the name of "prana" [life and life-force]. Prana takes mercy on oneself and enters Brahman, and [Hansa] takes on the name of "Brahman." That firstly mentioned Hansa is Itself Avinashi Brahman. That Avinashi is Itself kal, the Void, jiva [individual consciousness], Shiva, Niranjan.

In this body there are: mind, pavan, Shabda, prana, Brahman, Hansa, kal, the Void, jiva [individual consciousness], Shiva, Niranjan and such, whose residing places are: heart, navel, anahata [anahata chakra; heart center], Niranjan, Brahmanda [universe], gagan, lotus, Anupa, pavan, moon, sushumna. If the appropriate residing places are not there, then they are in: Anupa, Niranjan, above, Avinashi, Self, Avinashi, Self, the Void, Omkar, Shiva, Niranjan, in steps.

The vital aspect without which another aspect cannot remain – that aspect is called "jiva" [vital-life]. Such as: the "jiva" of mind is pavan – meaning: without pavan, there cannot be mind. And pavan – meaning: the Still vayu – its jiva is samnyas [abidance with] – meaning: without samnyas, vayu does not remain Still. And the jiva of samnyas is Shabda – meaning: if one does not listen to the Omkar Sound, samnyas does not continuously stay. Thus, if there is no prana, the Omkar Sound cannot be heard. Thus, it is prana that is the speech of the Shabda in jiva. And without Brahman, there is no prana. Therefore, the jiva of prana is Brahman. Without Hansa Great Void there is no Brahman. Therefore, the jiva of Brahman is Hansa. Without Avinashi, where is Hansa – meaning: without the par avastha of Kriya where is the Supreme Space? Therefore, the jiva of Hansa is Avinashi. Where is Avinashi without the Great Void? Therefore, the jiva of Avinashi is the Great Void. "Anupa" – meaning: the One Brahman Who has no comparison or resemblance – without that, where is the Great Void? Therefore, the jiva of the Great Void is Anupa Brahman. Without kal, where is Anupa Brahman? Therefore, the jiva of Anupa is kal. And where is kal without the jiva [individual consciousness]? Therefore, the jiva [vital-life] of kal is jiva [individual consciousness]. And without Anupa Brahman, where is the Void? Therefore, the jiva [vital-life] of the Void is Anupa.

As is jiva [individual consciousness], so is Shiva. Without Shiva, where is jiva? Therefore the jiva [vital-life] of jiva [individual consciousness] is Shiva. And without Niranjan, where is Shiva? Therefore, the jiva [vital-life] of Shiva is Niranjan Kutastha. Without the One Brahman, where is Niranjan? Therefore, the jiva of the One Brahman is Niranjan – meaning: the jiva [being] in the par avastha of Kriya is Kutastha Itself, because it there that there is samadhi in the intoxication.

Everyone says, "mind, mind." But most people do not actually know about the emergence of mind [from where and what, and how]. This mind emerges from breath, and its merges itself in pavan – meaning: the Still vayu – meaning: the merging is in the Still vayu Brahman in the par avastha of Kriya. Pavan – meaning: the Still vayu – comes from Omkar. And breath comes from pavan. Pavan – meaning: the Still vayu – dissolves into the Omkar Sound. And the Omkar Sound comes from prana and merges with prana. And prana comes from Brahman and merges with Brahman. And Brahman is from Hansa and merges with Hansa. And Hansa merges in dhyan [meditation]. And dhyan merges in Omkar. And Hansa is from the Void, and the Void merges with Omkar. Kal is from Omkar and merges in kal. And the void is from kal and merges in jiva. And jiva is from Shiva and merges with Shiva. And Shiva is from Niranjan and the merging is in Niranjan. And Niranjan Kutastha is from anila, and anila merges in the Form of the Self. And the Self [merges] in the Self.

EMERGENCE	MERGING
Mind from breath	In pavan
Pavan from Shabda	In Shabda
Breath is from pavan	
Shabda is from prana	In prana
Prana is from Brahman	In Brahman
Brahman is from Hansa	In Hansa, dhyan, Omkar
Hansa is from the Void	In Omkar
Kal is from Omkar	In kal
The Void is from kal	In the jiva [individual consciousness]
The jiva is from Shiva	In Shiva
Shiva is from Niranjan	In Niranjan
Niranjan is from anila	In the Form of the Self
	And the Self in the Self

One by one everything is cut away. What remains is: mind, pavan, Shabda, prana, Brahman, Hansa, dhyan, Omkar, kal, Shiva, Niranjan, [being] in the Form of the Self, the Self in the Self.

Mind is within the in-breath and out-breath. By doing pranayam and such Kriya, one should merge it into pavan – meaning: the Still vayu. Immediately after vayu is Still, if attention is given to that Stillness, One Omkar Sound in short, long and flooding waves is heard. Therefore, mind is from this breath itself, and pavan is from the breath as well. And the Sound of that Omkar Resonance is from prana. Therefore, upon the continuous performance of the Kriya of prana –

meaning: by continuously remaining locked, one merges in Brahman. And Brahman merges in Hansa Supreme Space. In dhyan – meaning: upon performing 1728 pranayams – there is merging in this body, which is the form of Omkar. Continuing to abide in time [kal], one stays [in oneness] at all times – meaning: there is merging in kal [time]. By merging in kal, there is Shiva – meaning: upon continuous abidance in Niranjan Kutastha, there is merging in the Form of One's Self. And One's Self remains in the Self – meaning: the experience of "Sohang Brahman" [I Am That Brahman] is realized. This experience of the True Form of Oneself is that which is described in the shastras [scriptures]. The Self knowing the Self is called "jnana" [divine knowledge]. It is in This that there is liberation.

CHARAK

Yogiraj Sri Sri Shyama Charan Lahiri Mahasaya

English translation by Yoga Niketan

Charak

Contents

CHARAK

(Translated from the original 1891
Bengali version which was)

Published by
Panchanon Bhattacharya,
a disciple following the guru-disciple
lineage of Sri Sri Gurudeva
[Sri Shyamacharan Lahiri Mahasaya]
and with His blessings

Calcutta
No. 11 Baburam Ghosh Lane
The year 1297 [Bengali Calendar] (1891 C.E.)

FOREWORD*

[*Translator's note: "Announcement" in Bengali]

[Translator's note: The term "prana" is usually written in lower case when it refers to vital airs. However, when the term refers to Life – the source of the vital airs, the word is then capitalized - "Prana." This "Prana" in Hindu terminology can also mean God, The Divine Mother, or the Supreme Deity. In this case, "Prana" can also be addressed with personal pronouns (as will be seen in the text). The author of the "Foreword" uses the different meanings of "prana" interchangeably and with interwoven meanings. For the sake of simplicity, we have chosen to use the capitalized form - "Prana" - containing all of the meanings aforementioned, with the exception of some instances which are obvious to the reader.]

[Translator's note: Throughout the entire book, any statement in parentheses - "( )" is in the original text, including the parentheses themselves. Any terms or phrases in brackets - "[ ]" - is from the translator, provided for the purposes of clarification for the reader.]

Brahman is Infinite and His Forms are also Infinite, and the attributes of the Forms are Infinite as well. As soon as one tries to describe the Infinite, finiteness comes into being. But those attributes do not have any end. For this reason, the attributes of substances [also] have no end - that which yogis have not been able to limit. Thus it is useless to talk about such things. Whatever God is making one speak – we are speaking that only. Speaking happens through Prana – this Prana-vayu. He resides in the heart. We are bowing to Him by His Power Itself – meaning: by Omkar Kriya. By whose controlling force everything is – meaning: if there is no Prana, then nothing remains, and the desires that come about via Prana are causing the actions that happen – all things and all actions (external and internal) are existing under the controlling force of that Prana. Externally – like this: a desire to obtain an ink-pot came about; via that very Prana, one took that ink-pot and put it near oneself; and as soon as the desire to write appeared, one went on to write via that very same Prana. That very Prana is the doer of all that was mentioned. Internally – it is because that Prana is there that all internal experiences are felt and known. Therefore, Prana is the Lord [or: Doer] of All in All. One should serve the Lord. For this reason, it is absolutely necessary to perform Kriya. And all phenomena that exist – the God of all is Prana. So what is there to serve this God-Prana by – meaning: other than Prana Itself, what else can be used to serve It? So that that Prana expands, it is absolutely necessary to do that [which expands Prana]. Expanding that is called "Pranayam." That Pranayam which is the direction followed by all intelligent beings and which is the thing of significance all of the scriptures. That is only the performing of Kriya and nothing else – that Kriya by which this body attains health. Thus, the performance of "sandhya"* [worship in a particular time] in the form of Kriya must be done every day. And everything is founded in Prana. And its container is this body. If that [the body] remains in a regular state, and stays in good condition through the practice of Kriya, then everyone is respectfully urged to perform Kriya with faith in the teachings of Guru. It is that which is the great and infallible medicine – meaning: abiding in the par avastha of Kriya after the performance of Kriya. Writing just this statement is actually having written everything that can be said. If this is just said as talk only – if one is just saying that becoming One is why one must practice Kriya – this is not the doing of Kriya.

*[*Translator's note: "Sandhya" - literally "dusk," or "transitional periods of the day and night. These are times of worship. The worshiping itself is also known as "performing sandhya."]*

Making everything One is what is called "shastra" [scripture], and all worship there is must be first preceded by Pranayam – meaning: should be performed in the par avastha of Kriya. One Essence, which is the Essence of all the essences, yet there is no essence in that Place – this is experienced by nearly all Kriyavans in the par avastha of Kriya. In the intoxication after that, Bliss Itself is known. But there is nothing at all there. For this reason, That is called "Asat"* in Vedanta.

*[*Translator's note: The usual meaning of "asat" is "non-truth," but in this case it means "void of existence and non-existence."]*

And everything is happening via Him alone, via His entering His Atom. It is He only – meaning Kutastha – by That He has become "Sat" [Existence]. From that Sat, the Prana-endowed creatures have come into being. It is He again Who is the Atom itself, the Atom that is the Atom of Brahman – He has become the infinitesimally subtler Particle within the subtlest particle. For this reason, if mind is concentrated on some external atom/particle, the experience of That Atom becomes known. If one says, "Why doesn't everyone see It?" Because of the lack of teaching from a qualified preceptor, and because of being entranced by the raja and tama gunas, one is not able to experience any of the supernatural/spiritual and wondrous Essence. Without internal experience (which does not happen without Kriya), the use of medicine and such is like throwing stones in the dark and not much more. It is making one type of effort [to cure]. But the effort that brings relief to all types of ailments (external and internal) – that Kriya of Omkar is of this Prana Itself – it is one's duty to perform this (meaning: inviting the Mind in via the mind). Without knowing that, one cannot know the past, present or future states of the illness. But if one performs Kriya all the time, suddenly that is known. If medicine and such are applied after that, it is possible that the illness will get better. Illness and death come about from the distortion of that Prana-vayu only. Therefore, practice steadiness/peacefulness, kindliness and eat proper food. It is He who is "Asat" [with no existence or non-existence] – the One Who is the Prana [Life] of prana [vital airs] – Who has no visible effulgence, and at the same time, Whose Light is revealed momentarily via the Power of Kutastha – the One Who is fire, water, food which is Brahman, Who is Gayatri [Divine Mother] – Whose Light/Revelation is within and without – if it is not revealed within, how can the appropriate medicine be ascertained? But by trying ten [solutions] one somehow hits – that's about all. Rain happens due to vayu and sound of crickets also happens due to vayu. The effective medicines and such – for internal and external uses – are all known. "Medicine" [is that which] destroys afflictions. "Vishashya vishamaushadam" ["poison kills poison" or "that which kills poison is 'medicine'"]. Whatever is the reverse of afflictions – internally and externally – that is "medicine." Without inner observation, one cannot know the attributes of all substances. It does not happen without doing inward directed Kriya. Therefore one must do Kriya. It is that Prana Itself which is "rita" - meaning Truth. Other than Prana-Kriya, all else is false, because not abiding in Truth means "false." This is what the sages say. And all of the talking that happens is from Prana only. It is important to practice beneficent and amiable speech. Thus, Self-Kriya is the ideal of all scriptures. It is one's duty to do that. Performing that, keeping mind on God, one should prescribe/apply medicine. Contemplating God is also the work of Prana. Death is of Prana only. So that that death does not happen – for this reason – Kriyavans – meaning "devatas" [deities] – worship that Prana Itself. Because of abiding in sattva guna [primal pure attribute], they become truthful and attain the Supreme Plane [or: have superior people around them]. Through the experience of this very Prana, the Great Form can be seen. And the one who is making that "seeing" happen is that Prana Itself. Thus, everyone is actually worshiping Prana only, some consciously and some unconsciously. Via this Prana are the sun and moon seen, and desire is of Prana Itself. All meridians are being exerting "prana" [vital airs] through and in Prana. There is only the difference in names and positions. Within "prana" and "apana" [ingoing and outgoing vital airs] is the Being. That Prana is the one who is coming and going. It is She who is called "Matarishvari" [Mother Goddess]. Everything is existing because of this Prana-vayu and everything is also founded/established in Prana. Thus, that Prana is residing in this body. One must do that which can save and sustain this body. So, we have extracted from Charak [the original full treatise] all of the methods which apply to the saving of the breath, and are disseminating this wisdom via the help of certain Kriyavans. To do good works in secret is even more virtuous. We are not disclosing the name of this noble person. His intention is beneficent. Women should know about the womb, and men should know about their particular parts of the body, and both should know about the other's physicality. It is extremely important to know the behavior of the menses [or: have knowledge of the menstrual process] for the sake of taking care of the body. To regulate the natural currents/urges in the body, one needs to know about that as well, in order to destroy afflictions. The subject material written here is from the essence of Prapathak 23, 11th Kanda, Mantra 3 of the First Anuvad of the Atharva Veda.

The Publisher

Sri Panchanon Bhattacharya

OM

CHARAK

[Translator's note: Throughout the work the word "Purush" [Person; Being] has been interchangeably translated as "Being" and "Person" [note the capitalization], depending on the quality of the Purush [Self as Person] expressed in particular passages.

Those who do not partake in austerities, fasting, the studying of scriptures, continence, observance of righteous vows and such things are subject to having intense afflictions [physical and mental] rise upon them – meaning: those who perform Kriya practically do not have illnesses. But it must be done according to injunctions.

"Dharma" [spirituality or righteous living], "artha" [material life], "kama" [sensual life] and "Moksha" [spiritual Liberation] have health as their root. But disease destroys all health [or: ease], and even destroys freedom and living itself. Thus, if Kriyavans practice Kriya properly and according to the teachings of Guru, the immunity-endowed Supreme Life-Force expands in their bodies, and eventually they attain Liberation. Therefore one must always follow the directives of Guru in order to preserve the health of the body. Those who have taken up the particularly the Kriya of sat [sattwa] guna instead of following raja and tama guna, and have become free via Kriya, and those who have the unobstructed knowledge of the past, present and future – because they have attained

Brahman and have attained Supreme Intelligence upon having mastered the "Chatushtaya Sadhana"* [fourfold practice of Jnana Yoga], including the practices of "sama" [equanimity in all circumstances], "dama" [self-control] and such – thus their wisdom is beyond the rajas and tamas gunas and is therefore proof positive. But among proofs, foremost is the proof of direct experience. Its sign is this: the Self enters into phenomena taking the senses and mind along. At that time, the knowingness/wisdom that becomes revealed is called "pratyaksha" [direct wisdom] – meaning: by subduing the mind via Self-Kriya, Kriyavans experience directly the Supreme Stillness in the paravastha of Kriya [post-Kriya state]. What is there that is more direct an experience than this! By remaining enjoined in that par avastha of Kriya, Liberation happens, because feelingful attachment to all things is detached via Kriya itself. The vital-air [vayu] is God Itself. So that the vital-air does not become corrupted, one should drink a solution of ghee and warm water. By drinking this, prana [life] is extended and the Self/self is saved [from premature death]. All afflictions arise from the Self/self. Therefore taking care of the body and Self/self is absolutely necessary.

[*Translator's note: "Chatushtaya Sadhana" is a fourfold practice in Jnana Yoga consisting of: "Viveka" [spiritual discrimination]; "Vairagya" [detachment]; "Shat-sampad" [six virtues, two of are the above-mentioned "sama" and "dama"]; and "Mumukshutva" [longing for God or Liberation].]

One should stop living recklessly and save one's life [or: life-force]. "Saahas" [literally "courage"; but in this case "recklessness"] - because life itself is the "person." That "person" is the same one who experiences the beneficent [or maleficent] fruits of one's own actions. Perform Kriya and do not put mind in other directions. Renounce all except the Self. Always take care of the body, because if the body is not there,

there is no place for the Self. And if the Self is not there, absolutely nothing is there. "Buddhimaan" [intelligent person] – meaning: one who abides in the par avastha of Kriya – many kinds of painful aliments can come about for him from indigestion and wrong eating. "Hitaashee" [benevolent person] – meaning: that by which wealth and lifespan increases – and that by which, for the sake of beneficence, wealth and lifespan increases – do that. And "mitaashee" [follower of moderation] – meaning: one who eats a moderate amount and one who eats at the right time – meaning: take your meals at regular times and become victorious over the senses.

The lifespan is affected by both "daiva" [extra-rational or unseen] and "purushkaar" [personal or evident] causes. These extra-rational and personal causes are of higher and lower types [or: better and inferior types]. The karma [in this case: "fruit of action"] that is the result of one's own actions in a previous life is called "daiva" [of "supernatural" causes]. The karma [in this case: "action"] that can be done in the present time is called "purushkaar" [doable by the person]. Therefore, in order to be free of the afflictions caused by both unseen and evident [daiva and purushkaar] causes, Kriyavans must be continuously and fully immersed in the practice of Kriya according to the instructions of Guru. This is substantiated in the [Bhagavad] Gita: "yathaidhaangsi samito'gnirbhaasmasaat kurutarjuna; jnaanaagnih sarvakarmaani bhasmasaat kurute tathaa" - "It is just as the blazing fire burns the lit wood into ashes, O Arjuna! In the same way, the Fire of Divine Knowledge destroys the ignorance known as 'karma'." The "Being" within the "daiva" and "purushkaar" [acts and results] is not associated with anything at all. What that Being Is, and all of the forms that arise from that Being – that is being expounded in a progressive manner presently.

1) How many kinds of mutations come about in the Being

when there is mutation in the [material] substance. 2) How does the Being become the cause. 3) From where does the Being arise. 4) Is the Being all-knowing or is It not all-knowing? 5) Is the Being Eternal or temporal? 6) What is Prakriti [creation and energy of creation] and how many permutations of [Prakriti] are there? 7) What are the signs of the Being? [It is said] that the Being is non-doing and independent, and that the Being is the controller, all-knowing, omnipresent, self-knowing and the knower of the field [existence] and the witness [is also] said. If the Being is "non-doing" then how is it possible that It knows God through Kriya [literal definition of "kriya" - an act]? And if you say that [the Being] is independent – meaning: abiding in Its own power and that It is God Itself – then how is it that the Being takes birth in a worldly womb? If the Being is the controller, then how is it that living beings' minds become forcefully enslaved to other directions? If the Being is all-knowing, then why does the Being not know the pains of others? If It is omnipresent – meaning all-pervading – then why can the self not see beyond when there is a mountain or wall in the way? "Knower of the field" - but the conflict is this: is the field there first, or is the knower of the field there first? Where is the self without the body? If the body is first, then the Self is temporal. And if It is the witness, then there is no other Lord other than him. Then who or what is It to be a witness of? These seven questions – such as non-doing etc. - are there.

1) The Self is immutable, then how can It become the pain-enjoined self? 2) Past, future and present – in which of these can [medical or healing] treatment for that self be administered? If treatment is applied for the future – well, that future has not happened yet. If treatment is administered for the past, then in that case it is "anagama" - meaning: that which is gone, that certainly does not come back. If treatment

is administered in the present – in that case it cannot be complete – meaning: the signs of illness are appearing gradually – meaning: in transition. All these conflicts are present. What is the cause of pain – meaning disease? And what is its recourse? Meaning: from what is it arising? Why does all disease go away and become extinguished?

Answer: 1) Know that the Being is enjoined behind these six: the five elements and mind. And the one Awareness Substance is also the Being – meaning the Supreme Person.

Again and again, via mutation in substance, the twenty-four-aspect-enjoined Person – i.e: mind and the ten senses [of perception and action], the five experiences – meaning: sound, touch, sight, taste and smell, and the eight substances of the form of Prakriti [creative energy/creation] – enjoined to these is the Person. Lack and fulfillment – these too are experiences in the mind. How do these happen? When the senses of the self and the experiences of the senses occur then there is arising [of appearance]. With that, because of special focus, mind becomes aware of something. This means: when mind enters into matter – meaning things – the things also enter the mind – meaning: for some time the thing remains reflected, and mind ascertains with surety as real. Partitioning atomically [absolutely minutely] and uniting [making one] are two qualities of the mind. And thinking, discrimination, swoon, contemplation and determination [goal-oriented-ness] are also qualities of the mind. Anything other that these that is known by the mind – know that as "vishaya" [matter; world; concerns; subjects; "samsara"]. This means: mind is able to enter the subtle, and the nature of the Person is oneness and immutable perception – meaning: contemplating the physical and the subtle, and discriminating between and within them. "Muhya" [swoon] – one is entranced in that itself – meaning: becoming entranced by seeing and being entranced in the par avastha of Kriya [the post-Kriya state]. "Dhyeya" [contemplative] – meaning: meditating on material subjects and meditating in the Subtle Brahman. "Samkalpa" [determination; goal-oriented-ness] – meaning: performing acts such as Kriya with the purpose of attaining Brahman and praying for physical things.

The acts of the mind are expedited by all of the senses – meaning: abiding in all [phenomenal] things in every way. And after such senses are restrained and after the process of good and bad according to acts of previous lives are analyzed, "param buddhi" [Supreme Intelligence] – meaning: "para buddhi" [Intelligence beyond mind] (the par avastha of Kriya) – arises. The senses present with the mind – via them, all sense-experiences – hearing, seeing, touching, smelling [and] tasting – are had – meaning: when Kriyavans are not in the actual practice of Kriya and are partaking in the matters of the world such as spouse/family, song, playing music and such, but still in that state [the state of the par avastha of Kriya] – all good and bad qualities of all that is happening is continuously known by the mind – meaning: Kriyavans sit on top of the path of Kriya and go on knowing the good and bad [of that which goes on]. Within such happenings of the world going on [and being in the spiritual state], the self-certain intelligence advises with certainty and one is secure in taking action – meaning: upon contemplating matters of concern to the heart and mind [chitta] – meaning: upon contemplating matters upon which to act – the certainty of knowing/Intelligence that comes about – by that Intelligence [the Kriyavan] goes about doing all works in the world.

Having become connected with the five elements and one [or more] sense[s], there is the experiencing of the five actions – from which knowingness comes about – meaning the experience of samsaric [sensory] phenomena of sound, touch, sight, taste, smell – the one who experiences this is mind. The five organs of action: hands, feet, anus, tongue, sex organ – the act of movement is through the feet; the two hands are for taking/receiving and holding, and the anus and sex organs are for expulsion – meaning: for the expulsion of excrement and urine [and reproduction], and the tongue is the organ of speech – for truth, light, "tama" and nectarous speech – know this. This means: words of Truth – meaning: about Brahman – the Light from the teachings of Guru – and "tama" - [being without] the divine sight had by Kriyavans in Kutastha – meaning: falseness – one is not doing Kriya and is staying [the consciousness is staying] in the matters of samsara. space, air, fire, water, earth – these are the five primal elements. Their qualities are sound, touch, sight, taste and smell [respectively].

All qualities before the quality of smell expand by a multiple of ten. This means: the quality of the subtle substance as come forth from the Atom/Particle of Brahman. Following this – the Atom/Particle of Brahman is one [1], 10 in space, 100 in air, 1,000 in fire, 10,000 in water and 100,000 in earth. In this way, with the qualities expanding by multiples of 10 – starting from the beginning – the world is created.

The quality of earth is hardness – meaning: that by which the tenderness of the body ends; the quality of water is the taste of food; the quality of air is motion, and the quality of fire is heat; the quality of space is sound. In time all of these signs have been shown – meaning: these are all "pariksheeta" [tested/proved].

The signs/indications mentioned are all perceivable by the sense of touch, and those touchable things that are dangerous can also be known by the sense of touch.

Qualities, elements, substances and such – the qualities of the body have all been pointed out. And their signs have also been spoken about. The matter of knowing the perceivable qualities of phenomenal existence has come about – qualities such as sound.

The intelligence that rises from the animal-species taking recourse in the senses which they use – by those very senses is that type of intelligence attained. And mental intelligence arises via the mind. Hearing by sound; touching is known by the sense of touch; vision is via sight; taste via the liquid/taste sense; smell from scent – taking recourse in all such senses brings about the type of knowledge associated with these senses. And mind is the super-sense and the cause. Its qualities are separate from the five senses of perception. Thus the intelligence that is of the mind can be called the "intelligence of the qualities of 'that' [mind]."

Because of the different types of acts by the senses towards the objects of the senses, many types of understandings come about. Because of the Self/self contacting the senses, mind and their forms, different understandings [or intelligences] come about one by one. And like when the striking of nails on the [strings of] the veena [stringed lute] create different kinds of sounds with different strikes on different tones – in a similar way, the adjoined intellect – meaning: the senses, self [ego], mind and the functions of the senses (sound, touch, sight, taste, smell) and the functions of the mind – because of two or more of these uniting with each other [in different ways], different types of perceptive understandings [intelligences] arise.

Intellect, senses, mind and their objects/functions – know that the One Who is greater than these is the yoga-endowed Brahman [or: Unity Brahman]. Know that it is He Himself who is the 24-aspect-enjoined Person. This is the answer to the first question.

2) The Person that is enjoined with raja and tama [gunas] has endless bindings happen. And upon releasing oneself from raja and tama [gunas], sattva-intelligence comes to being. With this intelligence, the awareness of the results of actions and wisdom are present. And within this are the natural aspects of life – delusion, pleasure, pain, living and dying are there – meaning: all of these reside in the sushumna itself.

One who perceives through this type of knowledge is the one who can know dissolution and emergence. And the necessary treatments and whatever else he wishes to know he can know as well – meaning: he becomes omniscient. If the Being is not there, then – light, darkness, truth, false, Vedas – no beneficent or maleficent acts take place. The Doer and whatever the Doer is coming to know – all these also do not happen – meaning: the Being is the root of all.

If the Being is not there then Supreme Knowledge – meaning the par avastha of Kriya – does not happen. Body, pleasure, affliction, movement, inertia, speech, scripture, birth, death, bondage, liberation – all of these do not happen. Thus, the one who is causing it is the Cause which is the Being. This is what the knowers of Brahman have said.

If the Self is not the Cause, then the Earth and all such things are causeless, and there is no possibility of sentience in living creatures. And there is no necessity for Earth and such, just as without the potter, a pot does not come about from earth, stick and wheel; and without a house-builder, a house does not come about by the acts of earth, straw and wood. One who speaks/thinks like this says the body has come about because of "cause." One who says that things are emerging because of an insentient cause and without a doer is someone who is devoid of reason – meaning: that which the shastras [in this case, Indian scriptures - specifically] state as "reason," and is "agam" [cannot access] – meaning he is without the wisdom of the shastras - such as the Vedas etc. – and devoid of reason. All analysis can prove that the Being is the Cause. This is experienced directly.

Some sages say that there is one Primal Person from whom humans have come displaying a similar form [as the progenitor], and then some other sages say that humans come about from the form that it is connected with previously – meaning: humans from humans, horses from horses etc. They make statements such as these. Those who believe in this way – that [living beings] come about from previous forms – they believe that humans and other species are without Soul/Self or God. (This is not good deduction.) Their reason is that the person is neither the doer nor the experiencer of the deed, and according to their opinion, the results of deeds done visibly by other humans are experienced by other humans. Those who believe in the Godless self say this. What is said by them is impossible, because the One Who is the Being is the Doer and it is He Who is the experiencer – just as: the actions of senses such as eyes and ears can be observed – these acts are emerging from One Being – sight via the eyes, hearing via the ears, taste via the tongue and such multitudinous things can be observed. But at the root of all is the Being. He takes the form of whichever form to which He attaches Himself, and acts according to that form. But regardless of whatever type of form doing whatever type of acts, the root of it is "Ishwara" [God in action]. Thus, whatever form is taken by humans, the Primal Root is that Being. One can see the differences in all of the acts taking place but the Doer is only that One Doer. The reason that doing comes about from the "functions" – meaning: by the union of the senses and the Doer, it is He Who is the Cause of all actions – meaning: upon connecting with senses such as the eyes and ears, [the Person] becomes aware of sight, sound and such. He is One Substance. It is only because of the difference in forms and places, [and] being connected to such, that different types of experiences are had.

For living creatures, at the time of death, death comes quicker than the blink of an eye. And if those who die are reborn, they do not get a different doer. The knowers of Brahman have stood by this. For this reason it is He Who is the Cause. It is He Who becomes aware as the Eternal Being at the time of experiencing the fruits of actions of living creatures.

The results of ego-based actions from past lives and the good and bad acts are remembered – in memory and movement – from one body to the next body – meaning: the results of good and bad acts of a previous life are accordingly experienced in another life.

Although the Beginning-less Paramatman [Supreme Self] does not actually emerge [or disappear], yet delusion, desire, repulsion [and such] do. The Person becomes aware of "raashis" [aspects; the previously mentioned 24-aspects]. Because of that aspect-aware and self-aware Person being yoked to all the functions (all the sense organs), perception [of the world] comes about. But because of the impure nature of those functions, or because of not connecting, perception does not come about. That which is seen or known – just as one can see a beautiful face clearly on a clean mirror, but if [the mirror] is dirty, it is not like that [one cannot see the face clearly], know that it is the same for the chitta [personal consciousness, or the knowing faculty].

The organs of the senses and the organs of action, mind and intellect – all of these act because of enjoining with the Operator of the functions and the knowledge of suffering comes about.

That One Who is the Self does not make anything come about. He experiences the results of essences of phenomena. All things come about through "samyoga" [intercourse or conjugation - in the broad meanings of the words]. Without contact/conjugation no substance can manifest. Another substance cannot come about just from a substance, and That Which has no cause (meaning Brahman), even That does not manifest. One's nature goes away very quickly, thus substance (meaning Brahman) does not change. The One Who is Beginning-less is the Eternal Person. The opposite of It is the "caused" (meaning non-eternal person). [The Eternal Person] is Truth. In the present, He is as "form." He is known as Eternal. There is no other cause – meaning: [there is no] manifestation of substances like the body and such.

It is the Beginning-less Person that is Eternal – and He is known through the "bhava" [inner experience]- causality. By bhava-causality (meaning "dharma" [spirituality]) He cannot be known because in order to know, there is "two." The emergence [of anything] can be known by the Causality ("Causality" meaning Brahman).   Know Him as that Beginning-less, "Avyakta" [Inexpressible-Intangible] and the Unimaginable [One] in the bhava-causality – meaning dharma-causality. Everything else is "vyakta" [tangible-expressible] – meaning: that which can be had by the senses and such is/are that Person as vyakta. And that which cannot be known by the senses and such is the Unimaginable, Inexpressible Being.

The One Who is the Inexpressible Self is the knower of the field, Universally Present (meaning [all-] pervading) [and] Indestructible. For this reason He is different from the aforementioned tangibility-expressibility [vyakta]. Vyakta and Avyakta are two different things – that is being spoken of here. In this, that which can be had via all of the senses – that is known as "aindriyaka vyakta" [tangibility through the senses].

And again that which is not that [different from that] is called "Avyakta," using "atindriya grahya" ["having" beyond the sense-functioning ways] – meaning: Kutastha and the par avastha of Kriya. The five elements such space, intellect, Avyakta, ahamkara [sense of "I"] - the nature of these eight elements and the sixteen permutations are being expounded upon.

The sixteen permutations are: five senses of the intellect, five senses of perception, sound, touch, sight, taste, smell and mind. Know that these are the sixteen permutations.

All of the mentioned fields, which have left the Avyakta, have been spoken about, and the One Who is Avyakta within these fields is called by the sages as "Kshetrajna" [the Knower of the field[s]].

The intellect [or knowingness] arises from the Avyakta, and from the intellect the feeling of "I" and its forms are felt, and "I" - meaning ahamkara [ego; individual "I"] - gradually begins the experience of everything.

Upon the ahamkara conjugating with the five elements and then when the entire body is manifested, that is called "jaat" [class, type or race]. And again when there is dissolution, there is union through the Divine. The Being becomes enjoined to elements and becomes vyakta from Avyakta, and again becomes Avyakta from vyakta. He goes round and round in this revolving wheel only because of taking on raja and tama gunas – meaning: those who reside in samsara [in this case spiritual samsara, not the physical living in the world itself] – it is verily they – because of acting from raja and tama gunas – who have to experience birth and death again and again. As long as the desires of samsara [and of worldly living] are not cast off, for so long there is no liberation.

Those who have become addicted to conflict and those who have become ego-oriented are the ones who have birth and death happen to them. But those who are not addicted to conflict and are not ego-oriented are the ones who do not have birth and death – meaning: if the par avastha of Kriya becomes constant and if they continuously perform Kriya according to the directives of Guru, they become "jivanmukta" [liberated while still living in the body].

"Iccha dvesham sukham duhkham prayatna shchetana dhriti; buddhi smriti ahamkaro lingani parmatmanoh" [desire, repulsion, pleasure, pain, endeavoring, knowing, holding to; intellect, memory, the sense of "I" are all adjuncts taken on by the Supreme Self]. These are the adjuncts taken on by the Supreme Self. Pranavayu, apana vayu, blinking and such, life, the movement of mind and the distribution of sense activities in their myriad forms – their taking up and holding onto; going far and wide to different lands during sleep, and death; and when one closes the right eye with the finger, it can be seen in the left eye; in that same way if the left is closed it can be seen in the right eye; desire, repulsion, pleasure, pain, endeavoring, holding to, intellect, memory, the sense of "I" - these adjuncts/characteristics are known because of being in the alive state. Upon death, these characteristics do not remain in the Self. For this reason great sages have said, "When the Self/Soul leaves, the five elements come to an end." Thus, because this body becomes non-conscious and empty – for that same causality it is called "panchatva" [five-ness]. It is called "panchatva" because of the Self/Soul leaving the body and the five elements coming to an end.

The mind which is in this body is non-conscious, and by the work of some other greater doer, it becomes conscious. And that mind, being enjoined to the Supreme Self, becomes the director of doing all of the activities of the Divine [meaning all acts] – meaning: mind becomes conscious from being non-conscious upon being enjoined to the Supreme Self, and experiences working in worldly existence.

Because of the Self being conscious, It is called "Kartaa" [Doer, Lord]. And as the mind is non-conscious, it is not called "kriyavat" [that which does] – meaning: it is the Self that is conscious. It is the Doer. Mind is enjoined to It and carries out the work of worldly existence.

Just as by one's own self the Self travels through all the different yonis [wombs], life [prana] distributes the life-force [prana] through itself. One is not the operator of another [being]. "Tantrak" [operator] – meaning: one who spreads/expands it around – meaning: when Kriyavans' selves come under Self-control through the practice of Kriya ["basheebhut"], they attain the state of all-knowingness, and can go from one living being to another living being, and can expand/spread prana through prana.

The "Bashee" [one who is under control] that does the act for which he has to experience the result of that act. The Bashee takes on the workings of the chitta [canvas of individual consciousness] and the Bashee casts off all things of the world. This means: through the continuous practice of the Guru-instructed Kriya, the chitta becomes pure, desires of samsara come to an end, and they go beyond the difference of Prakriti and Purush and [merge] in the Void and are in Oneness. This is why the self/Self can be called "Bashee" [in the power of Divinity as well as liberated].

As the Self is all pervading – through that same reason does one become "embodied" via contact with the senses. And because He remains in contact with all things, He is All. For these reason, the Self does not experience pain. As the Self is abiding in different ways in different senses, one sense is not able to know in the way another sense does, and [one body] is not able to know the matters of another body – meaning: when one is not "Bashee" [under the power of Divinity].

As the Self is everywhere and Great – thus the Self is Supernatural. And because of the mind being "resolved," the Self is able to know/see even while being covered [living an embodied life] – meaning: when one is perfected via Kriya and the concepts of the chitta end, then the Self is all-pervading, and keeps only a personal/functional connection with mind. All samskaras [latent tendencies] end; thus both become witnesses of each other – meaning: the par avastha of Kriya.

The Self That has become enjoined with the body and a mind according to karma [actions performed previously] – that Self is Eternal [but] becomes bound. Know that when there is settling in one yoni, the Self attains all yonis – meaning: as the Soul is enjoined with mind according to karma, one takes birth in a yoni according to the results [of that karma]. And when there is All Void and one become One and One only, then He abides in all yonis – meaning: all is Brahman.

The Self has no beginning and the field has no beginning. Thus, because of the "no-beginning-ness" of both, it cannot be said what is/was before.

(Jna) is the one who is the witness. (Ajna) is the one who is not the witness. Thus, know that the particular "dharmas" [ways] of every phenomena has the Self as their witness. This means: (jna) is the Self as a being and (ajna) is Brahman – the par avastha of Kriya which is Brahman, in which knowledge and ignorance cannot remain. Thus the Self is Itself all in All. Thus it is He Who is the Witness – meaning the par avastha of Kriya.

As the Soul of phenomena can never be experienced by any signs, that One which is so extremely subtle to perceive does not present any signs – meaning: upon the Kriyavans' continuous performance of Kriya, they attain the state of samadhi, when mind and Self/Soul become One – that is called One – whether it is one or two, they can know with certainty and understanding – meaning: at that time, neither any dharma or sign of the Self/Soul – none of that remains.

There is pain from the Person's desire; the creator/cause [of the pain] is singled out [from that]. Where there is constant pain, the creator/cause of that [condition] is singled out in that very place – meaning: the place where there is desirous activity of the Person/Self, it [the creator/cause of the result] is of that place, and where there is the dominance of vata, pitta and kapha [wind, bile and phlegm – respectively] it [the creator/cause of the result] is of that place.

The healer treats the pain of the three states of time; some say this using this type of reasoning. That reasoning is something for us to observe – meaning: healers treat past, future and present – the treatment is for the three states of time.

The headache comes; the fever arrives; then the cough becomes strong, then vomit comes up – by these prevalent statements, one admits the presence of the past. It is again seen that the medicine that is prescribed by observing the state of time – that [medicinal] substance is related to the pain of the past – that is what called "prashaman" [subduing] - meaning treatment.

The water that was there before – that water has come again. The seeds of creation that were destroyed before – in that way, bridges are made between all actions.

The act that can be performed by foreseeing the signs of mutation in the future – that act destroys the malady to occur in the future.

Maladies emerge continuously one after another, and applying that which brings about comfort/healing brings about comfort/healing.

The "dhatu" [substance] in the body that has become upset does not find equilibrium. The cause of [ailments or comfort] of all the states of time is born as "dhatus" of the body – meaning: humours, blood and such [comprising] seven "dhatus" – and vata, pitta, kapha [wind, bile, phlegm – respectively] – these are called the "dhatus" of the body.

The physician takes up this reasoning first, and treats the affliction of the three states of time. And the One Who Cannot Be Held and is Constant is actually the cure itself.

Suffering – the cause that is greater and beyond the things that contain suffering is called "upadhan" [that which holds]. When all "upadhans" are banished, all suffering is destroyed.

As the silkworm creates a thread that can kill itself, in the same way, the ever-ignorant take up thirst [desire and repulsion] in the midst of afflictions and worldly values – meaning: [just as] the silkworm goes on bringing out silk thread from within itself, thinking "I will now be happy" [but] in the end becomes bound by its own thread and dies, in the same way, the one who is ignorant takes up the thirst of want and repulsion from sound, touch and such [sensual experiences], and falls to death. The afflicted behave contrarily to the methods prescribed by the scriptures and become diseased. And Kriyavans who do not practice Kriya in a complete manner and according to the instructions of guru, become bound by the tethers of song and dance and such things of samsara, become afflicted, and die within a short time.

One who is (jna) – meaning: intelligent – knows the fire-like nature of that which is considered valuable by the world ["artha"] and become disassociated ["nivritti"] from that. The Person who is prior to the beginning of inter-exchange [with sensuality] – suffering cannot abide in Him.

One who has come to know Brahman by following [the spiritual path] via the grace of guru, he [knows] that "artha" is like fire – meaning: sound, touch, sight, smell – meaning: knowing the cause of the hell of sight, sound and such [sensual experiences], he remains disassociated from them. Having become a knower of Truth and having become disassociated from [sense experiences], desire, repulsion, beauty, suffering [and such] are not able to settle in him.

The destruction of intellect/intelligence and understanding/memory, the rising of "kal" [time and its inevitable march] and karma, the engagement in maleficent sights and sounds – know that these comprise the cause of all suffering/sorrow – meaning: the destruction of intellect/intelligence and such [beneficent aspects of the person], and the emergence of the results of karma from previous lives, and the indulgence in samsaric matters such as lust, greed and such – all these cause afflictions and sins.

One who attends to disturbing things – whether or not that disturbing thing is permanent or temporal, and whether or not it is good or bad – that is what is known as "buddhibhrangsha" [aberration of mind]. And the mind that looks at everything – meaning: being deeply into samsara and lust, gluttony, addictions and such – that is what is known as "buddhi vibhrangsha" [total aberration of mind]. And the Knowledge of Unity is called "buddhi" [intelligence].

Because of the destruction of "dhriti" [regular adherence or stability] due to maleficent substances [or: indulgence in things of maleficence], the mind is in a state of disturbance. That mind is not able to come to regular ways. Regularity is called "dhriti."

One whose "chitta" [overall personal consciousness] is covered with raja and tama gunas – his chitta's grasp of the Knowledge of Brahman is destroyed. That is called "smriti naash" [the destruction of understanding or the destruction of memory].

Upon having buddhi, dhriti and smriti destroyed, all of the non-beneficent acts that one does are called "prajnaparadh" [doing wrong against clear inner perception]. That "prajnaparadh" brings about the fury in all of the "doshas" [humours] - "dosha" - meaning: "vata" [wind], "pitta" [bile], "kapha" [phlegm] – meaning: disease forces previously non-existent toxins to come out; and to control those toxins whose force has become apparent, one attends to reckless kinds; one attends to sexual needs excessively; modesty and good character are taken away; and one speaks derisively and aggressively towards people one should respect. One who has come to know the "artha" [meaning, or value] of oneself – meaning: Brahman – does not attend to maleficent things, and having become great, he attends to that which brings spiritual ecstasy.

Being involved with friends' wrongful activities, and going about in wrong places at wrong times, and abandoning all of the [previously] mentioned good character that exists just prior to sense activity, and attending to envy, fear, anger, greed, addictions, delusions and all such aspects, and the disease-causing acts that are born of those things – attending to that affliction-filled body itself, and from that, that certain type action laced with raja and delusion [that happens] – that [person] is called by scholars as "byadhikaari prajnaparadhi" [causer of afflictions and wrongdoer against clear inner perception].

Knowing the particularities of disturbance-causing things and [still] presenting oneself to disturbance-causing things is called "prajnaparadh" [doing wrong against clear inner perception] - know this. That very prajnaparadh is perceived by the mind.

The time of emergence for afflictions and the spreading and growing of "pitta" [bile] and such have been addressed in the chapter on "hetu samgraha" ["Repository of Causes"]. And "shanti" [peace] has also been addressed previously.

Orientation towards falsehood [or false perception], orientation towards baseness, orientation towards extremes and the extremes of seasons such as the rainy season, and eating with little nutrition is this type of "kal" [time or state of illness and death], the type of food that is nearly devoid of any quality – the establishing of "kal" and "akal" [time as destruction, and wrong time] – these comprise the reason for disease, or the cause of their emergence.

In three particular "yaam"[s] [eighth of a day] of the day and in three particular "yaam"[s] of the night – all of the diseases that are certain to come about during those times – meaning: those that will inevitably be active [potentially or actually] – it is these that are called "kalajavyadhi"[s] [diseases of particular time periods] – meaning: all diseases that arise in the dawn, noon and end of the day and in similar times of the night as well – they are called "kalajavyadhi"[s].

"Dahagrahi" [having higher than normal body temperature] - "anyedushkaja," "tritiyak" and "chaturthak" types of fevers – these arise in the particular times of day and night with which they are associated and they gain in force at those particular times. "Anyedushka" is the fever that comes about at the same time every day; "trityak" [is] every other day; and "chaturthak" [is] every two days. These arise at the specific times of [the dominance of any of] vata, pitta and kapha, and gain in strength.

The One who knows the strength and times [of diseases] – via Him, all of those diseases and all of those "kalaja" [time-specific] disease do not appear and are curable.

Because of the movement of "kal" [time] all diseases that are normally associated with old age and death are seen. Those who are without Kriya are the ones who think of these as "natural."

Via divine word, all of the karmas connected with the previous body have been known, and the causes for the diseases due to the passage of time are also being known.

There is no act so high which does have as its end the experiencing of the fruits of that act. For this reason, all diseases that are karmic destroy the ability for action. When those karmas are eroded away, the afflictions caused by karma end and peace ensues. But there is no [usual] way to [act to erode these karmas]. Thus, those who practice Kriya well – it they who have their karmas destroyed. When karmas are destroyed, naturally the karma-caused afflictions are [also] destroyed.

Because of hearing extremely intense sounds, all kinds – meaning: [it is difficult to hear] any other kind of sound. And very weak sounds are not heard and "jada" – meaning: deafness comes about.

Harsh speech is terribly impure – and superficially sweet mirth/talk that one likes – when the ear associates with these "found" sounds – this is called "mithya yoga" [false or wrongful association].

Non-touching, touching excessively, and touching extremely little – about these touch oriented matters it can be concisely said that these are detrimental to the sense of touch.

All that are of poisonous ailments that become connected to oneself, and those that appear at the wrong times [or: unexpected times], and [excessive] caressing, or if there is contact with cold and heat at unnatural times – this is also called "mithya yoga" [false or wrongful association].

Looking at flashing light ruins sight, and looking at extremely subtle [extremely small, almost faded etc.] [eventually] makes it difficult to see all other things and because of such, sight is destroyed.

[Looking at] ghosts, evil spirits, terrifyingly ugly things, and looking at things very far away, affliction-causing [or afflicted] things, and looking at/in darkness – this is called the "mithya yoga" of sight.

And not experiencing tastes of complimentary types, accepting disturbances from tastes, and tasting very little is also detrimental.*

[*Translator's note: The word "liquid[s]" can be substituted for "taste[s]." The original word "rasa" has multiple meanings.]

Attending to very fine [or] very intense smells, and not paying attention to all types of smells is destructive to the sense of smell.

Foul scents, and "bhut" [elemental] – meaning – particular to yonis; "bish" [poison] – meaning: animate and inanimate beings; "dvishta" [repulsive] – meaning: unpleasant smells; "atibiheen" – meaning: very base smells – meaning: smells of the menses [and such] – if these contact the sense of smell, it is called the "mithya yoga" of [the sense of] smell.

These types of harmful associations to the senses and the concept of the three types of wrongs are being stated here [see next paragraph]. Know these to be what is known as "asadhya" [meaning in this case: incurable]; these do not allow the person to have a good state of being.

False/wrongful association, extreme association and weak association – know that the ailments of the senses that arise from these are called "aindriyak vyadhi" [ailments of the senses].

Happiness/well-being is caused by only one type of whole-association. But this has become extremely rare. But the cause of happiness/well-being and pain/suffering is not the senses or the objects of the senses – only wholly associating [good and bad] is the cause of happiness/well-being and pain/suffering. But four types of associations have been observed to be the cause of well-being and suffering. The senses and the objects of the senses are there but there no association happening with them, nor are there any afflictions.

Thus, if there is no knowledge of the four types of associations – Self, senses, mind and intellect – or if there is no [understanding of] specific ways of acting, well-being does not have a way of coming about.

Speak specifically according to how the state of well-being or suffering is in specific places. The experience of contact that arises from touch – it is the mind that is the subject of touch.

The cause of the rise of the touch of well-being and the touch of being is of two types. From that happiness and suffering – the desire-oriented and repulsion-oriented want – that arises from happiness and suffering.

The thirst which is the cause of pleasure and pain are being spoken about again – why that thirst is the home for the things that cause suffering.

[When] there is no contact – if there is no enjoining contact, pain is not experienced. And all of those things that make a home for pain – the mind and body which are there with the senses – meaning: unless these make the environment, it is not possible for afflictions to rise.

Hair, body hair, tips of the nails, food, excrement and urine [bodily wastes] – unless these make the environment, it is not possible for afflictions to rise.

Enjoinment [or association] is the common thing related to all ailments, and in Liberation, they do not arise.

"Nihshesh nivritti" [absolute and final release] is called "moksha" [liberation]. And inaugurator of "moksha" is called "yoga."

When the mind becomes Still by abiding in the Self, the engaging of the appropriate works related to the personal self, senses, mind and objects of the senses take place in order, as they work together next to each other. When there is no working for pleasure and pain, and there is release from pleasure and pain, one becomes "basheetva" [under Divine Power].

The knowledge of union that occurs with the use of the body – that is what is called "yoga" by the sages. From that "yoga" there is the going into [another's] "chitta" – meaning: entering into another's body and the knowledge of the objects of the senses – meaning: the knowing of sound, touch, sight, taste, smell, and Kriya while abiding in Brahman.

The yogis' vision, understanding, grace and the ability to vanish at will – these eight types of Divine powers are described.

Due to purity and goodness being realized, [powers such as] entering into [others] and such arise. And because of the absence of raja and tama [gunas] and because of the erosion of powerful karmas, Liberation comes about.

If there is the cutting out of karma-enjoinment, rebirth does not happen. Worship saints, and abandon [the company of] un-saintly people.

Observing vows [discipline], fasting, practicing different [good activities] and having thorough knowledge of the spiritual scriptures, and absorption in spiritual practice in solitude; and serving others and not engaging in [binding] acts, finishing out karmas already existing, exiting mind and ego, and seeing engagement [in worldly ways] as fearful, resolving mind and intellect, having complete vision of substantive knowledge - because of the existence of remembrance and understanding ["smriti"], all of these things come about. By serving Truth, one attains remembrance/understanding and steadfastness. Via "smriti" [remembrance/understanding] – remembering the characteristics of [all] tendencies and feelings, there is release from suffering ("duhkha" [suffering; pain; sorrow] – putting mind in other directions – meaning: [in directions] other than Brahman). That by which "smriti" can come about – those eight causes are being spoken about here.

By knowing causal forms and those forms of antipathy, and practicing the ways of holiness and purity, and listening again and again to Jnana Yoga [yoga of spiritual wisdom] – the remembrance [of the knowledge gained from these] causes "smriti" to become apparent.

Smriti arises from these eight causes: the causes of the emergence [of smriti]: (1) memories from past lives; (2) witnessing after having performed Kriya and being in the par avastha of Kriya; (3) abiding in Brahman; (4) from the Inaccessible; (5) seeing; (6) hearing; (7) experiencing; (8).* In order to have Liberation, for the sake of freedom these comprise the one and only road [to Liberation]. By that which one gains Knowledge and strength of understanding with remembrance, and never returns [to life and death] – that path of the yoga-oriented yoga is being explained again.

[*Translator's note: There is no matter written [to the translator's knowledge] regarding the eighth cause in the original. Only the number is written in the original and accordingly transcribed here.]

The path of Liberation through freedom – those knowledgeable beings who have taken up the way of Knowledge – they have been duly identified.

All substances that are there other than Brahman and all temporal substances comprise the cause of suffering. These have been identified.

Because that suffering is not caused by the Self but arises because of habit [or: characteristic acts of the personal self] – up to the point that True Intelligence does not come about – this statement "all that has been done [or: all results] is 'me'" is not there.

All these are as long as "I" am, not because of knowledge. The Self is making everything existent. Ending and submitting oneself in that Self, wholly knowing Knowledge and Supreme Knowledge, one is released from the root of all pain which had seemed to be endless. After that, Brahman is the phenomena. The experience that phenomena has a separate spirit no longer happens.

One Who transcends all experiences/feelings, One Who has no indications that can be known – Brahman is Itself the way for the knowers of Brahman. He is Formless and devoid of any signs. For the knowers of Brahman, This is Itself the place of Knowledge. But the ignorant are not fit to know that Brahman.

DISCOURSE ON HOW THE SELF/SOUL ENTERS THE WOMB

[Translator's note: Due to the particulars of the English language, the pronoun "He" and its conjugations ("Him, His") are being used to denote the Paramatman [Supreme Being/Supreme Soul] taking personal form. This is only for the sake of not having to write "It" (unless necessary) or "He/She." The Indian languages can address the Being (any being) without reference to any gender, as the languages have neutral pronouns which still indicate a being and not an object (the word "It" usually refers to an object or denotes something other than the aliveness of a being (i.e. when there is a reference to a child or a collective etc.). It should be understood by the reader that "He" is used here for the sake of convenience only and refers to both male and female incarnations taking place in the womb.]

Paramatman [Supreme Being] becomes enjoined to these four subtle elements - air, fire, earth, water – and begets Himself in a womb. How He settles in the womb and spreads/gathers the life-force, and how He creates the body, senses, bones, fat, flesh, sperm, blood [and such], and upon settling inside the womb, how He gradually grows the body, and how He makes the mind – which is greater than the senses – and the personal self His own – the explanation of all of these – and how to take safe care of the infant and the mother during pregnancy, and after birth, how to take safe care of the child and mother – what to do and for how many days – these are being explained in the following [pages] [or: successively].

Having joined – according to karma – with earth and such elements and the union of woman and man, the Self/Soul becomes endowed with time. The Self/Soul in the form of sperm and egg arrives from the worlds beyond, mixes with the four subtle elements [see above paragraph], and settles in the womb, joining with the subtle and physical/solid elements of the mother and father.

The Self/Soul merges with these substances - the liquids of the mother, the secretions of the father, and being enjoined with sperm and egg – as soon as It enters the womb, pregnancy takes place. The primary constituents of that womb [or: the purpose of the womb] is the [proper] development of the elements – ether, air, fire, water, earth – and the establishment of consciousness within them.   Firstly, upon entering the receptacle of the womb, the Self/Soul endeavors towards getting sattva guna. After getting sattva guna, the greatest guna among all gunas, He takes up space/ether. It is like the way God created the sky/space first after the end of the [previous] "pralaya" [[previous] dissolution of creation]; similarly, the Self/Soul/God first creates sky/space in the womb as well, and takes up air and such afterwards. Upon taking up the subtle elements followed by the taking up of physical/solid elements, the state of pregnancy ensues. But God accomplishes all of this in totality in a very short period of time. When all of these substances come together – the different manifestations and the particular months in which they take shape in the womb are being explained in the following.

In the first month, the substances and the Self/Soul merge and a gooey liquid comes about and settles in a dense form in one place. The Unmanifest takes form – meaning: the physical form and the person and individual identity, and the limbs of the body [and such] – all begin to come about. In the second month, matter becomes dense and takes a fleshy form – or "arbud" ("aab") [both words mean "tumor-like"]. In this is the cloudy [alternate meaning: cubic] form of the male and the flesh form (a fleshy disc) of the female, and the tumor-like form of the neuter [or: hermaphrodite]. In the third month, all senses and all limbs of the body come forth at the same time. In this month the fleshy limbs and such born of the mother and the nerves/arteries and such born of the father gradually become distinct from each other. Skin, blood, flesh, fat [or: humours], navel, heart, "klam" (where thirst occurs), liver, spleen, breast, "vasti" (the place for urine), the sex organs, the "northern" [upper] orifice (the opening of the small intestine), the lower orifice (the opening for excrement [anus]), the small intestine, the large intestine ("nadi" [biological passageway]), the body-structure, that which can support the body-structure – meaning: settling and the nerves which support the settling – all of these come from the essences of the mother. And hair, tears, nails, body hair, teeth, bones, nerves, tendons, arteries and veins and semen – all these are from the father. Because the womb is inhabited by the Self/Soul, the movement of the womb, the visible features of the embryo, and the specific operations of each of the senses – all of these take place. And, according to karma, the lifespan and the capacity of intellect grow. There can be no action or [ordinary] knowledge for the "doer" without the senses. After the third month, it can be seen that certain actions are being performed by the senses through the use of certain substances – meaning: the qualities [gunas] of the space/ether element – the space/ether-oriented sound, hearing, lightness, subtleness, piercing analysis/discrimination; the air-oriented – meaning: the qualities [gunas] of air – touch, touching/feeling, sensitivity, emitting, and the ability to break matter, and physical strength; the fire-oriented – meaning: the qualities [gunas] of fire – the visible, sight, light/revelation, order, and fiery nature; the water-oriented – meaning the qualities [gunas] of water – taste, tasting, coldness, muddiness, affection, filth – all of these take place; the earth-oriented – meaning: the qualities [gunas] of earth – scent, smelling, pride, steadiness, inclination. In this way these emerge upon union of these and the Being.

All that is in the Supreme Person is also in this body. All of the substances that come forth upon the birthing of the now whole child is being revealed. Teeth, nature, the femaleness [or: female sex] and the maleness [or: male sex] are seen, and the neuterness [or: hermaphrodite] is seen. In the fourth month of pregnancy, stability [or the embryo and the womb] comes about, at which time the mother begins to become heavy. In the fifth month – more than any other month, there is a great increase of flesh and blood in this month. As blood and flesh settles in the womb, the mother takes on a kind of emaciation in her appearance. And in the sixth month, strength and shape increase in the womb. For this reason, the mother loses some strength and shape. In the seventh month, through the use of all of the substances, the womb suddenly expands. For this reason, the mother experiences extreme tiredness. In the eighth month, a passage from the mother to the womb and from the womb to the mother comes about through which ojas* [food energy] is exchanged. As the womb is not completely sufficient with supply, when the mother draws ojas from the womb she feels energized, and when the womb draws ojas from the mother, she feels exhausted. Thus the ojas substance is incomplete [or: insufficient]. Because of this, a feeling of unsettledness takes place in the womb. For this reason, there should be great care taken by everyone in attendance for the safety of the womb. And if all of these [following] procedures are steadfastly and without deviation implemented during pregnancy, the womb remains safe. When pregnancy has settled in, do not work with heavy things, hot things or anything fear-causing. Do not use intoxicants. Do not get on vehicles [or: carriers – such as horses]. And do not do acts which create adversity for the eyes, ears, nose and other senses. And give to the mother whatever she wants to eat without any delay, otherwise many kinds of wrongs can take place in the womb. Therefore, it is very necessary to give [the mother] the foods that she wants.

[*Translator's note: There is no accurate translation for "ojas" in English. An approximate be the vitality-feeling/substance that is in food and the sexual energy in the body.]

Now the discourse continues on the period from the beginning of the ninth month until the tenth month and the time of birthing and the formations. If there are abnormalities in the womb at this time, this gives birth to a child with abnormalities in the body. The abnormalities of the body will be according to the abnormalities in the sperm and egg. If there is too much heat in the seed of the man and if at the same time there is delight between man and woman during intercourse, a hermaphrodite is born. If the sperm is dominant, there will be a male in the womb, and if raja [guna] is dominant, there will be a female. And in this way, the many different proportions of the combinations of raja and sperm bring about the great number of bodies [alternate translation: the many differences in greater and smaller proportions of raja and sperm control the creation of big bodies and such]. Disregarding unimportant matters, the necessary matters are being presented for the betterment of the normal body. As the sign of pregnancy becomes evident in the first month, a proper amount of raw milk should be taken frequently, and [the mother should] eat regularly at dawn and dusk. In the second month, [the mother should] take milk mixed with kakali, kheer-kakali and gulancha. All of these foods – mix: 2 tola milk, ½ poa water, 1½ poa end ½ poa – if it is prepared like this and thus taken, the child becomes strong and beautiful. In the third month, drink a mixture of milk, honey and ghee. In the fourth month, a mixture of milk and butter in the amount of 2 tola should be fed [the mother]. In the fifth month, 2 tolas of ghee should be mixed with milk and be fed [the mother] at dawn and dusk. In the sixth month, milk, kheer-kakali and ghee should be mixed and fed [the mother.] In the seventh month, a 2-tola mixture of milk, ghee, kheer-kakali and gulancha should be fed [the mother]. In this month, hair appears on the infant in the womb and gives heat to the mother, and at this time [the humours] vata, pitta, and shleshma [phlegm] arise in the child and give heat to the mother. At this time, the mother will experience itching sensations. To give her relief from that, dried jujube soaked in water, a mix of gulancha, kheer-kakali and butter, with ½ chatak [about one ounce] of water should be fed [the mother] at dusk and dawn. And make a paste made of crushed red sandalwood and lotus stalk and rub it into the breasts and the belly; or rub crushed "triphala" [three myrobalans] paste. This will relieve the itching. In the eighth month, [the mother should drink] a mix of stone-ground wheat powder, milk and ghee. By doing this the newborn child is endowed with strength, good form, good voice and a firm body.

In the ninth month, a mixture of kakali and kheer-kakali with sesame oil should be applied inside the yoni with a piece of clean cotton. By doing this, the mother will not experience any kind of suffering during labor. And oil makes the opening of the womb soft and relaxed; thus there is no suffering during the exiting of the baby.

By the application of the procedures described pertaining to the period from the first to the ninth month, the mother's belly, hips, sides [and] back find ease; air goes downward, and excrement and urine evacuate normally. And the skin and nails are healthy; there is an increase of strength along with the growth of the body, and in due time [the mother] gives birth to a superior child in that race. In the ninth month, the birthing-room should be prepared, which should be on a good piece of land without pebbles and shards. Make the door either to the east or the north. And keep the wood of the bel or mangosteen or catechu [plants/trees] for fire when necessary. In order to ward off the fear of evil spirits and malevolent beings, do not wear red clothing at this time [or: the mother should not wear red clothing at this time].

Immediately after the beginning of the tenth month, go into the birthing room. Just before the time of birth, all these signs come about: the whole body becomes slack – including the mouth and the closing of the eyes. The womb loosens downward. The lower part of the body becomes heavy, and the thighs, urinary bladder, hips, sides and back experience discomfort, and liquid comes forth from the yoni [and] there is no desire to eat – right then you can know that the time of delivery has arrived. Immediately after that there is "aabee" – meaning: labor pains begin. Then make a soft bed on the ground and have the mother take the bed. And a spirituous (with alcohol) type of liquor should be given [to the mother] to sip; and women of similar age, breeding and character should surround the mother to help, and they should repeatedly encourage the mother to open and push. If there is delay in this, "kut," big cardamom, powdered bach, powdered natyabeej – whatever among these can be found – have the mother repeatedly smell these; and bhurja leaves, shingshupa [timber tree] (shamee tree), resin – make and burn incense from any of these that can be had; and from time to time rub warmed oil on the hips, sides, back, thighs in the direction of the front of the body. Through these techniques the womb opens downward. Immediately after that, the binding of the heart becomes unlocked and the bladder goes up into the belly.

Upon seeing the contractions becoming frequent signaling that the baby is ready to quickly come out, tell the mother to push flowingly ("kontani" [pushing similar to the time of bowel evacuation]).

Immediately after this, the empathic women should continuously tell the mother things so that she feels good. Afterwards, when the baby has come out, if the "amara" – meaning: the umbilical cord – does not want to come out – to bring it out, the attendant should put his/her right hand on the mother's navel area and strongly push while putting the left hand on the mother's back and give slow shakes, and someone should slowly massage the legs/feet, sides, "shroni" ("kati" [hips]), and slowly push [without jerking] the lower abdomen. If this is done the "amara" will come out quickly. And send smoke burned from either bhurja leaves or "sarpanimok" – meaning: the shed skin of a snake - in the direction of the mother's yoni. And make a "juice"* from the powder of crumbled palm leaves, and mix it with either strong liquor or pureed "kalai" [a type of pulse/bean] or pureed figs and have the mother drink it. Either that or make a juice* from these: small cardamom, fig, beet salt, jaggery, chnoi, black cumin – make a juice* from these and have the mother drink it. Serve the drink with whichever of the substances according to availability. Make one "matra" of juice.* When there are 2 tolas of "churna" [two meanings: powder, or calcium carbonate] - ½ tola. And make an oil mixture with lotus flower, "knud" [a type of jasmine], "madan" fruit ("mael" fruit), asafetida – soak a piece of cotton in this oil and enter it into the yoni. If this is done, there will relief from pain, discharge and the relief from being opened wide. Hereafter, after the umbilical cord is out, take two stones and hit them against each other near the child's ear[s]. Throw sprinkles of either cold or warm water on the child's face. If this done, the child's prana will awaken from having been bottled up. And fan the child with the leaves from verbena. Upon doing this, when it is seen that the child's life-force is flowing normally, then begin to massage the child's "talu" [the peak of the skull], lips, throat, tongue. Wrap cotton smeared with ghee around a finger – with trimmed nail – and massage. After this, feed one or ½ "rati" [about 1.9 grains] of rock salt to the child and induce vomiting. After this, in order to cut the umbilical cord, measure eight fingers' length on the cord from the point of the navel. Make a mark at that eight-fingers' length end point. Then, cut the cord in an upward way with either a gold, silver or iron cutting instrument or with some other type of cutting instrument. Immediately after this, take a bunch of thread and close the torn cord still on the child by tying the opening and keep the excess thread on the collar of the child. If that cord has an improper wound or if it becomes infected, then make a powder of hard dried licorice and hard turmeric mixed with sesame oil, and smear it on the child. And sprinkle oil and that boiled powder-mix [alternate translation: boiled calcium carbonate coagulation] on the wound. This will cure the infection of the navel. And if the cord is not cut according to the aforementioned proper procedures, then the navel will be either excessively large, large, prominent and round like a ball in the mid-region, and it will be subject to constant change – meaning: it can be seen that it grows sometimes and sometimes becomes smaller. Therefore, do not cut the cord in improper ways. If the procedure to cut the cord is done as written here, then there will be no need to fear any future problems due to an improper operation of the cord. Right after the cutting of the cord, wash the child's body with warm water, and feed the mother ghee and honey, and have the child feed from the right breast first. And cover all four sides of the lying-in-room with the leaves of catechu, "seaakul," "phalsa." And spread mustard, tamarind and grains of husked rice. And make several cloth bundles with "bach," "kud," "atab," husked rice, mustard, grains of husked rice and hang it on the cross-plank of the doorway of the lying-in-room, and tie a small cloth bundle [with the same substances] around the necks of the mother and the child. And keep these near water-pots, sitting places and tie them on the windows and such as well. And continuously keep a fire lit in the room with woods such as catechu.

[*Translator's note: The word "juice" is written exactly as the English word "juice" with Bengali letters in the original – a transliteration of the English word through the Bengali alphabet.]

And for 10-12 days keep the child in the lying-in-room under constant care, and perform beneficent rites, such as oblations, as well. And if the new mother gets hungry: fig root, chnoi, fig, "chite" (blood) [alternate translation: red flattened rice], dried ginger, ghee with calcium carbonate, oil, bone marrow – make a mix of whichever of these are conveniently available and feed [the mother]. And after the mother takes ghee, put oil and ghee on the body [of the mother]. And wrap the belly firmly with a long piece of clothing. This will help the vayu to be settled in the belly and not cause problems such as distention, and then there is no need to fear that the belly will enlarge unnaturally. Some people, because of a lack of good advice, do not wrap the belly and the stomach bloats out. Thus, wrap the belly firmly. This will alleviate the fear that the belly will enlarge. When that ghee begins to run out, boil figs or some such fruit, and grind old stone-ground wheat and husked rice into a powder. From that, take ½ poa of the powder and 14 times that amount of the water used to boil the aforementioned fig or some such fruit. Take a fourth of that and give that to drink, and serve that at dawn and dusk. And before drinking in the morning, bathe the mother in warm water. After bathing, ghee should be taken first, and then the gruel. Keep this procedure of drinking [these products] strictly in this way for 14-15 days. These procedures are given here in order to regain and maintain the new mother's health. Deviation from this can cause health problems for the new mother. If afflictions occur during the time of menstruation, that affliction may prove difficult to heal or nearly impossible to heal [at that time]. Therefore, after menstruation, take extra care when carrying out the procedures [mentioned]. And use nutritious and strength-giving foods, and give the mother body-rubdowns and such. The substances used for the rubdowns can include mustard [possibly ground mustard], milk, dried ginger and powdered wheat. Afterwards, on the tenth day, give the new mother the aforementioned powder with mustard and such mixed with aloe [not clear whether its the wood or the liquid] and white sandalwood, and rub the body with this mixture. Right after this, bathe the mother and have her put on new [or fresh] clothing that is thin in material.

Later, the mother can wear gold or silver jewelry according to her wish. And after clothing the child, lie it with the head either in the easterly or northerly direction. And upon entering the house, do pranam to deities and Brahmins and such. Afterwards, during the time of naming the baby, give it two names: one astrologically based and one that has meaning [understood by everyday people]. But if that name has been used within three previous generations already, there will be a maleficent effect. Worthwhile names are of the stars and deities with four letters of deities' names [unclear in the original] adjoined to the name.

After this check the lifespan of the child. In order to make a discernment about the lifespan of the child – if these signs are observed, whether the lifespan is short or long can be ascertained.

If the newborn child's hair is not dense, and is light, little in amount, soft, with strong roots and black [or dark] – these are all signs of a long lifespan. And the firmness and thickness of the skin is a great indication; and the total soundness of the body-form is somewhat of a proof, and an umbrella-like [or: domed] head is excellent. And if the "shankhasandhi" ("rog" [temple]) is firm, thick and well formed, and broad and "upachita"] full ("vriddhi" [expansive or broad]), and a half-moon shaped forehead [are all] excellent. And somewhat long and of even size and big eyebrows are best. And if the two eyes have equal radiance [or: color] and are properly separated and filled with energy and have beautiful "upanga" (the corners of the eyes) – this is best. And strong and long breaths ("chidra" [nostrils]) which together are like bamboo [the whole nose], and the front portion is slightly bent downward – this type of nose is best. And a large, straight type of face is best. And a long and wide, with the color of a slight amount of white mixed with pale red (mix of white and red colors), tongue is best. And if the palms are soft, thick and warm. The red [rosy] colored palm is best. And a great, strong, pleasant, resounding, somber sounding and steady voice is best. And not extremely thick but not extremely thin, wide, with a color of muted red – these are best for lips. And a round but not extremely long neck is excellent. A strong, prominent jaw is best. And a "byudh" (wide, filled with flesh), "gudh" ("gupta" [hidden]) "jakru" ("kantha kup" [pit of the throat]) is excellent. And the back is best in this way. A prominent and wide chest is best. And steady and like banana leaves are best regarding the two flanks. Round, full and long arms, and [similarly] from the thighs to the feet and toes are best. If it is like this, it is best. And wide and full hands and feet are best. And firm and soft skin, and the nails shaped like the top of a tortoise are excellent. And a clockwise looking raised navel, and if there is one-third of the flesh and space of the breast at the area of the lower abdomen – these are excellent. And round, firm, fleshy, not very high up – this is excellent for buttocks. And gradually tapering and round and full thighs are excellent. Not too full, and like the legs of a deer, with hidden veins and joints, the thighs [possibly meaning lower legs - unclear] – excellent. And too much flesh in the area of the ankles is not good. And similar to the tortoise like form mentioned before – this is best for the two feet. And if there is natural functioning of wind, urine, the sex organs, anus, and if there is normal crying from waking up from sleep, [normally] feeding from the mother's breasts – if these show signs of being completely natural and normal, then there will be a long lifespan. Whatever has not been addressed here should also show signs of working normally. If there are abnormalities, these could be the cause [or: signs] of a short lifespan.

Now, how the wet-nurse is, and how the milk she milks from the breasts of the mother is, what kind of taste will indicate that the child will be without illness, those sings, and the signs of abnormality, and the procedures to cure – these are being explained in the following. Firstly, if the wet-nurse mother is of the same type of body as the mother, young, intelligent, not ill, beautiful, has had a son, knowledgeable about biological matters, and if the mother has breasts that are "avapanna" (pure milk), with breasts of medium size, from a good family-lineage, with breasts of milk [or: with breasts of the same shape], without afflictions in the body, with pure nature – if this type of wet-nurse and mother feed the child [or: rear the child], the child does not experience any physical troubles. Now, this type of breast-milk is excellent – like: the color, smell, taste and consistency to the touch should be natural/normal. And milking the breasts into a clean, white-colored vessel containing pure water will make the milk mix into the water completely. This is because milk has a particular similarity to water in nature. This type of milk is immunity-building and nutritious. And the type of milk that is affliction-causing or without nutrition – I am explaining that in the following: the breast-milk that has a slightly blackish-tint, is slightly red, if tasted has an astringent taste, if it is smelled there is a rough scent, and it has lumps and foam and is not very tasty – if the child drinks this the body will dry up; the head will become heavy; it is possible that there will even be coughing; there will be indigestion as well, and after that there can also be diarrhea. This is first. And the milk that is black, blue, yellow, or brown and tastes bitter, sour, pungent; and if it is smelled there will be a foul smell, and the smell of blood, and too warm to the touch – this type of milk will cause the child to have diarrhea, indigestion, spitting up, excessive heat in the body and will cause fever. This is second. Then, the milk that is too white, when tasted has a salty taste, and when smelled has the scents of ghee, oil, fermentation, marrow, and feels slimy to the touch, and can be observed as being stringy, and when put in a vessel with water, the milk will sink [instead of mix] – this type of milk will cause the child to have coughs, repulsion to milk [feeding], and looking upwards with no motion in the eyes, and there will be phlegmatic fever. These are the three types of bad milk. To resolve this, first the mother has to be treated. In the following, the medicines [and procedures] are being described.

The one to whom the corruption of breast-milk has happened – give that new mother all these things to eat: barley, wheat, rice with red "skin" on it from "shalee" grain, rice from "sethe" grain, mung dal, "matar" [a type of split pea/legume] dal, "kurti kalai" [another pulse] dal, liquors – give the mother all these things to eat and drink, and "aknadi" (special wood [also could mean specially dried "aknadi"]), dried ginger, "debdaru" [a kind of pine], "suchmukhi," "guduchi," "chireta" [a bitter medicinal plant], "betoshak" [leaves from a cane plant], "mane" fruit [could also mean – "betoshak" – meaning its fruit], "katki," "anantamul" [a medicinal plant] – give these things. Serve it with the liquid [from cooking] absorbed in the food and not in a watery way. Other than this, "neem" [margosa leaf], "potol" [a type of small squash], cane tips and such bitter edible substances should be served in a pureed form. By these procedures, the causes of aforementioned three types of bad breast-milk are destroyed and the breast-milk is purified. If there is no milk being produced by the woman, or if there is very little milk – in order to make more milk, prepare the medicines as explained below.

First, give the one who needs to have more milk created in her body some rice or liquor from jaggery/molasses to drink [alternate translation: some liquor made from either rice or jaggery/molasses]. And wild meat, meat from aquatic animals, spinach, grain, meat, and with sweet and sour salt – a good amount of food should be eaten. And peepul fruit, banyan fruit, fig and "anantamul" – a puree made from these should be given in 2 tola amounts at dawn and dusk.

And "shyamak" (meaning "shyamaghas" [literally: black grass]) and "sethe" grain, "rakta shalee," sugar cane, "nata," "ulu" [a kind of grass], "kusha" hairs ["kusha" grass] – drinking the essences of this creates more milk in the mother. And the pure milk-giver should drink milk. If the breast-milk is not completely pure, then make a puree from one or two – whatever is conveniently available – of the following: "rakhalolsha," "brahmi" leaves, and white and yellow colored "durba" [a kind of grass], cow's hoof, "karkati," "gulancha," myrobalan fruit, "katki," white "berela" – of 2 tolas and feed the milk-giver one-fourth of this [puree]. After that, the milk-giver should have the child face the east and be fed with the right breast. Thus the procedures for the milk-giver have been stated.

Now, the way of preparing the house with the child, so that all will be safe and sound, is being described in the following.

In order to prepare the house – firstly, a house is excellent. Otherwise, an older house that is designed from traditional culture is charming. The child's room should be decorated with many kinds of pictures and visually attractive things. It should not be dark and it should not be drafty. But from one side of the room/house there should be a flow of air. There should not be mice and such or their holes, and flying insects and such should not be able to enter. That house should be divided [into rooms] as necessary and one extreme side should the area of the toilet and the completely opposite extreme area of the house should be the place to keep [drinking] water and kitchen.

And there should be a beautifully decorated sheet for the bed, and in that house there should be highly beneficent substances. Well educated elderly women and other women should all be there and the house should always have a beautifully fragrant scent. And burn incense for the child's clothes and things with these substances – barley, white mustard, "atasi" [flax] ("masne" [linseed or flax]) flower, "hingu," olibanum, "bach," "brahma yashti" [a type of licorice], "jatamangsee," "chaam" grass, shed snake skin – mix ghee with however many of these that can be obtained and burn this as incense. And dress the child with jewelry. And the right horn of rhinoceros, deer, cow, ox – but from live animals – should be taken and kept in the house. Other than this, follow the procedures or use of medicines as prescribed by holy/sagacious men. And keep many types of visually attractive and charming toys that make sound as well. But these toys should be light in weight, and should not be overly solid or fearful like a lifeless [toy] deer and such. And never scare the child, but when the child cries or eats, then take the names of monsters, dark spirits and ghosts and such. And if any ailments arise in the child, then, upon analyzing and discerning the affliction, its function and cause, treat the child accordingly with the medicine of the country and the land that is inhabited at the time. Stop the use of any unhealthy things and utilize good things. If done this way, the child will get strength, form/beauty, lifespan and success. And if the aforementioned disciplines are well attended to until the time of youth – and keep mind always in the way of dharma – if this is done, the offspring will remain affliction-free. Those who deride others and without righteousness and hateful – they can never establish themselves in the world, and their children cannot have long life and be free of afflictions. Therefore it is necessary to practice dharma.

It has been previously said that this world has been created with the six substances. How they are connected and the relationship of the body with the Universe – meaning: people have claimed that the body is itself the microcosm – how this unity is, is being explained. By the union of the five elements and Brahman, the Person has come into being. That person's (form) – earth; (liquidity) - water; (power) – fire; (life-force) air; (openings) space; (inner Self) Brahman. Brahman in the Universe – the Divinity of Brahman in the inner Self; the Divinity in the loka [plane; or: Universe] – the Divinity of Brahman in the body; "prajapati" [lord of creatures] in the inner-soul-being; "Indra" [energy] in the pure loka – "I"-ness in the body; sun in the loka – having/engulfing in the Person; fiery energy in the loka – passion/anger in the body; moon in the loka – peacefulness in the body; "vasu" [wealth] in the loka – pleasure/happiness in the body; "ashvini kumarodvaya" [sunrise and sunset] in the loka – beauty in the body; "marut" [wind] in the loka – enthusiasm in the body; all deities in the loka – the senses and the objects of the senses in the Person; "tama" [inertia guna] in the loka – delusion in the Person; light in the loka – knowledge in the Person. As it is in the lokas such as the heavenly abodes, so it is in the Person from the womb. Satya Yuga in the loka – childhood in the Person; Treta Yuga – youth in the Person; Dwapara Yuga – old age in the body; Kali Yuga – the afflictions in the body; the end of the yugas – death of the body. Because there is this direct connection with the Universe and the body, the body is called the "microcosm." And the Self is verily the Primary thing in this body. It is He Who watches and does [or: makes happen] all. And it is He Who is the cause of pleasure and pain – the karma-based causes. Having been united to causalities and such, knowing "sarvaloka aham" [I Am all existence], the first thing that arises in order to have liberation is knowledge. Because of being connected to that Person, that loka gets sound [alternate meaning: the "Holy Sound"]. And the subtle six substances are in all. The causality ["hetu"] [and constituents] of that "all" are: "utpatti" [emergence], "vriddhi" [expansion/growth]; "upaplava" [breakdown/destruction]; "viyoga" [subtraction/absence]. The cause of "utpatti" [emergence] is called "hetu" [causality] and the birth of a thing is called "utpatti." "Vriddhi" [expansion/growth] [to] "apyayan" [annihilation] – meaning: growth eventually goes to "upaplava" [destruction] – the pain aspect of the six substance-oriented creation. That which is called "viyoga" [subtraction/absence] – this is called "jivapagama" [the departure of the sentient being]. The stopping of the life-force and breaking down is in the nature of the outer world. Death and the root cause of death and all destruction is "pravritti" [engagement]. "Nivritti" [reversal of engagement] – meaning:

"upaplava" is "pravritti" – pain; "nivritti" – happiness. The Knowledge that arises from that happiness is called "Satya" [Truth]. That Truth is the subtle unity in all. Because this Knowledge is the subtle unity, that Knowledge of the subtle unity requires initiation that is of the subtle unity.

The processes/acts/procedures of that pravritti and nivritti are being elucidated: the acts bound by delusion, desire and repulsion are rooted in pravritti [or: are the root of pravritti]. From that pravritti come "ahamkar" [egoism], "sanga" [connection to; attachment], "samshaya" [doubt; conflict], "abhisamplava" [unconscionable self-importance], "abhyadhahpata" [mine and theirs], "vipratyaya" [untrustworthiness; unreliability], "avishesha" [indiscriminateness; non-specificity] and "anupaya" [having to manage forces beyond one's control; acts to appease forces beyond one's control]. Just as a massively branched tree expands crushing a new tree growing under it, in a similar way, pravritti runs over purity and spreads in the Person. In this: race, beauty, wealth, high status, intellectualism, personality, saying "I" with the pride of lineage-roots and haughtiness [and such] are called "ahamkar" [egoism]. And all acts that are done through mind, speech [physical energy] and body – and not by Grace – these are called "sanga" [connected to; or: attached to]. And that by which there is doubt about whether things such as fruits of karma, liberation, Being, after-world – whether these types of spiritual realities exist or not – this type of thinking is called "samshaya" [doubt; conflict]. And when, in every situation, the "I" is predominant - "I" am lord and creator of all, "I" am verily the perfect nature; "I" am verily the body, senses, intelligence – when I keep in this particular way – this type of reckoning is called "abhisamplava" [unconscionable self-importance]. And that by which one feels "my" mother and father, brother, spouse, child, friend, dear one, servant – that all of these people are "mine" and I am "theirs" – this is called "abhyadhahpata" [mine and theirs].

And that by which – duty, that which is not to be done, good, bad, beneficent, maleficent – approaching these things in precarious ways is called "vipratyaya" [untrustworthiness; unreliability]. And not properly seeing the real nature nor distortions of knowledge, ignorance, pravritti and nivritti is called "avishesha" [indiscriminateness; non-specificity]. And that, because of which one performs rituals such as "prokshana," "anashana," "agnihotra," "triyavan," "abhyukshana," "avahana," "jala/agni pravesha" and such [Vedic rituals such as cleansing, fasting, sprinkling of water on idols, fire ceremony etc.] - is called "anupaya" [having to manage forces beyond one's control; acts to appease forces beyond one's control]. Going this way, steadfastness and understanding are enmeshed with egoism; strength is compromised by doubt and unconscionable self-importance; intelligence falls to the sense of "mine and theirs" – from that there is the pursuit of indiscriminate trivialities by looking in other directions [than the Divine], going on wrong paths – this is the root of all suffering in the tree of the body. One who has become captivated by sins such as egoism – he cannot ever get beyond pravritti. But that pravritti is actually the root of sin. And nivritti is called "apavarga" [salvation]. That "apavarga" is called – the Peace Beyond. That Inexpressible Brahman is liberation. The path that will lead those who desire liberation to that abode is being described.

One who has become aware of the errors of society [alternate meaning: one who has seen the errors of phenomenal existence] must first go to a guru [preceptor] and should investigate according to the teachings/practice. And one should cultivate fire. One should act according to righteous principles and the scriptures, and upon having becoming aware of their wisdom, upon becoming inextricable with those righteous ways – after that, one should practice the instructed Kriya, and worship/cultivate "sat" [truth-oriented ways] and cast off "asat" [bondage-oriented ways].

And [have your heart] in Truth, feel all people as wonderful, and have no opinions, speak carefully and at the right times, and see yourself in all beings, and do not become absorbed in worldly matters. Do not endeavor for or pray for worldly things. Cast of lustful relations and abandon all conflicts. In order to have clothing and food, take simple substances [to eat and] wear. In order to sew bed coverings and blankets, take up the needle [sewing]. And for cleanliness, keep a "kamandalu" [water-pot used by sages]. And take up a staff. In order to cultivate begging for alms and in order to keep alive, beg only that which is excess and consume it the same day. And in order to get rest and relief from laboring, take dried fallen leaves from trees, and grass, and make bed and pillow from them. And in order to meditate, practice yoga asana. And let go of passionate desires and anger. And in order to have good sleep and be well in travel, be regular in eating, exercise and recreation. And tolerate affection, praise, derision, humiliation. And be tolerant of hunger, thirst, travel, labor, cold, heat, wind, rain, pleasure, pain. And do not harbor grief, distress, hatred and vanity [or: shame]. And do not take intoxicants; do not take up greed, desirousness, jealousness, fear, anger and such. Think of fashionable clothing and such as burdensome. Be barely noticeable to people and be vigilant about the possibility of dutiful work not getting done. And at the time of beginning yoga practice, do not constantly have grief [and such] in the mind. And for the sake of salvation, take up enthusiasm, intelligence, concentration/focus, and strength of memory/understanding for Truth/purity.

And the senses should be disciplined. The chitta's in the chitta, the self's in the Self – in this way, control all the senses. And through the [understanding of] substance-differences keep the limbs of the body in check. And suffering is caused by all [worldly things] but this personal activity is not forever. And pravritti [engagement with attachment] in everything is "duhkha samjna" [knowing pain], and nivritti [reverse of pravritti; non-engagement without inertia] is "sukha samjna" [knowing happiness]. This is called "abhinivesh" [profound attention]. This is the "hetu" [causal element] for "apavarga" [salvation]. "Apavarga" is something other than worldly matters/sense matters. Worldly things are blasphemous and the cause of hell. Thus the path has been systematically explained for the sake of attaining Brahman.

By the practice of the aforementioned pure discipline, the sattva becomes pure in every way and thing, as a mirror is perfectly cleaned by oil, cloth and small chips of particular substances. And in the way a house receives sunlight when there is no covering by clouds, dust, smoke and fog – in the same way, when there is no impurity in the body, the sattva is pure, and the body is filled with Light. And in the way the still flame of a lamp fills a room with light – in the same way, by the union of the pure-sattva to the Self, and secretly being in the passage, there is Light. Great power comes about from the Truth-Intelligence that rises from the pure-sattva. The great delusion of tama is destroyed. And by that, the knowers of the nature of the Self become desireless in all matters, and absorption in yoga comes about. And there is Knowledge, because of which egoism does not come about. And there is no worship of the causalities making things happen. And by that, there is no more inner association with any of the things of the world.

And by that Truth-Intelligence, there is renunciation of all things of samsara. The Eternal Brahman is attained. Brahman is ageless, Peace, Inexpressible/Undefinable/Indestructible. That [Brahman] by which all of this is attained is called "vidya" [knowledge], "siddhi" [attainment], "mati" [perception], "medha" [intelligence]. It is That which is called "jnana" [knowledge/wisdom] – [sages] call That [by such terms and know It as so. And the Self is expanded everywhere in the Universe. And people are seeing – within the Self – the "other" and "this and that." This ruins the root of peace and wisdom. And one who is seeing all things at all times and in all phenomena, and if he has become Pure Brahman-Substance, then there is no "samyoga" [enmeshing]. And because all causalities are known in the Self, all signs are known. When that Self is without all causalities, that can be called "mukta" [liberation]. That "mukti" [liberation] is called "vipapa" [sinless], "viraja" [pure; or: free from passions], "shanta" [peace], "para" [beyond], "akshara" [inexpressible; or: indestructible], "avyaya" [inexhaustible], "amrita" [eternal; or: nectar, ambrosia], "Brahman" [Absolute], "nirvana" [final release] – by all of these ways, one attains Peace. All of this is known through "vijnana" [spiritual wisdom; or: [spiritual] science]. Liberation is through "jnana" [[spiritual] Knowledge]. By becoming devoid of doubt, raja and tama [gunas], and by being established in Kriya, may Kriyavans attain Nirvana [Final Release].

Thus ends [this section]

ASCERTAINING THE LOCATION OF THE SENSES IN THE BODY

AND

THE MANNER OF LIVING LIFE IN THE WORLD THAT WILL BRING ABOUT BLESSINGS IN THIS AND THE AFTER-LIFE

ALL OF THESE PRINCIPLES ARE BEING DISCUSSED HERE

This body is made of five elements. Five senses, the objects of the five senses, the positioning of the five senses, the intelligence of the five senses – there are statements about these aspects of the attributes of the senses. And mind is "atindriya" [beyond the senses]. Some call it "sattva" [pure; neutral]. All senses are the subjects of that mind and strive to fulfill it. And the knowledge aspect of the senses is called "cheshta" [effort; endeavor], And each senses' individual purpose, their resolve, their characteristic behavior appears in the many things experienced by the Person. Mind is verily one. When raja and tama [gunas] unite in sattva, mind ([which is] sattva) is not [seen as] many. Mind is one and is subtle. For this reason, it cannot engage in many things at the same time. It succumbs to one thing at a time. For this reason, all senses do not get engaged [fully] at the same time. And the guna that follows the Endless Being is called "sattva." Superimposed on

447

that foundation is "hetu" [causality]. The sages give teachings
on "sattva." And because mind moves prior to all senses, the
senses are able to take up all the different forms. What those
senses actually are - that is being explained here. Eyes,
hearing, smelling, tasting, touch – these five; and space, air,
energy, water, earth – these are the objects of the five senses.
The location of the five senses – eyes, ears, nose, tongue, skin
– these five. And sound, touch, sight, taste, smell – these are
the "artha" [purposes/reasons/functions] of the five senses.
And the intelligence and such of the eyes [and such] – all of
these intelligences of the senses [are there]. All these, and
again the [further] "artha" of sattva and the Self – [and] closely
related [or: connected] to these is momentariness and certainty
– that twenty-five forms – these: 1) mind; 2) the objects
["artha"] of mind; 3) intellect; 4) the self; (qualities of the
subtle substances) – these are collectively presented in a
condensed manner. And the "hetus" good and bad, pravritti
and nivritti are stated. And the acts that are of the substances –
that which is called "kriya" [acts] – that is also being stated.
"Dravya" [substance] – meaning: [in this case] "Atman"
[Self]. Five senses, the objects of the five senses, the homes of
the five senses, the "artha" [see above] of the five senses, and
the intelligences of the five senses – these are the twenty-five
distinctions of the senses. Within this, the "great phenomenal
mutations" can be ascertained, covering everything. Presently,
as far as the senses: energy is with the eyes; space is with the
ears; smell is with earth; taste is with water; air is with touch –
the particular elucidations are being made here. Within these
particularities, as the particular sense is, [and as] the particular
endowment [to that sense is], so is the form that follows. After
that there is the particular nature/characteristic, and the "hetu"
[causality] that spreads. The enjoining of the "arthas"
[functions/purposes/objects] with "atiyoga" [excessive
attachment] and with "mithyayoga" [the attachment to the

false; illusion], brings about the the mutation of "aapanyamaan" ["I"-orientedness] Immediately, whatever the intelligences of each are, those begin to head towards their own destruction ["heenayoga"]. And again, upon uniting with "samayoga" [attaching completely], the "I'-oriented chitta makes the tendencies of each spread out. And the function of the mind is thought – that "thinking" – in mind and intellect – with "samayoga" [uniting completely], "atiyoga" [uniting excessively]; "heenayoga" [uniting in lowly/destructive ways] and "mithyayoga" [uniting with delusion] – [that thinking with all these] becomes the causality of mutations of [original] nature. When [original] nature mutates – for the sake of maintaining the natural state's equilibrium and normal pressure, take care via all of these "hetus" [causalities]. All of these hetus are beneficial for the self. Attend to all of the substances conjoining and expanding in all works, and by their application and by observing the place, time, particular qualities [of each thing], and their opposing forces – endeavor with care to make the mind be in its natural state. In order to do this – meaning: for the sake of the natural state, those who are desirous to benefit the self – meaning "yogis" – should keep the memory oriented mind in a steady state and perform the "samvritta" [associated acts]. What that "samvritta" is will be explained in the following. Worship deities, cow, Brahmins, guru, the elderly, sages and teachers. Along with everything travel with fire – meaning: go on while continuously doing Kriya. And take up beneficial medicines – meaning: abide in the par avastha of Kriya. Bathe in the day and in the night. Bathe in the "triveni" upon doing Kriya and be fulfilled. And cleanse the places [in the body] where wastes accumulate and the feet, and clean the mouth, clean and cut hair, beard, nails three times during one period. And wear whole clothes every day. Always be in the garb of a sadhu. Cut the hair on the head. Always oil the head, ears, nose and legs/feet. Light incense every day. When meeting with people, speak sweetly, and greet the other person before they greet you, or even if they do not greet you. And in treacherous paths be intelligent. Do oblations – meaning: do Kriya. Perform the acts of "yajna" [fire ceremony]. Give Kriya to others. Perform Omkar Kriya. Via Kriya, take away the maleficent power others may harbor. Be reverential to guests. Meditate in the Kutastha. According to the time [and place], be of nectarous speech. Control the personal self. Have mercy on phenomena [or: spirits]. And have the desire for the cause, but do not [have desire] for the fruit. And be without worry, without fear, [be reverent to the] learned, prosperous – meaning: be reverential to those who are: modest, greatly enthusiastic, capable, forgiving, righteous, God-believing, humble; [be reverential to] family, elders, sages and teachers. Carry an umbrella. Carry a staff, and be "mouni" [silent]. Be anonymous. When walking on the road, look at ground the distance of four feet's length ahead of you. And always be of beneficent nature. Crumbs, bones, thorns, disgusting things, hair, ice, pebbles, ashes, puddles, sand, mud – avoid them. And do not exercise just before the commencing of laborious work. See all living beings as friends. Be forgiving towards angry people. Give assurance to those who are in fear. Give counsel to those who are downtrodden. Always carry yourself in truth [or: in purity], and always be watchful. And tolerate the harsh words of others. Destroy sorrow via Kriya. Attend to that which brings Peace – meaning Kriya. Destroy that which causes the emergence of desires and repulsions – meaning: end raja and tama gunas – meaning: be without desire. Do not speak falsely. Do not take the wealth of others. Do not lust after the spouse of another. Do not desire after other lovers [than the one with you]. Do not have enmity with anyone. Do not do any sinful acts. Do not keep the company of those who commit sinful acts. Do not speak ill of others. Do not try to know the secrets of others and do not speak to people about the secrets of others. Do not sit with people who are not righteous or those who are out to cause civil strife. And do not keep the company of drunkards and addicts, those who have fallen to wayward ways, those who perform fetal abortions, lowlifes and miscreants. And do not eat grain which is not robust. And do not kneel or sit on hard seats. Do not lie in a bed that is not spread enough, without pillows, not long or wide enough, or that is on uneven ground. Do not travel on mountain peaks or where it is difficult to breathe. Do not climb trees. Do not bathe in a river with torrential current. And do not take the shade of trees that are at the edges of bodies of water. And do not go around and about in locations where there is uncontrolled fire. Do not laugh loudly. Do not go out in howling winds. Do not yawn, sneeze, laugh and such things without covering the mouth. Do not pick the nose. Do not grind teeth. Do not click fingernails. Do not clap [just for its sake]. Do not dig the earth [without need]. Do not tear grass. Do not trample on egg shells [alternate meaning: do not rub the scrotum]. Do not perform acts in meritless company. And do not constantly look at fiery, bright, shiny things which are impure and maleficent. And do not roar. And do not cause transgressions under the benedictory holy shade of the "chaitra vriksha" [trees under which worship is done]. And when it is night, do not travel in sacred places, "chaitra vriksha" – meaning the trees in a village under which worship is performed [during the day and evening], or courtyards – meaning: unguarded groves. Do not enter into empty homes alone. And do not get into "atavee" [jungle] – meaning: those plants and trees that grow on their own – like a jungle. Do not aspire for sinful tendencies, lustful relations or associations of servitude. Do not go against the excellent. Do not worship lowly ways. Do not behave crookedly/insincerely. Do not take up with people of ill-repute. Do not cause fear in anyone. And do not follow the ways of recklessness, oversleeping, staying awake in unhealthy ways, excessive bathing/pampering, excessive drinking and excessive eating. Do not lie flat [on the back] or with knees raised for excessively long periods of time. Do not follow behind snakes. Do not go towards fanged or horned ones. Do not be excessively exposed to forceful winds, excessive sun, dew, storm – all such. Do not argue with anyone. In proper places, perform the worship of fire. Do not care if there rejection from anyone. Do not heat anything in low positions. Do not bathe without having gotten rid of exhaustion, without having washed the mouth/face, and also not completely naked. After getting up from bathing, do not go about with the wet bathing clothes worn on the head, and do not pull forward the hair on the forehead. And do not wear the wet clothes from bathing [after the bath]. And do not go out of the house without having touched things such as jewels, ghee, sacred and beneficent things and beautifully fragrant things. And do not go while keeping sacred and beneficent things on the left side. Things other than these aforementioned types can be kept on left side and one can move forth. Do not go about any place without having jewelry on the hand, without bathing, without having changed out of old and worn clothes, without having chanted, without having performed oblations to the deities, without having ascertained the lineage (Kutastha), without having offered to gurus or to guests, without having smelled good scents, without wearing a mala [garland; or: rosary], without washing hands, feet and face/mouth, without cleaning the face, without washing the mouth with water [alternate meaning: without having taken holy water by the mouth], and without having eaten, without being refined, without being cleansed and while hungry. And: without a dish, or with a dirty dish, or in an ugly/disgusting place, at the wrong time and in an wide-open place, without having given the first portion to fire (not having offered to the five vayus), without the ritual sprinkling of water, without having become mantra-sanctified by having said mantras – meaning: not having given offerings to the five deities internally via Kriya – and foods that are unhealthy - do not eat such things or in such ways. Eat without having said bad things about others and without derision to yourself.* Do not eat day-old food [or: old food] other than raw meat, dried leafy greens and fruits. Other than milk, honey, salt, powdered pulse, do not eat any other foods too much. Do not take dairy products at night, and do not eat pulses only by themselves. And do not eat much [or: many things] at night. And do not eat without having drunk water first. Do not eat sitting in a crooked position. Do not lie down immediately after eating. And do not do any work with anxiety. And, towards air, fire, water, moon, sun, brahmins, guru – do not spit, pass wind, excrete or urinate towards them. And do not spray urine on the road. And do not blow phlegm out of the nose in populated places, at the times of eating, chanting, oblations, studying, worship or during any acts of beneficence. Do not insult women. Do not trust too much. And do not reveal that which is meant to be secret [or: that which is meant to be private]. And do not let anyone rule over you. And do not have sexual intercourse under these following conditions: if the partner is a woman who is menstruating, if the partner is sick, dirty, maleficent, with evil countenance, with evil behavior and evil character, antagonistic, without appropriate desire, desirous of others, spouse of another, sexual partner of another, non-sexual. Do not have sexual intercourse after having become impure in places such as: a bier, porch, place of leatherworks [alternate meaning: a square], grove, cremation grounds, near water, near medicine, in the places of brahmins, gurus and deities – or during the two transitional periods of the day and night or in forbidden places of pilgrimage. Do not have sexual intercourse if: medicine has not been taken, one is without a proper resolve, one is without the presence of real sexual desire, one has not eaten at all, one has eaten too much, one is in an unhealthy place for breathing, one is afflicted with problems of excretion and urination, one is afflicted from labor, one has: tiredness from exercise, lack of energy from fasting, sleepiness – or if the couple is in an exposed place [visible to others].** Do not insult sages and gurus. Do not become engaged in doing maleficent acts – meaning: do not bring harm to others through the use of mantras (Kriya) and such; do not become exposed to things such as ceremonies on a bier and its objects, and the studies of such. And do not study under these circumstances: when there is lightning, when there are rain clouds, when there is not any clear vision in all directions, when there is uncontrolled fire, when there is earthquake, when there are massive celebrations, when cinders are flying, during the time of "mahagraha upagaman" – meaning: when there is a comet, at pilgrimage places which are not favorable to the moon, at dawn or dusk, if the material has not come from the mouth of a guru, if substances have not been brought down, when taking an excessive amount of time and with an ugly voice, and without having the matter actually there, too quickly, too slowly, too weakly, by shouting or with an excessively quiet voice. Do not waste time. Do not go against disciplined ways. Do not go to other lands at night. And at the time of dusk [or: the time of worship – usually dusk], do not eat, study, amorous relations, sleep or serve. And do not become excessively friendly with children, the elderly, the licentious, the ignorant, the afflicted and the weak. And do not have desire for alcohol, games, consorting with prostitutes. Do not reveal things that are meant to be secret. Do not be disrespectful of anything. Do not be egotistical. Capable, non-antagonistic – meaning: do not insult those who do not oppose or those who do not insult others, or those persons who are of harmonious nature. Do not hit cows with sticks. And do not denigrate the elderly, gurus, associates and rulers by insulting them. Do not speak too much. And do not oust from the house friends, those who help in times of trouble and those who know your secret/private things. Do not be unduly unsettled or excited. And do not be attracted to acts which either make or nurture suffer – meaning: any worldly thing. Do not just trust everyone. And do not fear anyone. And do not be judgmental all the time. And do abuse the time of work. Do not enter into anything without testing it. Do not become enslaved to the senses. Do not go about everywhere with a restless mind. Do not rely excessively on the senses and intellect. Do not be dilatory during work. Be vigilant with anger and delight at all times. Do not be enslaved to grief. When there is success, do not become overly delighted. When there is no success, do not express sorrow. Practice the remembrance of Infinite Nature. And make strong effort for cause with certainty, and perform acts related to cause every day. Do not give assurance to anyone by saying, "I will do the work." Do not ejaculate semen. Do not harbor insults you may have received. And do not make oblations of these without fire: impurities, intoxicants, ghee, sunned rice, sesame seeds, grass, mustard seeds. Give assurance to yourself by saying, "There will be beneficence for me," and [by saying] "may the fire and air sustain my life and not cause wrongs in my body. May Vishnu – meaning: settled existence – give me strength. May Indra (Kutastha) give me the Seed; and may water nurture by body." And massage the body during twice during the day [once at each of the two divisions of the day and night]. And bathe after having massaged oil on the feet and hands. May there be appeasement through the water of the powers that bring about wellness to one's heart, head; that bring about knowledge, generosity, friendliness, empathy, "harshapeksha" (meaning that which carries delight). Water – meaning: the waters of causality. May the aspirant take up all of the dutiful acts and establish them. May the aspirant be praised by the sages and be prosperous in society and live more than a hundred years. And may the aspirant enjoy spiritual and material well-being and friendships equally fully. For this reason it is the duty of verily every person to perform the beneficent acts [mentioned here] always. And as far as the beneficent acts that are not mentioned here – one should perform and be established in them upon hearing about them.

THE END [of this section]

[* and **Translator's note: Out of the need to keep the sections on eating and sexual intercourse understandable in English, the phrasing for these sections in this translation was split in two or three consecutive parts. The injunctions relating to the aforementioned subjects in the original Bengali are compiled one after the other with only one reference to the subject itself. We have had to mention the subject more than once because of having to group the different categories of the stated injunctions associated with the same subject. Although the grammar is clear in the Bengali, a literal representation of that grammar in these asterisked sections would not be functional in an English translation.]

KNOWLEDGE OF THE SEASONS

Always abide by the rules of the seasons – meaning: if eating and activities are done completely and according [to the seasons], lifespan is increased and the body remains without disease. For this reason, the ways of eating according to each season, the manners of recreation, and the particular things by whose use according to the particular seasons bring about well-being – that is being explained here with specificity.

[Translator's note: The six seasons of the Hindu calendar are: "Shishir" [cold and dewy] – mid-January to mid-March; "Vasanta" [spring] – mid-March to mid-May; "Grishma" [summer] – mid-May to mid-July; "Varsha" [rainy season] – mid-July to mid-September; "Sharat" [autumn] – mid-September to mid-November; "Hemanta" [winter] – mid-November to mid-January.]

That which is called "year" on Earth is divided into six parts because of the seasons. In this, when the sun travels in the northern trajectory [north of the equator], that is called "uttarayan" [also the name for the summer solstice]. The duration of this period is from the time of "Shishir" through the time of "Vasanta" and "Grishma" [see note above]. And when the sun moves in the southern trajectory [south of the equator], that is called "dakshinayan" [also the name for the winter solstice]. This period begins at the time of the "Varsha" season and remains until/through the "Sharat" and "Hemanta" season [see note above]. This ["dakshinayan"] is also called

457

"visarga." And "uttarayan" is called "adan." In these two, extremely dry/harsh vayu [air property] does not dominate during the visarga period, but during the adan period, there is a dominance of dry/harsh vayu. And during the visarga period, the moon has unimpeded power, and through the rays of the dews, she fully nourishes all of the things of world. For this reason, the "visarga" period is called "saumya" [pleasant]. And the sun, vayu [life-force in air], moon – these obey the natural processes of that time, and initiate the causes of the activities of the subjects of time and the seasons: the six "rasas" [tastes or humours], and vata, pitta and kapha [wind, bile and phlegm – respectively – in the body], and the physical attributes of all things, and the capacities of the bodies of living beings and the causes of their emergence. In all of this, during the period of "adan," the sun sucks all the softer things of the world and vayu is intense and dry/harsh at this time. During period containing Shishir, Vasanta and Grishma, dryness/harshness gradually becomes present, and there is the expansion of the bitter, astringent, pungent rasas in a harsh form and brings about weakness in human beings.

During the period containing Varsha, Sharat and Grishma, the sun in its southern trajectory becomes established during [that] time, and by vata [wind property] and the rains, the heat pressure becomes subdued. And with unimpeded power via the auspicious, moist, peaceful and comfortingly warm moon, there is imbuing of everything with sour, salty, sweet, moist rasas. During this period human beings gradually gain strength. During visarga and adan, human beings are weak at the beginning of visarga and at the end of adan. And during the middles of these two periods, human beings have a medium amount of strength. And at the end of visarga and at the beginning of adan human beings have the greatest strength. And during winter, regarding the strong ones, because of the touch of the vayu of winter [or: cold vayu], fire remains contained in the intestines and gives strength. For this reason, during winter, all living beings such as human beings begin the losing of weight in the flesh. In the winter that fire does not take the form of digestive fire [as much]; then that fire begins to attack the humours in the body. In the winter, the cold vayu comes about from those impure humours. For that reason, in the winter, eat pure meat accompanied with softeners such as ghee, along with tart and salty sauces or liquids. And eat the meat after masticating it well, like the way the "vileshaya" (animals who live in holes) eat meat and birds and such that they have acquired for food. And during this period liquors called "madira" and "sidhu" (madira with good breeding) and honey should be used regularly. And substances made from dairy [alternate meaning: from the juice of mangosteen] and sugar-cane juice, coagulated substances, oils, and rice cooked from new rice grains should be used, and warm water should be imbibed − if this is done, then the life-force will never decrease, it will gradually increase.

And massage oil during the winter in an "apatan" manner − meaning: thoroughly rub it in. Massage oil on the head. And sweat − meaning: take steam-baths. And take in the heat of the sun. Live in a place made of earth, or in a warm cave home. During the winter, cover your body while lying, while in asana [or: while sitting] and while moving. And cover yourself with sheets, deerskin, grass-bed, blankets and such. If the body is light in weight, cover it with thick comforters. And at the time of sleeping lie embracing a lover − covered in a comforter − who is greatly affectionate, full-breasted and lithe in form. And during the entire time of Shishir, continuously enjoy pleasures with each other. And take light and airy (vayu dominant) substances, and the air from the easterly direction. If the time of eating has passed [and one has not eaten], then eat lightly and do not eat "mantha" (mashed) food. And the particulars are these: the rising of dryness/harshness during the period of adan [from the end of] Hemanta and [the starting point of] Shishir, and the cold that is carried with the cloud-vayu causality [during the period of visarga].

THE END OF THE BOOK

Dedication

"Dadu"
Sri Sailendra Bejoy Dasgupta
(1910-1984)

Exalted direct disciple of Swami Sri Yukteshvar Giriji Maharaj

Dadu,
We are your children surrendered at your feet.
Thank you for guiding us with your light.
Please accept our quiet offering.

Titles available from Yoga Niketan

Kriya Yoga by Sri Sailendra Bejoy Dasgupta

Paramhansa Swami Yogananda: Life-portrait and Reminiscences by Sri Sailendra Bejoy Dasgupta

The Scriptural Commentaries of Yogiraj Sri Sri Shyama Charan Lahiri Mahasaya: Volume 1

The Scriptural Commentaries of Yogiraj Sri Sri Shyama Charan Lahiri Mahasaya: Volume 2

The Scriptural Commentaries of Yogiraj Sri Sri Shyama Charan Lahiri Mahasaya: Volume 3

Srimad Bhagavad Gita: Spiritual Commentaries by Yogiraj Sri Sri Shyama Charan Lahiri Mahasay and Swami Sriyukteshvar Giri

A Collection of Biographies of 4 Kriya Yoga Gurus by Swami Satyananda Giri

Kriya Stories by bala

Made in the USA
Middletown, DE
27 October 2023

41471338R00269